One-Arm Boy
in a Two-Arm World

One-Arm Boy
in a Two-Arm World

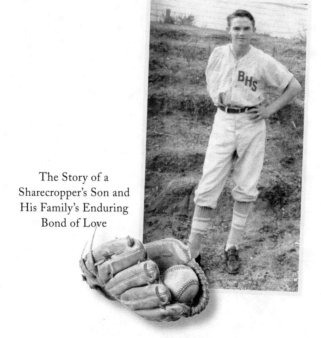

The Story of a
Sharecropper's Son and
His Family's Enduring
Bond of Love

Nancy Bone Goff

TATE PUBLISHING & *Enterprises*

Published by Tate Publishing & Enterprises, LLC
127 E. Trade Center Terrace | Mustang, Oklahoma 73064 USA
1.888.361.9473 | www.tatepublishing.com

Tate Publishing is committed to excellence in the publishing industry. The company reflects the philosophy established by the founders, based on Psalm 68:11,
"The Lord gave the word and great was the company of those who published it."

Book design copyright © 2010 by Tate Publishing, LLC. All rights reserved.
Cover and Interior design by Stefanie Rooney

Published in the United States of America

ISBN: 978-1-61663-057-7
Biography & Autiobiography, General
10.02.19

Dedication

This book is dedicated to the memory of
my parents, *Willie* and *Adell Culpepper Bone.*

Acknowledgments

Special thanks to my brother, *DM*, and
my sister, *Imogene*, for sharing their memories.

Table of Contents

Foreword

Nancy Bone Goff is a fascinating writer. From the beginning of her stories to the very end, you feel as if you are a part of the story. Her storytelling is vivid and descriptive. One feels as if he is going back in time, experiencing the same joy and hardships as the actual characters themselves.

One-Arm Boy in a Two-Arm World will capture you from the very start. It is a book you will not want to put down. If you've ever enjoyed just sitting back and listening to your parents or grandparents tell stories of what some call "the good old days," you'll feel right at home with this book. Take a trip back in time with the Bone family and discover why people who lived during that time did not always see them as the good old days. Read about the struggles and hardships families faced during the time of the Great Depression. Learn about the struggles of a sharecropper and his family as they faced everyday life, working to survive.

Today, people take many of life's simple pleasures for granted, like being able to get in their car and run to the store to buy a loaf of bread, a gallon of milk, a pound of butter, or a bag of flour. Imagine having to raise and prepare these items by hand from the crops the family grew by the sweat of their brows, or riding on a mule-drawn wagon into town for those supplies. Fall back to a place in time where everyday life was not taken for granted and life's simple pleasures were looked upon much differently.

One-arm Boy in a Two-arm World will make you sad and perhaps even shed a tear. However, it will also make you smile and rejoice in a young boy's accomplishments. In the end it will make you realize how fortunate we are today for all the modern conveniences and technology at our fingertips.

—Linda Cynan Majors

Prologue

Every person, every family, has a story to tell. Some stories are funny, some are sad. Some stories tell of great fortune and how it was obtained; others speak of poverty. My family's story is one of survival—not one of surviving a particular event, but rather, one of surviving from day to day.

I was born in 1951. I was the last child born to Willie and Adell Bone. My mother was thirty-nine, my father forty-eight. There were seven children in all. Julius Earl was the oldest. Next in line were Willie Charles and Delene. They were my half-brothers and half-sister. I had one full-blood sister, Imogene, and two full-blood brothers, DM and Wilfred. There was a twenty-eight year age difference between Julius and me. Because of the age difference my sibling's lives remained somewhat of a mystery to me. I was not a part of much of their previous lives.

When I was growing up, Mama would tell me stories about what life was like before I was born and how hard times were for them. I can remember lying beside her in the stillness of the night, sharing the same bed, listening to her every word. I would try very hard to visualize my siblings as children growing up. It was hard. I had never picked cotton or been without electricity. I had never plowed with a mule or dug a well in order to have water. I had never washed clothes in a creek using a scrub board or made lye soap in a black wash pot.

I knew my family was poor, and I knew there were a lot of hard times they had endured. They had lived through the Great Depression. There had been much sickness in the family. However, it was not until I was grown and found myself no longer physically able to carry out my lifelong profession as a hairstylist that I truly began to ask questions.

By the time I became obsessed with learning about my family's background, Julius, Willie Charles, and Delene had already passed on. My father and mother had also passed. The siblings who were left were getting on up in years. I needed to know what made them tick. I wanted them to share their memories with me.

Imogene was the easiest to talk to. In the past I had spent more time with her than with DM or Wilfred. She was like a second mother to me. Her three daughters, Teresa, Vicky, and Debra, were more like my sisters than my nieces. Teresa was two years older than me, Vicky was six months younger than me, and Debra was two years younger than me. Other than being an aunt to Teresa before I was even born, I was also an aunt to two older nephews, Richard and Travis, and another niece, Lee. Richard and Lee were Willie Charles's two oldest children. Travis was Julius's one and only child.

It was my brothers who eluded me the most. DM was eighteen years my senior, and Wilfred was ten years my senior. During my growing-up years, their lives centered around making a living for their own families. I had very little knowledge of who they were or what had brought them to the place they were now.

I began to ask questions, questions about their childhood, my parents, grandparents, uncles, and aunts. To my surprise, DM offered to take me on a sightseeing trip back to the places my family had once lived and worked. Before we began our day-long trip, I decided to carry along a tape recorder. I knew I would never remember all the information I hoped would come out. I put in new batteries and brought along several ninety-minute tapes. I didn't want to miss a single word he had to say.

The long-awaited morning finally arrived. I hoped it would be the first of many. He arrived fifteen minutes earlier than our designated time of 7:30 a.m., which was fine with me, as I had been ready since six thirty. He drove a beautiful late-model red Ford truck accented with white and white leather interior.

At the time, DM had turned sixty-nine on his birthday in February. His close-cut salt-and-pepper beard was more salt than pepper, and so was his hair, at least what I could see of it. A camouflage ball cap covered most of the hair on his head, and his matching camouflage jumpsuit covered his corpulent stomach. As I climbed into the oversized cab of his truck, he smiled his usual crooked grin and bid me good morning.

"Good morning," I responded with a return smile. "Great truck."

"Thank ya," he said.

Reaching across his body, he grabbed the gearshift knob and placed it into the drive position. "I'm going to take ya to the cemeteries first; then I'll show ya where we lived when I was young."

"Sounds good to me," I replied.

There was so much I wanted to know about this man. I knew about his arm. I knew he had worked in the roofing business most of his life. I knew he was married, had five children, several grandchildren, and even great-grandchildren. Other than knowing those facts, I didn't really know my own brother. I hoped our day together might change that.

After locating the various graveyards where our mother and father's people were buried, he drove on down the road farther, eventually pulling into a yard where an old, faded-green, weathered house stood seemingly abandoned. A thick growth of bamboo cane surrounded what was once the backyard. The tin roof was rusted in spots, and the outbuildings were either gone or in disrepair.

DM reached through the steering wheel and switched off the ignition. "This is the Walter Patrick Place," he said. "This is where we lived when my arm was taken off."

I watched the look on my brother's face as he reached deep inside the memories of himself as a child. His stories were of hard times, happy times, sad times, and some just plain awful times. I was so glad to have my recorder with me; the information was often too much for me to take in and then sort out in my mind.

At one point he became so emotional his voice cracked and his chin began quivering. I could sense the deep pride he felt in where he had come from to get to where he was now. I felt that same pride in all my siblings. I knew they had lived through tremendous hardships, yet all of them turned out to be good citizens and good people.

This book is about those hardships and how my family endured.

Willie and Adell Bone, my parents

Men of the cloth will tell you that God will never give a person more than he or she can bear. Those who are strong in their faith will withstand through any hardship. Some people are born with a natural inner strength and a will to survive. Giving up is not a part of their character. When faced with adversity, they meet it head-on rather than letting it get the better of them.

The Walter Patrick House

The Walter Patrick Place

Farm life in rural Alabama in the 1920s, '30s, and '40s was that of survival. Most of the people who farmed were poor. Farmwork was hard, backbreaking work. If a farmer was lucky and the weather cooperated, he was able to feed and clothe his family. He seldom had any money to speak of. Luxuries like electricity and indoor plumbing were only for the well-to-do. Food was grown by the sweat of his brow, caught from the creeks and streams, or hunted and killed in the woods.

Willie Onzeal Bone was born July 17, 1902, to Oliver and Katie Lou Bone. He grew up on a farm. He was used to hard work. He grew up learning how to cut wood with a crosscut saw, lead a mule behind a plow, dig wells, milk cows, treat sick animals, and butcher meat. He was taught how to survive off the land.

Willie's first wife, Fannie, died from complications of childbirth one week after their youngest child, Delene, was born. His two sons, Julius Earl and Willie Charles, were seven and five. After Fannie's death, Willie moved back to his parents' home with all three of his children.

Willie had two brothers, Isaac and Andrew, and four sisters: Josie, Lena, Myrtle, and Lera. His sisters, along with their husbands and children, were already living back home, mainly because they were too lazy to work. After Fannie's death, they readily stepped in to take advantage of Willie's situation, supposedly helping him by taking care of the children. Most of what they did was eat the food Willie brought home for his children. In all honesty, they were simply living off Willie much more than they were assisting him. For nearly two years after Fannie's death, he more or less supported the entire family in exchange for their help with his children.

Willie took jobs wherever he could find them. His skills were basic, but his back was strong. Much of his time was spent working in the sawmills, which had sprung up along the creeks and rivers of nearby townships. His days were long, working from sunup to sundown. The pay was poor. If he earned fifty cents a day he considered himself lucky. Oftentimes he would be gone for a week at a time, coming home only on weekends to see his children and bring home what money he had made. To make matters worse, his brothers and sisters worked sporadically and only when they felt they had no choice.

Willie was a tall, handsome, dark-haired, brown-eyed widower. Two years after Fannie's death, he met his second wife, Adell Culpepper. Adell's older brother, Barry, was married to Willie's sister, Josie. In fact, Barry and Josie were responsible for introducing them to each other. Willie was nine years older than Adell, but the pretty, petite, blond-haired, blue-eyed farm girl won his heart right away. After a rather short courtship, they were married December 23, 1929.

Adell was no stranger to hard work herself. She grew up on a farm. From the time she was old enough to carry a tote sack, she worked in the fields. She was the daughter of William and Lula Bell Culpepper of White City, Alabama. She had four brothers and five sisters: Dee, Carrie, Barry, Cora, Annie, Buck, Babe, Emma, and Ruth. They lived their entire lives in and around the same area. Adell's world centered around her family and home life. All she had ever known was hard work and being poor.

Taking on a ready-made family was a huge responsibility for the young bride. To make matters worse, Willie's family resented Adell from the very beginning. For nearly two years, Willie had earned the living for all of them. Once he married Adell, the free ride his siblings enjoyed abruptly ended. Truth be told, had Josie known the two of them would have hit it off so well, she would have never introduced them in the first place. She and Lena tried their best to end the relationship between the couple. For as long as the newly married couple remained in the same house with his family, there was constant turmoil among them.

Adell quickly found herself not only taking care of three stepchildren but at times, Willie's entire family. By marrying the man she loved, she had become an instant wife, mother, and maid to a house full of lazy people. Eventually, Willie knew he would have to get as far away from his family as he possibly could if he wanted his marriage to work. He moved his new bride, along with his sons, to the John Burkhalter place, just outside the small town of Billingsley. Delene stayed with Willie's mother, where she remained most of her childhood life.

Willie could barely read or even write his own name. He had given up on going to school when he was barely in the second grade. Book learning was second on the list for most young boys of this era. They were needed at home to help with the farmwork. Consequently, most of what Willie knew how to do was farming. Because he owned no land of his own, he was forced to become a sharecropper, which meant whatever crops he made had to be divided fifty-fifty with the landowner as a means of payment for using the land.

Adell completed sixth grade at Oak Grove School in White City. The one-room schoolhouse was over a five-mile walk from her parents' house. Oftentimes there was little or no money for school supplies or even shoes for the family of ten. She was forced to quit after her sixth year in order to work on the farm. This also saved money needed for the younger children to go to school.

Adell was glad to be moving away from Willie's family, although it also meant moving away from her own family. Without them around, she felt alone for the first time in her life. She had no friends and no one to turn to except Willie. He continued to work away from home through the winter months, leaving her alone with only the two boys. To top it off, she became pregnant right away with her first child. Julius and Willie Charles defied her in every way possible, making her life even more miserable. When they were told their stepmother was going to have a baby, things got even worse.

Adell was into her sixth month of pregnancy. She was becoming more and more tired every day. One day she decided to lie down for a while to rest. It was midafternoon. A cool spring breeze blew through the open window beside her bed. She lay down crossways on the bed and quickly dozed off to sleep. A short time later, she was awakened by the crackling sound of wood burning and the distinct smell of smoke. Alarmed, she quickly sat up on the side of the bed.

There in the middle of the floor between the two beds was a pile of blazing sticks and twigs. Her first reaction was to grab a quilt from off the bed to try and put it out. Fortunately, she was able to smother the fire before it had a chance to get out of control. As she and the two boys were the only ones there, she immediately knew who was responsible for setting the fire.

When she confronted them, they readily confessed that Josie and Lena had told them to do it.

Adell couldn't believe her ears. She knew Willie's family didn't like her, but she never expected they would resort to burning her alive. She was devastated. Immediately, she sat down and wrote her mother a letter telling her of the incident, pouring out her every fear and the loneliness she felt. When the letter was finished, she folded it and placed it between the pages of her Bible. She would mail it one day when she had an extra penny to buy a stamp.

In 1930, Willie and Adell's first child was born. They named her Imogene. No middle name, just Imogene. When her birth certificate arrived in the mail, the people at the Board of Vital Statistics had listed her with her first name being Imo and her middle name Gene. A correction was made and a new certificate was issued. She was a pretty child with dark hair and brown eyes, like the Bone side of the family. It was obvious from the start that Julius and Willie Charles were jealous of the new baby. They were resentful of the fact that their full-blood sister, Delene, did not live with the family. Imogene's birth only added to the hard times they were already giving their stepmother.

After a year or so, the family moved from the Burkhalter place to the Farmer Epperson place. Adell tried very hard to love her husband's sons, but their resentment toward her daughter and her made it very difficult. They would not mind her at all and sassed her terribly when Willie wasn't around. They knew not to sass her in front of him, as he would have whipped them severely.

Three years passed when Adell realized she was pregnant for the second time. They had just made another move from the Epperson place to the Jack Davis place. Times continued to be really hard. The Great Depression held the entire country in its grasp. Between thirteen and fifteen million people were unemployed. Crops were poor. They were barely able to keep food on the table. Adell knew adding another child to the family at that point in time would only make things worse. She worried constantly about how they would get by, often falling into a deep state of depression. Willie could only assure her things would get better, as did the new president of the United States, Franklin D. Roosevelt.

The year was 1934. Times continued to be hard. Roosevelt adopted emergency measures to meet the economic crisis. Talk among the locals over at the mercantile was about how the new democratic government was going to help the poor and needy in the South as well as the entire country. Adell knew little about what the rest of the nation was going through. She only knew of the hardships in her own little corner of the world. However, despite all the worries about how they would get by, in February of 1934, their second child was born. This time it was a boy. He also had dark hair and brown eyes the color of coffee beans. They named him simply DM.

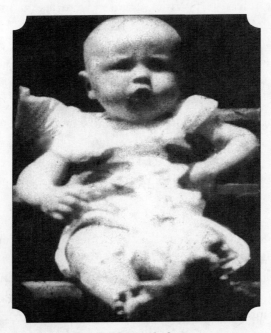

DM as a baby

On May 11, a terrible dust storm from the Great Plains swept across the Eastern states, leaving everything covered in a layer of dust. The newly sprouted fields of corn disappeared below the thick blanket of dirt. It did no good to sweep the floors or dust the furniture, for within an hour after doing so, it was back just like it was before, covered in dust. In 1935, Willie moved his family from the Jack Davis house to a forty-acre farm on Autauga County Road 24. Walter Patrick, a local merchant from Billingsley, owned the house and land. The wood-frame house had no electricity or running water. After moving in, one of the first things Willie did was dig a well out back of the house so the family could have water. Kerosene lanterns supplied light at night. Kerosene cost money, of which they had little. More often than not, the family went to bed as soon as it got dark to reserve their meager supply.

In most rural areas there were few indoor toilets. The two-seater outhouse near the field out back was always plagued with spiders, wasps, and even an occasional snake. During the coldest winter months they kept a porcelain chamber pot beneath their bed to use during the night. It smelled, but it was better than going out into the cold night air to the outhouse.

A tin roof covered the house. Sometimes when it rained, the rain came down so hard on the tin roof they could barely hear themselves talking. Along with the wood cookstove in the kitchen, a stone fireplace in one of the three rooms provided heat. In the winter they carried in wood from the woodpile out back and stacked it behind the stove, on the back porch, and by the fireplace. A pile of pine wood kindling was stored in a wood box near the back door. The pine, resin-filled splinters were used to start the fire each morning.

During the hot summer months, a huge cedar tree at the front of the house helped to shade the front porch. A row of cedars grew along the roadside, their branches filled with the nests of small birds. A thicket of bamboo cane grew along the fenceline out back. Several hickory trees growing nearby dropped their nuts in the fall of the year. A huge oak tree directly across the road from the house dotted the ground with acorns.

Next to the oak tree was an old, weathered barn where Willie kept his mule, Ben. Ben was as strong as an ox and faithfully plowed the ground each year for planting. The barn also housed the milk cow and a variety of barn cats. Alongside the barn was a pig lot where hogs were raised for meat.

Adell did most of the milking. Regardless of the weather, milking the cow was one of the first things she did each morning. The cats learned quickly to come running when they heard the clanging of the bail against her milk pail. They knew she would share what she could with them. The family also raised chickens for eggs and an occasional Sunday dinner of fried chicken, chicken and dumplings, or cornbread dressing.

A field of corn was planted to provide meal for bread and also to feed the animals. The familys' half of the cotton crop was sold to buy coffee, sugar, salt, flour, and what clothes they could afford. Adell handmade most of their clothes from flour sacks or feed sacks. She made quilts from scrap material and worn-out denim overalls. When she wasn't cooking, washing clothes, or tending to the children, she worked in the fields beside Willie, knowing all too well that if the crops failed it meant even harder times for the family. Every waking minute of the day was spent caring for the crops, the farm animals, and themselves. It was not a question of working to earn money. It was a question of working to survive.

In the spring, when the fields were plowed and ready for planting, Willie purchased seeds and fertilizer on credit from Mr. Patrick's mercantile. Through the summer, he and Adell chopped the cotton to thin out the plants and plowed the corn to keep the weeds down. They planted a garden filled with peas, butter beans, potatoes, green beans, onions, and tomatoes. As soon as Imogene was old enough, she and her mother spent many long, hot hours over the wood-burning stove, canning the vegetables for use during the winter.

Each year, sugarcane stalks saved from the previous year's crop were extracted from the ground where they had been buried for the winter. The stalks were then laid down in rows and covered with fresh-plowed dirt. Each joint of the stalk would in turn produce another stalk of cane. Ribbon cane syrup made from the sugar cane was a vital part of the family's diet.

For all the hard times the family had seen in previous years, it seemed as though 1935 was going to be different. Willie always said, "Nothin' lasts forever, good times or bad." Things were looking up. By late August, the cotton crop looked the best it ever had. The crib was full of corn, Adell's pantry was full of canned vegetables, and the sweet potato crop proved to be one of the best they had ever raised.

Fall was harvesting time, and the fruits of their labor were divided with Mr. Patrick in exchange for the use of the land. It was difficult to keep up, much less get ahead. It seemed as though nearly every cent they made was spent before they ever got it. Once the credit account at the mercantile was paid off, there was little to nothing left. Each year that passed meant doing it all over again just to make ends meet. Sharecropping was a no-win situation. In reality, sharecroppers were simply white slaves to the landowners. Farm life was difficult, but it was all they knew.

Some three years passed while living on the Patrick Place, and each year the family toiled in the fields. It was springtime once again, and the new cotton crop was well underway. It was also Saturday, washday. Adell gathered their one change of clothes and started a fire under the black wash pot in the yard. Using a scrub board and lye soap, she scrubbed the dirt and grime from Willie's overalls, shirt, and socks. She then added her plain cotton dress and the children's clothes to the pot to boil, stirring them with a long wooden paddle. Once the washing was finished and the clothes were hung on the barbwire fenceline, it was time for Adell and the children to go to the field.

Adell put on her flowered sunbonnet her mama had made for her from a printed feedsack. The bonnet helped to shade her eyes and face from the sun. She also wore a long-sleeved shirt to keep the sun off her arms. With her fair complexion, she was easily sunburned, so she wore as much protection as possible to cover whatever skin was exposed. While Willie plowed the corn, Adell used a long-handled hoe to chop the cotton. This process was necessary to remove the smaller plants of cotton to allow the bigger ones more room to grow.

Imogene was seven years old, too young to do much hoeing. Her job was to bring water to her mama in the cotton patch and to her daddy and older half-brothers in the cornfield. She was also required to keep a watch over three-year-old DM, who was playing in a nearby wet weather run. The run was at the base of the hill, about a quarter of a mile north of the house.

Willie had made DM a small slingshot for Christmas, which he used to shoot at birds, frogs, and anything else that dared to cross his path. The spring rains, which trickled steadily down the run, were an ideal harbor for tadpoles, frogs, and lizards. DM was busy filling his overall pockets with tiny rocks from the edge of the water when suddenly a small green lizard emerged from the cluster of thick bushes, making a beeline for the water. DM spied it immediately, picked up a small rock, and flung it at the unsuspecting reptile, striking it in the head. Stunned but not dead, the lizard raced back up the side of the red clay bank for the safety of the thick bushes. A barrage of rocks, one right after the other, followed the poor, defenseless creature as it scampered to get away.

"DM, ya leave that poor lizard be," Imogene fussed. "He ain't botherin' ya."

Suddenly DM grabbed his right arm. "My arm hurts," he said, frowning.

"That's what ya get for throwin' rocks at that lizard," Imogene scolded.

DM quickly scrambled up the side of the embankment. "It was hurtin' before I threw the rocks," he protested.

Adell looked up from her hoeing just in time to see DM running toward her across the cottonfield.

"Mama, my arm hurts," he called to her as he shuffled through the small green cotton plants.

When he reached her side, Adell looked closely at his arm. There was no sign of an injury. "You're just havin' growin' pains," she reasoned. "You'll be fine. Y'all go pick some blackberries down by the ditch, and I'll bake ya a cobbler for supper."

DM and Imogene loved blackberry cobbler. Imogene fetched two syrup buckets from the house. The two of them spent the next hour picking the sweet, juicy berries that grew along the ditch while dodging the honeybees that swarmed around their heads.

The blackberry bushes growing along the banks of the wet weather run were full of berries. The berries were as big and juicy as Imogene had ever seen them. Meticulously, she picked the dark, sweet berries and placed them in the syrup bucket she carried across her arm. Beads of sweat began to run down her thin face and drip from the ends of her dark, straight hair. The hot afternoon June sun warmed the earth beneath her bare feet. A tiny stream of water from yesterday's rain shower made babbling sounds as it trickled across the rocks at the base of the run.

Her small hands became dotted with dark purple stains as she continued to pluck the berries from the sticker vines. Occasionally a sharp briar pierced her hands and arms, causing a red streak of blood to appear on her tanned skin. She didn't worry about the scratches; they were just a part of picking berries. The thought of a fresh, hot cobbler for supper made the small abrasions and stains well worth it. Before they knew it, it was midday.

From the nearby field, Adell called to the children, "Let's go to the house and get some dinner. Imogene, see if ya can round up Julius and Willie Charles and then go down to the lower field and tell your daddy it's nearin' time to eat."

DM continued stuffing his mouth with handfuls of berries. "Imogene, my arm is hurtin' worse," he called to her between bites.

Imogene reached for DM's bucket. "Let me see how many berries you've actually picked. I think you've eat more than ya put in the bucket."

Peering inside, she could see DM's bucket was less than half full. She was about to scold her little brother. However, when she saw how silly he looked with his purple-stained lips, she shook her head and smiled. "I think we have enough for a berry cobbler. I need to take some water to Daddy anyway. We'll tell Mama about ya arm again. She'll know what to do."

DM and Imogene slowly walked the two hundred yards back to where Adell continued to thin out the young cotton plants. He was beginning to fret more and more about his arm. By the time he got to his mother he was starting to cry. Adell threw down her hoe and rushed to his side. "What's the matter with ya, DM?" she asked.

"He says his arm still hurts, Mama," Imogene answered for him. "He's been throwin' rocks at the lizards again."

Adell carefully examined DM's arm. "This boy came here throwin' rocks,—she paused—"though it does look a little swollen. After ya take your daddy and the boys some water, take him up to the house and let him lay down. Get some camphor out of the cupboard and rub on it. I'll be up there in a minute after I finish this here row. After ya get DM settled, wash them berries real good and add some wood to the fire in the stove. I'll get the cobbler ready to cook when I get there. I'll need to put on some cornbread to cook too. Tell your daddy dinner will be ready in about half an hour."

After dropping DM off at the house and rubbing his arm with camphor, Imogene drew a fresh bucket of water from the well then high-tailed it to the cornfield, where her daddy was plowing the rows of young green corn. "Daddy," she called, "Mama says it's almost time to eat."

Willie looked up to see his young daughter standing at the edge of the field holding a bucket of water. "I'll be thar in a minute," he answered. "Soon as I finish this here row."

Imogene dipped the long-handled dipper into the bucket, filling it with cool, fresh water. "Do ya want some water, Daddy?"

Continuing with his plowing, he answered back, "Not right now, honey. I'll get some when I'm finished. Just leave the bucket where it is. I'll carry it back to the house."

Imogene placed the dipper back into the bucket and headed to the house. Along the way, she spied Julius and Willie Charles playing in the corncrib. "Y'all ain't supposed to be playin'. You're supposed to be workin'," she scolded them.

"Ah, shut up!" Julius yelled to her. "Ya can't tell us what to do."

Imogene shook her head. "Mama says it's time to come eat."

"We'll eat when we git ready to eat," Willie Charles scoffed. "Adell can't tell us what to do neither. She ain't our mama."

Imogene stomped away. "Fine then. Don't eat. I don't care. It just means more for the rest of us."

The ground between the rows of corn was soft and black. Much-needed rain had fallen the night before, making it easier to move the single-edge plow down the long row of young green cornstalks. When Willie got to the end of the row, he laid the plow on its side and took out his handkerchief from the pocket on the front of his faded-blue denim overalls. Dipping it into the bucket of cool water, he wiped his face with it. Although it wasn't as hot as it was going to get in the Deep South, sweat poured from his brow, and his shirt was soaked. He placed the wet handkerchief around his neck and then picked up the bucket of water.

Before leaving the field, he gave his mule, Ben, a good long drink of water and then unhitched him from the plow. Willie led him to a nearby tree at the edge of the woods and tied him to one of its branches. It would provide shade for Ben until it was time for him and Willie to return to the field. As Willie walked toward the house, a slight breeze blew over his body, helping to dry the sweat and cool him down. As he neared the house, he could smell the cornbread Adell was cooking in the wood-burning stove. His stomach growled at the thought of the warm bread covered with fresh, creamy butter and the pot of fresh turnip greens his wife had cooked first thing that morning.

When he got to the backporch, he poured the remaining water he was carrying into a small tin dishpan and splattered some on his face. A bar of lye soap they had made last fall when they killed a hog lay near the wash pan. He grabbed the soap and washed his grimy hands. He dried them on the sun-dried towel hanging on a nail by the back door. As Willie entered the kitchen, Adell was just taking the hot, golden-brown cornbread from the oven.

"You're just in time," she told him. "There's some hot coffee left from breakfast if ya want some."

Willie took his seat at the head of the table. "I think I'd rather have some buttermilk," he answered.

The kitchen contained a wooden table, several straight-back chairs, a wooden bench that sat against the wall next to the table, an iron cookstove, and a storage safe with a wire front. The table was set with a variety of plates and glasses collected from various sources.

Willie scooted his chair closer to the homemade wooden

table. Julius, Willie Charles, and Imogene were already seated on the wooden bench along the wall. DM was on his knees in a chair with the back facing the table, making him tall enough to reach his plate.

Adell dipped Willie a glass of fresh made buttermilk from the churn.

DM held his arm out toward his daddy. "Daddy, my arm hurts," he said to him.

Willie looked carefully at his son's tiny arm. "What's the matter with it?"

Adell dipped a portion of turnip greens onto Willie's plate. "He started complainin' 'bout his arm hurtin' when we was down in the field," she told him. "I looked at it, but I don't see a thing wrong with it."

"You're havin' growin' pains, son," he told DM. "It'll quit hurtin' afore long."

In a short time, they finished their noonday meal. Willie went back to his plowing. Adell poured hot water from the kettle on the stove into the dishpan to wash the dishes. Imogene took her place beside her mother, drying the dishes as her mother washed them. After the dishes were clean, dried, and put away, Adell got ready to go outside to work in the garden.

"Mama, my arm hurts bad," DM complained again.

Adell looked once again at his arm. She realized it was beginning to swell. "Did somethin' bite ya?" she asked.

"No."

"Maybe ya strained it playin' with that slingshot," Adell said. "Go inside and lie down on the bed. Imogene, get some of that liniment from the cupboard and rub on his arm again. That might make it feel better."

Two rooms of the house contained beds. Julius and Willie Charles slept in one room on separate beds. Willie and Adell shared a bed with DM in the room with the fireplace. Imogene slept on another bed in the same room. Imogene helped

DM onto her mama and daddy's bed. The room was slightly stuffy, so she raised the window beside the head of the bed and placed a stick beneath it to hold it open.

The headboard and footboard of the beds were made of iron. There were coil springs and a homemade cotton mattress on each. The sheets were made of four two-hundred-pound fertilizer sacks sewed together. Adell had washed and bleached them, but they still remained rough to the touch. The quilts were homemade too, made mostly from old clothes and scraps from the sewing box. Next to the bed, an extra set of clothes hung from nails hammered into the walls and on the back of the doors.

It won't be long before it'll be time to take on the bedbugs, Imogene thought to herself. She hated bedbugs. The very thought of one of those nasty, little creatures sucking the blood from her body made her shiver. In a month or so, when the weather was good and hot, they would pull all the beds, mattresses, and furniture out into the yard. The hot sun would almost immediately kill the bedbugs hidden in the bedsprings and on the mattresses.

Getting rid of the chinches on the inside of the house was a different story. First, they would draw water from the well, enough to fill two big, black iron wash pots. Her father would build a fire under the pots to heat the water until it was boiling hot. He and her mother would carry the hot water inside and dash it into the cracks of the wood-plank walls. The hot water caused the bugs to explode. The water would run red with the blood from the bedbugs. After all the chinches were dead, they would then need to clean the floor with a shuck mop and lye soap. It was an all-day event, one Imogene truly dreaded. But it was also good to know she wouldn't have to worry about being bitten at night by the nasty, little critters.

Imogene found the bottle of liniment and rubbed DM's arm and shoulder. The liniment, made from camphor and whiskey, smelled really bad, but it seemed to soothe the pain. Soon DM fell asleep. Imogene kept watch over him while reading a book to help pass the time.

As evening approached, the bright noonday sun edged its way downward. Adell spent the afternoon in the garden. Mrs. Friday, their nearest neighbor from down the road, had given her some collard and onion sets. Adell walked along the freshly hoed rows, making a hole in the dirt with her forefinger. She then placed a single plant into each hole and pulled the dirt in around it. The garden was coming along fine. Soon there would be fresh black-eyed peas and butter beans to go along with the rattlesnake beans, which were hanging in clusters on the vines.

Willie finished plowing the corn. On his way back to the barn, he decided he would try his hand at catching a few fish for supper down on Swift Creek. After rubbing down Ben with a burlap sack, he shucked and shelled several ears of dried corn, which he placed in Ben's feeding trough. Taking a shovel from the barn, he dug red worms from the ground near the cow lot. Placing them in a bucket, he grabbed two cane poles and went to the house to see if DM wanted to go with him. When he got to the back door, he leaned the poles against the house and sat the can of worms on the step. Upon entering the house, Willie realized DM was asleep.

"How's his arm?" he asked Imogene.

Imogene looked up from her book. "I rubbed some liniment on it like Mama said. He cried awhile about it, then finally went to sleep."

Willie rubbed his hand across his day-old whiskered chin. "I was gonna see if he wanted to go fishin' with me, but I reckon I better let him sleep."

Imogene jumped to her feet, excited at the prospects of joining her father. "I'll go with ya, Daddy. Let me go fishin' with ya."

"Naw, Imogene, ya'd better stay here with your brother. Your mama's busy in the garden, so you'll need to see after him."

Imogene stomped her foot in protest. "I don't never get to go nowhere. How come boys always get to go fishin' and girls have to stay at home? It ain't fair."

"Ya mind your manners, little girl," Willie scolded. "Girls ain't supposed to fish. They're supposed to stay home and take care of the house and family."

Imogene dropped her head. Her dark, reddish-brown hair fell across her disappointed face. "I'm sorry, Daddy. I'll stay here with DM."

Willie placed his rough hand gently under his little girl's chin, lifting it upward so he could see her beautiful brown eyes. "Daddy will be back soon. I'll bring ya a big catfish you and your mama can fry up for supper."

Imogene disappointedly sat back down in her chair beside the bed. "Yeah, well, I'd sure rather help ya catch 'em than help Mama cook 'em," she replied.

Willie laughed and kissed his little girl on the forehead. "Why don't ya get some onions out of the shed and chop 'em up so we can have hush puppies with our fish? Daddy sure would like some hush puppies."

Imogene knew there was no more need to complain. Her daddy was going fishing, and she was going to chop onions while she watched her brother sleep. It didn't seem fair to her, but that was the way it was. She decided right then and there, being a boy was a whole lot more fun.

In the early 1930s, antibiotics were the medicines of the future. When a person got an infection anywhere in the body, there was little known about stopping it or even treating it. The body healed itself, or the patient died. People usually doctored themselves using what home remedies they had on hand. When these remedies didn't work, they depended solely on the advice of their doctors as to what to do. When faced with a truly life-threatening infection, it was up to the doctors and the good Lord to heal it.

The pain in DM's arm persisted throughout the night, growing stronger by the hour. Willie didn't own a car, so he called on his neighbor, Junior Mims. He told Junior about the pain DM was in and asked him if he would carry them to the doctor in his automobile. Junior agreed. The next morning, he drove Adell, Willie, and DM to see Doctor Joe Moore in Clanton.

The doctor's office was located in one room of the doctor's house. The examining table was covered with heavily starched white sheets tucked in neatly at the corners. A row of bottles lined the shelf along one wall. Some were filled with pills, while others contained different colored liquids. White porcelain cabinets along another wall held rows of drawers filled with cold, shiny doctor's instruments. The room smelled strongly of disinfectant. It was the first time DM had ever been to see a real doctor.

Dr. Moore was a tall, thin man in his midforties. His hair was brown and thinning on top. His eyes were deep set with dark circles under them, as though he hadn't slept in days. After examining DM's arm, Dr. Moore took some pills from one of the bottles, placed them in a small envelope, and handed the envelope to Adell. "Give him one of these pills every four hours. They will help with the pain. I don't think there's anything to worry about. He should be fine in a few days."

However, as the days passed, the pain continued. The skin darkened as the swelling increased. The pain became almost unbearable. DM began to cry and complain almost constantly. Even during the few precious hours when he was able to sleep, he moaned.

Adell lay beside him on the bed, awake, unable to sleep. Willie lay on the other side of him, also unable to sleep. Both of them were worried. Finally Adell spoke first. "We've got to do something," she insisted. "I don't know how much more pain this youngun can take."

Once again, Willie called on Junior Mims. Junior gladly drove DM and his very concerned parents to Dr. Moore's office. Upon seeing DM the second time, Dr. Moore realized he would need a specialist. He immediately sent them to see Dr. John Blue at St. Margaret's Hospital in Montgomery.

St. Margaret's was a Catholic-owned hospital located at the corner of Ripley Street and Adams Avenue. It was the biggest hospital DM had ever seen. It was painted solid white with a screened-in porch running along the outside of the building. Rooms were set up on the porch to house those patients who needed treatment but who were unable to pay for it. A bed was prepared for DM in the ward. A nurse dressed in a nun's habit removed DM's clothes, replacing them with a child's hospital gown. The smell of disinfectant filled his nostrils. The cry of people in misery echoed throughout the room. Unbeknown to him or his parents, this was where DM would spend the next two months of his life.

Dr. Blue, Dr. George Hill, and four other doctors on staff quickly became involved with DM's case. Dr. Blue was a short man with broad shoulders and a square face. Dr. Hill was tall with a rather large overhanging stomach. All six doctors gathered at his bedside. Each of them examined DM's arm. By then the arm had become extremely swollen and was beginning to turn black. After the examination was complete, the doctors silently left the ward. After consulting with the team of physicians, Dr. Blue met with Willie and Adell in the waiting area.

"Mr. and Mrs. Bone," he explained in a professional but somber manner, "we believe your son has an infection called osteomyelitis. It is an infection of the bonemarrow and the lining around the bone. Has DM had a hard blow of some kind to his arm in recent weeks?"

Adell thought back to the terrible thunderstorm they had experienced a short time back. "He was in a house that was struck by lightnin'. Could that have caused it?" she asked.

Dr. Blue looked puzzled. "What do you mean 'struck by lightning'?" he asked.

Willie recalled the afternoon the storm occurred. "It came up a bad lightnin' storm a while back," he explained. "We were all down to Mr. Richard Thomas's house visitin'."

Adell quickly chimed in, "Lightnin' was strikin' everywhere ya looked. It struck the house we were in. Came right down the chimney. It was like it went right through our bodies. I was holdin' DM in my lap. He went to hollerin' like a banshee."

Dr. Blue began to pace back and forth, rubbing his chin as if he was in deep thought. "That is a possibility, Mrs. Bone. However, I was thinking more along the lines of taking a direct hit to his arm by an object."

"Well, he did have a window to fall on his arm," added Willie. "He was playin' at the window and knocked the stick out that was holdin' it open. The window came down on his arm pretty hard."

Adell thought hard. "He also got a hard lick to his arm when he and his sister was playin' in the cotton house," she reminded Willie. She looked at Dr. Blue. "The wind caught the door, throwin' it back against his arm."

Dr. Blue stopped pacing and scratched his head. "It could well be caused by any of these things you've told me, perhaps a combination of all three. Regardless of the cause, we have to release the pressure on the arm. The other doctors and I have discussed it. We have decided the arm needs to be opened up to allow the infection to drain."

Willie looked Dr. Blue straight in the eyes. "Do what ya have to do, Doc. Just make sure ya get my boy well."

"We'll do our best," Dr. Blue promised.

Shortly afterward, DM was placed on a gurney and wheeled into an operating room. Ether was administered to put him to sleep. A slit was made in the arm from his elbow down to his wrist. A stream of infection the size of a match stem flowed continuously from the opening. A day or so later, another slit was opened up from the elbow up to his armpit. Nothing else could be done but wait.

The smell of sickness and death from DM and the other patients in the ward attracted buzzards. The flesh-eating vultures persistently circled the hospital. Green flies clung to the screens, searching for a way to get in. Cries of pain could be heard throughout the night. For seven days, DM continued to suffer as Willie and Adell sat diligently by his side. On the seventh day, doctors met with them again.

Dr. Blue and the other doctors looked extremely concerned as they approached the bed where DM lay writhing in pain. "Mr. and Mrs. Bone, we are at a loss as to what to do at this point," Dr. Blue explained. "DM is quickly losing his battle with this infection. As I'm sure you've noticed, he is growing weaker every day. At this point, the other doctors and I think the only thing left to do is amputate the arm. I know this is a huge step, but we are in fear of the infection spreading. If this were to happen, he would surely die. Hopefully by removing his arm, we can stop the further spread of the infection to other parts of his body."

Adell gasped. She clasped her hands to her face. Tears of despair fell from her soft blue eyes.

Willie put his arm around Adell's shoulder to try to comfort her. He looked at Dr. Blue. "Will cuttin' off his arm save his life?" he asked.

"We don't know, Mr. Bone," Dr. Blue replied truthfully. "However, it's his only chance for survival that we can see. Despite all we've done, the infection is spreading, and it is spreading rapidly. If the infection goes to his brain, there will be nothing left to do but watch him die. If we remove the arm now, he at least has a chance. If we don't remove it, we feel he will surely die."

Willie removed his arm from around Adell's shoulders. Slowly he walked over to the window. Looking out onto the street, he could see the people as they passed by on the street below. These people were going about their daily routines, completely unaware of the decision he had to make regarding his son's future. What would his son's life be like with only one arm? How could he make a living for himself? How would he get by? Yet by not allowing the doctors to remove his arm, he would die. What choice did he really have? Willie turned to Dr. Blue. "Do it," was Willie's only reply.

Doctor Blue silently nodded his head. He and the others then turned and left the room. Adell wept. Willie held her in his arms, comforting her as best he could. Neither one spoke to the other. Adell felt numb inside. Willie felt as though he had sentenced his son to the hardest life he could imagine—a life with only one arm.

A short time later, several nurses came to DM's bedside. One of them carefully lifted the small, frail boy onto a hard metal table on wheels. Adell and Willie watched through tear-filled eyes as the nurses pulled up the guardrails on either side of the gurney. One of the older nurses looked at them sadly. Adell reached out and took her son's right hand in hers. It was to be the last time she would ever feel that hand.

"It's time to go," the old nurse said.

Adell leaned over the gurney, kissing DM on his hot, sweaty forehead. "I love you, DM," she whispered.

Willie touched his son's hand for one last fleeing moment. "Everything's gonna be all right, son," he assured him.

While their precious son was being wheeled away to the operating room, they each prayed a silent prayer.

Minutes turned into hours as the family waited. Willie passed the time by rolling and smoking one Prince Albert tobacco cigarette after another. Adell stood at the window, looking out onto the street below. Her tears had stopped. There was no room for them now. What seemed like an eternity of waiting finally came to an end when Dr. Blue entered the room.

"DM has survived the surgery. We removed the arm a few inches below the shoulder," he explained. "The main source of the infection has been eliminated. We'll be returning him to the ward soon. The rest is up to God."

The pain was almost unbearable for the tiny boy. A heavy bandage covered the stub where his arm used to be. Every few hours, nurses came to his bed to change the dressing. Each time the bandages were removed, DM screamed in pain. Adell wept with her son but tried not to let him see. She never left his side. Patiently, she remained beside his bed hour after hour, trying desperately to comfort him as best she could. His thin, frail body became skeletal. Dark circles surrounded his weak, deep-set eyes. The hospital staff brought him food, but he refused to eat.

Willie went back and forth from their home to the hospital as often as he could. With no means of transportation other than help from his neighbors, the visits were limited. He was torn between keeping up the farmwork and spending time with his son. Adell stayed with DM constantly. Because DM was being treated as an indigent patient, the hospital provided for his care only. Adell was given neither food nor drink, other than water. At times, two or more days would pass before she had so much as a soda cracker to eat. Occasionally one of the nuns would take pity on her and hand her a leftover piece of bread from off the serving cart.

Cora Huett, one of Adell's sisters, lived some forty miles away from the hospital at Babe Oaks Crossing between Prattville and Marbury. Cora was a hefty woman with dark, wavy, shoulder-length hair and powder-blue eyes. Even though she was a large woman, she bore a pretty face with a smile to match. When Cora could somehow come up with money to buy food, she would thumb her way to the hospital in Montgomery to bring Adell a hot dog or hamburger. Often, this was the only food Adell would have all week. Although she felt hunger, the constant lump in her throat made the food hard to swallow. She remained in eternal fear of her son dying.

Day after day, Adell remained close to her young son as he rolled and tumbled from side to side, writhing in pain. Green flies tried steadfastly to land on the place where DM's arm used to be. She kept a discarded rolled-up newspaper close by to swat them away. At times she felt as if she was dead herself. Her arms and legs felt limp from exhaustion. The only sleep she was able to get was when Willie or someone in the family came to relieve her for a few precious hours; even then her sleep was fretful.

While DM remained in the hospital, Imogene stayed with Adell's mother, Lula Culpepper, and her Aunt Cora at Babe Oaks Crossing. Imogene didn't like staying with her Big Mama, as she was called by her grandchildren, but she had no choice. Big Mama was very strict and had peculiar ways. Imogene worried about her younger brother and prayed every night that he would get better so they could all go home and be together again.

One day a few weeks after DM's surgery, Imogene was helping her grandmother snap a bowl of green beans. "Big Mama," Imogene asked, "is my brother gonna die?"

Without stopping what she was doing, her grandmother answered bluntly, "I don't know, Imogene. The Lord takes us all when it's our time to go. They've cut his arm off, but if it's his time to go, cuttin' his arm off won't do no good a'tall."

Imogene thought her grandmother to be hard-hearted and

hoped it wasn't DM's time to go and that he would get better soon. She missed her mama and daddy. She missed her little brother. She even missed Julius and Willie Charles. She also missed being at home, where she felt safe. Alone at night, she prayed.

Slowly DM's body began to heal, and he was allowed to go home for the first time in over two months. Their prayers had been answered. He had looked death in the eye and survived. However, his survival was just the beginning of the challenges he would have to face. He was now a one-arm boy in a two-arm world.

To complicate matters, an x-ray the doctors had taken of DM's spine revealed a malformation. His spine was growing crooked. Dr. Dawson, a pediatric specialist in Montgomery, believed this was caused as a direct result of the infection that occurred in his arm. Before leaving the hospital, a plaster cast was placed on DM's body from his shoulders down to just below his hips. Although he was healing, his body remained frail from lack of eating.

"DM is still very weak," warned Dr. Dawson. "It is extremely important to get nourishment into him any way you can. Feed him anything he wants, regardless of what it is or when he asks for it."

Although DM was very glad to be home with his family, he still refused to eat. His frail body was down to mere skin and bones. Adell tried everything. The two things he would eat were boiled eggwhites and an occasional biscuit with sugar and butter on it. On the rare occasions when DM asked for food, Adell fixed it for him.

After DM returned home from the hospital, Willie's mother, Katie Lou, came to visit the family. Katie Lou was a strict woman. She thought giving DM food when it wasn't mealtime was completely unnecessary. She and Adell were seated at the kitchen table, peeling potatoes for their evening meal. Katie Lou began talking to Adell about DM and his not wanting to eat. "If ya wouldn't feed that boy all durin' the day," she scolded Adell, "he'd eat when everybody else eats."

Adell politely ignored Mrs. Bone's comments. A few minutes later, DM called to her from the other room, asking for some boiled eggwhites. Adell immediately reached for a boiled egg and began peeling it. DM hobbled into the room just as she finished peeling it. When all the tiny pieces of the shell were completely removed, she broke the egg apart, removed the yolk, and handed DM the boiled eggwhite he had asked for.

Katie Lou shook her head in disbelief. "Are ya gonna give him that after what I just said?" she asked sarcastically.

Adell turned and looked directly at her mother-in-law. Although she had been taught never to be disrespectful to her elders, she answered her emphatically, "Yes! I'm gonna give him these eggwhites. I'm gonna give 'em to him anytime he asks for 'em and anything else he wants, for that matter."

That was the end of that.

During the time Willie and Adell stayed at the hospital with DM, the crops had fallen into disrepair. The grass and weeds had taken over. The farmwork was completely out of control. Willie knew there was no way he could get the crops back to normal by himself. He worried constantly about how he would feed his family the coming winter.

Folks in the community decided the Bone family needed their help. Friends and neighbors organized a day to work the fields. Some came by wagon, others by automobiles. They brought plows, mules, hoes, and rakes. Some worked in the cottonfield, others in the cornfield. It was hot, exhausting work, but everyone knew it had to be done if the Bone family was going to survive. They also knew that had the shoe been on the other foot, Willie and Adell would have done the same for them. There were so many people who showed up to help they were able to get the situation under control in only one day's time. The corn was harvested, the cotton picked, and the field readied for next year's planting. Willie and Adell felt extremely grateful and blessed. Although a dark shadow had loomed over their family, the kindness shown by the community gave them a new light on which to focus.

Regardless of the fact that it had been a very hard year for the Bone family, Mr. Patrick still wanted his half of the crops. Although Walter Patrick was a good man, he was a businessman first. The farmer did the work, and in exchange Mr. Patrick got his half for the use of his land. Some folks in the area felt he should have forgiven that year's debt, but Willie knew Mr. Patrick had always done right by him. He didn't begrudge Mr. Patrick for taking what was rightfully his. Life goes on regardless of the hurdles there are to climb.

Day-to-day life slowly returned to normal. Wood needed to be chopped and stacked on the porch. Adell had canning to catch up on. Imogene would have to help. After all, she was now eight years old. As soon as a cold spell came along, there would need to be a hog killing.

A month or so before hog killing time, the hog was fed as much as he would eat in order to fatten him up. Every part of the hog was used for something. Lard cooked down from the fat was needed to cook with, hopefully enough to last the year. Lye soap made from the fat was needed for washing the clothes. Cracklings, the leftover results of cooking down the fat, could be added to cornbread before baking. It gave the bread a wonderful flavor, not to mention added nourishment.

The meat from the hog was salted down then hung in the smokehouse over a hickory fire and smoked to preserve it. The head was boiled to make souse. The feet were either pickled or used for seasoning. The liver was boiled and mashed along with added spices to make liver pudding. The hog's intestines, called chitterlings, could be fried and scrambled with eggs. Even the casing that surrounded the intestines was cleaned out and used to make links of sausage. Nothing went to waste at hog killing time.

As everyone went about their daily chores, DM was busy relearning everything he'd ever learned. When faced with this type of adversity, it is much easier to let others do for you, but DM came from good stock. Although it was hard for Willie and Adell to watch him struggle, they knew he would have to figure out how to face these hurdles on his own. Everyone in the family had to pull their own weight regardless of their circumstances.

What some people looked at as a disability, DM looked at as a hindrance. He was young yet determined to be like everyone else. Therefore, he found ways to handle almost anything that came his way. When wood needed chopping, he knew he would have to figure out a way to chop it using one arm. If the crops needed tending, he would have to tend them with one arm. When the cow needed milking, he would have to do it with one hand. When it was time to slop the hogs, he would need to carry the slop bucket to the pen with only one arm. If he wanted to climb a tree, he would have to climb it using one arm. The fact was, he had one arm and he would need to face every task with a dauntless determination if he wanted to survive and prosper.

Shortly after returning home, one of the first encumbrances he had to conquer happened when he asked for his slingshot.

"I'm sorry, son," Adell said to him. "There ain't no way ya can shoot a slingshot with one arm."

DM dropped his head.

Willie saw the disappointment on his young son's face. "Give him his slingshot, Adell," he said. "He might just surprise ya."

Adell looked at Willie with dismay in her eyes. Reluctantly she reached for the slingshot hanging on a peg next to the back door and handed it to him. DM took the slingshot out back. Adell watched out the kitchen window with tear-filled eyes as her tiny son, still wearing the thigh-length body cast, struggled to find a way to shoot a rock with it.

Imogene was watching too. She felt sorry for her little brother. He had always loved shooting his slingshot. Now with only one arm, shooting it was next to impossible. She wondered how he would cope with this reality. Suddenly it came to her. She bent over, picked up a small round rock, and handed it to him.

"Ya don't need that old slingshot," she told him. "Ya can throw a rock better than anybody I know. Throw the rock instead of shootin' it from a slingshot."

DM threw the slingshot on the ground and did as she suggested. As he had been born right-handed, throwing a rock with his left hand was somewhat awkward. The first time, the rock went about ten feet then landed with a thump. DM started to cry.

Imogene reached for another rock and handed it to him. "Here. Try again," she insisted. "You'll get it if ya just keep tryin'. Surely ya ain't gonna let some old rock get the better of ya, are ya?"

Through sniffles and tears, DM did try again. The next time, the rock went a little farther, and the next time even farther. That was how it was. He learned to try. If one way didn't work, he tried another. Every task was a trial and every trial a task. More often than not, his persistence won out. Before long, DM learned to carry his own weight around the farm.

While DM was still confined in his cast, he would often sit for hours on the wood-plank front porch steps, watching and listening for cars and trucks to go by their house. Mr. Al Deason and a crew of men were logging down by the swamp near their house. Mr. Deason had several older logging trucks he used to haul logs. Years of wear had rusted out the mufflers. One of DM's favorite things to do was sit on the porch and listen for the big trucks as they topped the nearby hill. When the trucks changed gears, they often backfired, making everyone within earshot jump; this was much to the delight of the young, mischievous boy.

Every so often, a plane could be heard flying overhead. It was a rare occurrence and a special treat for everyone. If the family was in the house, they all ran outside to find where the sound was coming from. Once the plane was located, they watched until it was completely out of sight. DM would sit and dream about what it might be like to fly high above the clouds in one of the big, shiny planes.

After six months, the family made a trip back to Montgomery for DM's cast to finally be removed. His back was straight, and he seemed to be getting better. Anxiously, DM and his parents waited to see what Dr. Dawson would have to say. DM sat near his mother, holding tightly to her arm. He hated going to the doctor. Doctors usually meant pain, and DM wanted no part of it. He hated the smell of disinfectant. The cries of other young patients in the room next to his were reminiscent of the cries he had heard nightly in the ward at St. Margaret's. As soon as Dr. Dawson entered the room, the very sight of him frightened DM, and he began to cry. In order to get DM to sit still, Dr. Dawson made him a promise.

"If you will be a good boy, DM, I will give you a bright, shiny dime."

Money of any kind was hard to come by, and a dime was a lot of money to a four-year-old. Although the pain was hard to bear and having the cast cut off his body was scary, DM held back his tears so he could get his dime.

With his dime in hand, DM wanted to spend it as soon as they left the doctor's office. Down the street from Dr. Dawson's office was a small mom-and-pop grocery store. Willie and Adell took DM into the store to let him choose what he wanted to buy. Everything looked delicious. It took him a while to decide. Finally he chose a bag of cookies. The delectable shortbread cookies were topped with marshmallow cream and coconut, filled with a cherry filling. Once he tasted them, he was pleased with his choice. They were the best cookies DM had ever tasted. The cookies were the first food in a long time that actually tasted good to him. He didn't stop eating until every cookie was gone.

DM seemed well on his way to being his old self again until one day a short time later, Adell discovered a knot on the back of DM's head. She immediately panicked. "Oh my God!" she screamed to Willie. "Look at this knot! What do ya think it could be, Willie? Surely it's not the infection come back. They've cut off his arm, but they can't cut off his head."

Willie tried to console Adell, but with little luck. Once again, Willie called on Junior Mims to drive DM to see yet another doctor. Dr. Skinner was a bone specialist as well as a surgeon. Dr. Skinner carefully examined the swelling on the back of DM's head.

"It appears to be a lesion," he said. "I will need to lance it. He will need to be put to sleep for the procedure."

As Doctor Skinner thumbed through DM's medical records, DM clung to his mother's side. "It says here on his medical records that he is having trouble with his tonsils," Dr. Skinner continued. "While he is under the anesthetic, we might as well remove his tonsils at the same time."

"Do whatever ya think is best, Doc," Willie replied.

DM was put to sleep, the knot lanced and his tonsils removed. The infection on his head cleared up, and DM slowly grew stronger.

One day, Willie and Adell went out to the corncrib to shuck and shell corn, which would later be taken to the mill to have ground into cornmeal. DM wanted to help so Willie handed him an ear of corn and told him to feed the chickens. DM sat down at the edge of the corncrib floor. He managed to knock off a kernel or two of corn at a time with his one good hand and throw it out to the chickens in the yard. A large, dark red rooster strutted around boldly among the hens. He was a mean rooster and had twice before flogged Adell on her legs when she was trying to gather eggs.

The rooster took a position about thirty feet away from the corncrib. Suddenly and without warning, he charged straight for DM's head. Holding onto DM's hair with his beak, he spurred him directly in his face. His long, sharp talons tore open a gaping hole near the corner of his eye. DM screamed in pain. Blood flew from his open wounds. Adell grabbed for her son. Willie grabbed for the rooster.

Fleeing for his life, the ten-pound fowl flew from the corncrib. Willie flung several ears of dried corn at him, which he somehow managed to dodge. Willie called to his dog, Nero. "Catch 'im, boy!" he yelled. Obediently, Nero chased the rooster around the yard several times. Once when he ran him past the corncrib, Willie picked up a brand-new washtub and threw it at the rooster. The tub hit the ground with such force it split open at the seam, ruining the $1.25 washtub. That made Willie even angrier. Eventually Nero cornered the old rooster, and Willie was able to capture him. Straight away, he carried him to the chopping block. That night, the family ate him for supper.

As DM regained his strength, his will to accomplish more grew stronger too. As the days turned into months, he continued to improve. Willie continued to insist he carry his weight around the farm, which meant bringing in stove wood, carrying in water from the well, and picking cotton. It was hard, but DM was determined not to let his disability get the better of him. Whatever the chore might be, DM figured out a way to do it using his one good hand.

However, by no means was DM a perfect little angel. He had his mischievous moments, just like the rest of the children. Imogene called him downright mean. She often accused her parents, especially her mother, of letting him get by with things she would never let the others get by with. Deep down, Imogene knew it was because he'd lost his arm, but in her eyes, that still didn't make it right.

Cats were never one of DM's most favorite animals. He loved dogs, but cats were altogether different. There were always cats around the farm. Most of the time they stayed around the corncrib or near the barn, in search of mice. One of the mama cats had recently delivered a litter of young kittens. They were around six to eight weeks old. Adell had drawn a washtub full of water from the well earlier that morning. It was sitting near the back steps. DM decided it would be funny to throw one of the kittens into the water to see if it could swim. However, as soon as he threw it in, it managed to jump right back out. He caught another one of the kittens and threw it in the water. It too jumped out as fast as he had thrown it in.

The third kitten was harder to catch, but its fate soon became dire. This time he decided that instead of just throwing the kitten in the water, he would hold it under the water to see what it would do. DM managed to hold the poor kitten under the water for maybe five seconds. Terrified, the kitten retaliated by biting DM's hand with her tiny, razor-sharp teeth. Fighting desperately to get away, the frightened kitten clawed at his hand with her back feet, leaving bloody claw marks up and down his hand and wrist. Immediately DM threw the half-drowned kitten to the ground, began to cry, and ran into the house.

"Mama! One of them stupid kittens bit me!" he yelled to her.

Adell laid down the shirt she was mending and reached for his hand. "Bit you?" She gasped. "Let me see."

Adell wiped the blood from DM's hand with her apron. Four teeth marks were clearly visible where the kitten had bitten him. His wrist was covered with claw marks.

Willie knew his mischievous son all too well. "What did ya do to make it bite ya?" he asked.

DM dropped his head. "I didn't do nothin'," he lied. "It just bit me for no reason."

Adell immediately became concerned. "Reckon 'em cats got rabies from somewhere and gone mad?"

Willie ruffled the hair on DM's head and grinned. "It's more likely he did something to it to make it bite and scratch him like that."

DM continued to fret. "I didn't do nothin'. I swear. It just bit me for no reason."

Willie and Adell decided they should look for themselves. If the cats did have rabies, they would have to be destroyed. After searching for nearly ten minutes, the kittens were finally located. They were sitting on the windowsill at the front of the house, licking themselves dry. All three of them appeared to be soaked to the skin with water. Willie knew then exactly what had happened. The wet ground around the washtub and three soaking-wet kittens were all the proof Willie needed. It wasn't rabies that had driven them mad; it was DM trying to drown them. Ordinarily he would have been given a whipping for what he'd done but, Willie and Adell decided he'd been punished enough by the kitten. After all, he was going to have a mighty sore hand for several days to come.

~~~

Sometimes in life, it seems a fellow just can't get any luck at all. Willie Bone was one of those fellows. Shortly after spring planting, he was busy cutting up stove wood when his ax flinched off a stick of wood, striking him directly in the foot. Willie always kept his tools razor sharp. When the ax hit, it went clean through his boot, all the way to the bone. Adell wanted to take him to the doctor to have it sewn up, but Willie wouldn't hear of it. "Doctors cost too much," he said. "It'll heal sooner or later; just bind it up."

Adell wound a strip from an old bedsheet around his foot as tightly as she could to stop the bleeding. For several weeks, Willie remained immobile. While he was down, Julius, Willie Charles, and Adell tended the crops. As soon as he could walk again, Willie went back to work.

———

In late summer and early fall, cotton, which was the main crop in the area, was ready for picking. Everyone in the Bone family had to help pick the cotton. Once it was picked, it was loaded onto a mule-drawn wagon and hauled into town to Cleave Billingsley's cotton gin. It was not unusual to see fifteen to twenty wagons around the gin at one time waiting to unload. Once the cotton was ginned and the seeds blown into a holding barn, it was sent to Selma to be pressed and graded.

During cotton-picking time it was rare for any of the Bone children to get to go to town. Usually they remained at home to continue picking cotton. However, on occasion Willie would let one of the younger children go with him. Since DM was too young to pick cotton and still weak from all he'd been through, he was allowed to accompany Willie to the gin. He loved going to town with his daddy. If the cotton was bringing a decent price, he could sometimes talk his daddy into buying him an ice cream cone.

The road into town was rough. Ben ambled along slowly, pulling the heavily weighted wagon through sandpits and over ruts. As Willie and DM neared Billingsley School, Willie noticed Ben's right front shoe was loose.

"Looks like Ben has a loose shoe," Willie said.

"Does that mean we'll be goin' to see Mr. Dill Dall?" DM asked with anticipation.

"I reckon that's what it means all right," Willie answered.

Dill Dall Gray was the town blacksmith. He was a big man with massive arms and chest. He was an older man with a big, burly beard. His salt-and-pepper beard always had tobacco stains at the corners of his mouth. Although he was a white man, it was sometimes hard to tell. He was always covered in black soot from the smoke and ashes bellowing from the forge. He was a kind man with a jovial personality. DM liked going to Mr. Dill Dall's blacksmith shop to watch him work.

On their journey into town, P. L. Donahue's store was the first building they came upon. It was just past Billingsley School. As they neared the long, narrow, wooden plank store, Willie turned to DM "We'll stop up here at Pink Donahue's store. I'll see if I can tighten Ben's shoe good enough to get us to the gin."

DM liked Mr. Donahue, or Pink, as everyone called him. He was a tall, thin, wiry-looking man. He also had quite the knack for playing tricks on folks. DM recalled the day a traveling salesman came through town. The rather short, chunky salesman was trying to be funny.

Looking up at the nearly seven-foot-tall storeowner, he placed his hand to his mouth and yelled, "How's the weather up there?"

Rather than finding it funny, Pink became irritated by the young man's comment. Rather peeved, Pink looked down at the short, little man and replied, "Well, there's a telephone on my butt. Why don't ya call up here and see?"

DM laughed every time he heard his daddy tell that story.

Willie stopped in front of Pink's store long enough to tap

down three of the nails holding the horseshoe to Ben's hoof. When he was finished, he crawled back onto the seat of the wagon. "That will have to do till we can get to the blacksmith shop," he said. Picking up the reins, he slapped Ben on the rump. Slowly, the heavily loaded wagon began to move forward, and they were once again on their way.

As Willie and DM drove past the gristmill, they saw Joe Jones, the owner of the mill. He was out front helping to unload a wagon filled with bushel baskets of corn. Unlike some gristmills that were powered by running water, Joe used a tractor motor to pull the wheels, which in turn ground the corn. He worked on toll with the farmers, which meant he took 10 percent of the corn as payment for his services.

As they passed, Joe threw up his hand and waved good morning. "How's it goin', Willie?"

Willie tipped his hat, and DM waved and smiled. "Got a mule with a loose shoe," Willie answered. "Soon as I get this cotton to the gin, I'll be headed over to Dill Dall's place to get him to make us a new one."

"I 'spect he's pretty busy these days," Joe said. "Lots of folks been comin' into town this week with their cotton. Seems like everybody's havin' problems with broken wagon wheels, loose shoes, or plows that need sharpenin'." Joe reached for another bushel of corn. "Y'all take it easy now, ya hear."

Willie nodded.

Down the road a little farther, they came to the L. C. Lewis filling station. There weren't a lot of people in the area who owned automobiles. The few who did usually purchased their gas at Mr. Lewis's store. Out front was a frame lift used to drive the cars onto in order to change the oil or work on the underside of the car. He also owned a one-and-a-half-ton truck, which he used to carry people into Prattville. He charged them fifty cents to ride with him into town. However, folks were more than happy to pay it when they needed something they couldn't get in Billingsley.

A barbershop located in the back of Mr. Lewis's store was run by Leon "Shortie" Seymour. You could get your hair cut for a dime, buy an ice cream cone for a nickel, and catch up on the town gossip all at the same time. As they passed, DM and Willie waved to Shortie and several other men who were standing out front of the store. DM could almost taste the ice cream cone one of the men was eating.

By the time they arrived at Cleave Billingsley's cotton gin, several wagons were already ahead of them. The gin was run by a steam engine. DM remembered well the day he stepped barefoot onto one of the steam lines running between the gin and the blower. His foot was severely burned, leaving huge blisters along the bottom of his bare foot. From that day forward he learned to steer clear of the hot steam lines.

Once the cotton was ginned, a blower was used to blow the seeds into a holding barn next to the gin. One of the workers told Willie it would be a while before they were ready for his load. Willie decided to unhitch Ben from the wagon and head on over to the blacksmith shop.

Willie put DM on Ben's strong back so he could ride to the blacksmith shop. DM liked riding on Ben. It made him feel big. Things looked different from atop the mule's back. It was kind of like when he rode on his daddy's shoulders. It was as though it was he who was tall, and he liked feeling tall.

Up the hill was Walter Patrick's store. Mr. Patrick's store was where Willie's family bought most of their supplies. Mr. Patrick was a well-to-do man and stayed quite busy with his affairs. Cooter Headley ran the dry goods store for him and later purchased the store himself. DM secretly hoped his daddy would stop so he could get an ice cream, but he didn't.

"We'll stop by here on our way back," Willie said as he

passed the store. "Your mama wants me to pick her up a sack of flour. Got to have 'em biscuits every mornin'."

As they passed by the town hall, several men were sitting out front on a long wooden bench. Ira Huett was one of them. Ira was known for two things: his ribbon cane syrup and his smooth-as-silk moonshine whiskey.

Ira spit a stream of amber onto the ground. "Mornin', Willie."

"Mornin'," Willie replied. "'Bout time to start cookin' up some syrup, ain't it, Ira?"

"Won't be long," Ira said, spitting another streak of amber. "I see y'all got a little horseshoe problem."

"Yep. We're on our way up to Dill Dall Gray's now."

As Willie continued up the road, Ira called after him, "Tell Dill Dall I'll be comin' by to pick up my wagon wheel as soon as I git rested a bit." Willie threw up his hand and nodded his head to let Ira know he had heard him.

Just past town hall was John Will Patillo's store. He was Ira Huett's main supplier of sugar and the parts needed to keep Ira's moonshine operation going. Most everyone around Billingsley knew about this arrangement, except for the revenuers, of course. Mr. Patillo and Ira did their best to keep it that way. Bug Durden ran the store for Mr. Patillo.

Next came Richard Thomas's store. DM liked going to Mr. Thomas's store. He had a BB gun on display that DM wanted badly. Every time he got the chance, he would ask Mr. Thomas if he could hold it.

"Ya ought to buy that gun for your boy," Mr. Thomas would say to Willie.

"Maybe one day," was all Willie would ever say.

A short distance past John Will Patillo's store was a small store with living quarters above it. Mr. Claude Patilla owned the store and the sawmill in town. He was a wealthy man who also owned a good bit of property in the area.

Across the road from the main part of town was the train depot. Several people stood out front waiting for the arrival of the first train of the day. As DM rode past them on the back of old Ben, he wondered where these people were going. Some of them he recognized; others were faces he'd never seen before.

The main entrance to the depot faced the side street running perpendicular to the main street in town. Across this street was the post office. DM noticed several people going in and out of the building carrying letters and packages to be mailed.

Past the post office on another street that ran parallel to Main Street was Billingsley First Baptist Church. DM loved hearing the church bells ringing on Sunday morning. When his family attended church, this was where they usually went.

On the next street over were the offices of two small-town doctors, Dr. Downs and Doctor Campbell. Both of the doctors had their practices in the homes where they also lived. Dr. Campbell's house was always very dark and dreary with long, heavy curtains hanging over the windows. Neither of them was a specialist, but they served the community well for things like colds, broken bones, stitches, and delivering babies.

The sound of a motorcar coming down the road caught DM's attention. The roads were sandy and rutted, making driving the gasoline-run engines difficult. DM immediately recognized the pickup truck owned by Mr. Robert Wilkins as it came rumbling down the dusty dirt road. It was the first brand-new truck he'd ever seen. He'd heard the men in town talking about how Mr. Wilkins had paid eight hundred dollars for the truck. That was more money than DM could ever imagine. Mr. Wilkins waved to them as he passed, leaving dust and dirt flying through the air.

Just out of the city limits was the sawmill, owned and run by Mr. Al Deason. Mr. Deason was the wealthiest man in Billingsley. His mill had the capability to take a log from raw cut to a finished piece of lumber. He also owned several logging trucks used for hauling logs to the mill. These were the big trucks DM listened for while he was recuperating from his surgery. DM was glad none of those trucks was nearby at the time. Ben hated it when they backfired. It always scared him half to death. Sometimes he would take off running like a cat with its tail on fire. One time when one of those trucks back-fired, Ben ran off, and it took his daddy nearly half the day to find him.

When Willie and DM finally arrived at the blacksmith shop, Dill Dall was busy hammering out a long rod of hot steel on his anvil. The heavy cross-preen hammer Dill Dall was using sent tiny sparks from the red-hot steel spitting into the air. Fiery crimson coals burned hot in the forge.

When Dill Dall had the steel shaped to his satisfaction, he lifted the flattened steel with a pair of tongs then immersed it in the quenching vat to cool. Pushing his protective goggles off his eyes onto his forehead, Dill Dall looked up. "Howdy, Mr. Bone," he said. "Didn't hear ya come in."

"My mule has a loose shoe," Willie said. "I was wonderin' if ya could take a look at it."

"I'd be glad to," Dill Dall replied. Dill Dall walked over to Ben and lifted his foot. "Yep. He's gonna need a new shoe all right."

There were a variety of shoes hanging on pegs along the shop wall. Dill Dall walked over to the wall and selected the size needed for Ben. After comparing the shoe to Ben's hoof, he carried it over to the forge and placed it inside to heat. When the shoe was red hot, he removed it from the forge with a furrier's tong. Holding it securely atop the anvil, he began striking the shoe with a steel hammer. Hot sparks danced into the air like tiny fairies. Once the shoe was properly propor-tioned to his satisfaction, he doused it in the quenching vat, allowing it to cool before attaching it to Ben's hoof.

Once the shoe was cooled, he lifted Ben's leg, placing it

firmly between his knees. Arranging the shoe in place, he made a cleat on each end of the shoe opening to hold the shoe in place and keep it from slipping; this was done by bending about a half inch or so of the shoe around the back of Ben's heel. He then reached inside his leather apron and took out several horseshoe nails. Being careful not to injure the frog of the mule's foot, the nails were then hammered into the hard part of the hoof. Once the nails were all the way through, Dill Dall clipped the ends of the nails and bent them over to hold the shoe securely in place. Using a sharp pair of clippers, he then clipped the rough edges off the hoof, and the job was done.

Dill Dall patted Ben on the rump. "Thar ya are, old feller."

"Thank ya, Dill Dall," Willie said. "I shore do appreciate ya doin' that for me."

Willie paid Mr. Gray. Then he and DM started back toward town. They stopped long enough at Mr. Patrick's store to pick up a sack of flour and buy DM a cone of ice cream and a penny jawbreaker. By the time they got back to the gin, the wagon was unloaded. Willie stood around for a while, talking to some of the other men who had also brought their cotton in to have it ginned. DM sat on the wagon seat, listening and sucking on his jawbreaker, taking it out of his mouth every so often to check its size. By noon they were on their way home. It had been a good morning. Little DM had enjoyed his trip to town. As he put the somewhat-smaller round ball of candy back into his mouth, he looked up at his daddy on the wagon seat beside him and smiled.

DM was around six years old when Willie insisted Adell make DM a pick sack for picking cotton. Regardless of his handicap, he had little choice but to pick right alongside the rest of the family. Adell used a twenty-four-pound flour sack to make the pick sack. DM was young, it was hot, and he hated having to pick cotton. He balked at the job at first, but Willie made him stay in the field anyway. He might not pick more than five to ten pounds of cotton all day, but pick cotton he did.

Families who lived in the same community helped each other. When one family's crop was ready for harvesting and the other family's was not, one would help the other in exchange for helping them when their crops were ready. Such was the case with the Williams family.

It was time for Will Williams' cotton to be picked. Ample rain during June and July had made the plants lush and green. The rainy months were followed by a hot, dry August, which made for perfect growing conditions for cotton. The bolls held huge mounds of white, fluffy fibers. Had it not been a sweltering ninety-eight degrees outside, one would have thought the fields were covered with snow.

The Williams' lived just down the way, behind the Patrick Place. Libby was Will's wife. She was known to be extremely strict on both her children and her grandchildren. Her youngest son, Morris, and one of her grandsons, Joe Moore, were supposed to be helping her pick their cotton. Instead, they were doing more playing around than picking.

"All right, Morris, and ya too, Joe," Mrs. Libby warned sternly. "Ya younguns best quit all your foolin' around and git to pickin' this cotton. It shore ain't gonna pick itself."

DM was also there that day to help pick the cotton. He knew all too well not to agitate Mrs. Libby. He had laid witness to her temper way too many times to count. He also knew his daddy would skin him alive if he didn't give Mrs. Libby an honest day's work. Steadily, DM continued to pick. He watched out of the corner of his eye as Joe and Morris proceeded to goof off instead of work. He knew how Mrs. Libby was, and he suspected she wasn't going to stand for that kind of foolishness for long.

Soon, just as DM had expected, Mrs. Libby warned them a second time. "Ya younguns best git to listenin' to me 'fore I have to git' ahold of ya. Ya best commence to pickin'. Don't make me have to get a stick after ya."

Through all her fussing at Joe and Morris, she never once uttered a word to DM. He knew to do what he could and stay busy. At the end of the day, when all the cotton sacks were weighed up, the truth was told. Although DM had only one arm, he had picked way more cotton than Joe and Morris put together. Mrs. Libby was as mad as a wet settin' hen at the two boys. In retaliation, she picked up a cotton stalk and beat the fire out of both of them. Joe and Morris blamed DM for getting a whipping. Both of them would hold that against DM for years to come. DM figured it was their own fault for not pulling their own weight.

Earlier that same year, the Williams had helped the Bone family chop their cotton. Flora Anne, one of the younger William's girls and Dee Anne, her sister, were helping too. All the children were playing around more than they should have, including DM. Jokingly, DM ran up behind Flora Anne to scare her. Unfortunately, at that very same moment, she drew back her hoe. The edge of the hoe caught DM squarely in the middle of his head, cutting a gash about an inch long into his scalp. Blood quickly covered his neck and back. The kids panicked and made a beeline to where the older folks were working.

Adell saw DM first. "Oh my Lord, DM!" she yelled in a panic. "What in the world has happened to ya now?"

Dee Anne was sobbing, frightened by the amount of blood flowing from the gash. "Flora Anne hit him on the head with her hoe."

Mrs. Libby angrily reached out, grabbing Flora Anne's dress collar. "Did ya do that, Flora Anne Williams?" she yelled, raising her hand to strike Flora Anne.

Flora Anne began to cry. She knew her mama was going to tan her hide good. "I didn't mean to, Mama," she cried as she tried to back away. "It was an accident."

DM quickly intervened. "It's okay, Mrs. Libby," DM explained. "It was partly my fault. Flora Anne didn't mean to hit me. I came up behind her. She didn't know I was there."

Flora Anne was grateful to DM for taking up for her. He kept her from getting a whipping from her mama and maybe even another one from her daddy. Had he not taken up for her and told the truth, she would have been punished severely; the scars on her back from previous beatings were proof of that.

The cut on DM's head was bad, it should have been stitched up by a doctor. However, folks didn't go to the doctor for just any old reason. Adell took DM back to the house, where she washed the wound out with soap and water as best she could. She then poured an ample amount of one-hundred-proof moonshine into the open cut. DM hollered so loud you could hear him all the way down to the Williams' place. To stop the bleeding, she covered the gaping wound with tar salve and a white cotton rag. Eventually it healed, leaving a scar that would remain with him for the rest of his life.

DM was around seven years old the first time he actually made money picking cotton for someone else. It was on Mr. Earl Friday's land. Mr. and Mrs. Friday were both good, honest, hardworking folks. They lived just down the road from the Patrick Place. His cotton crop was fully open, just right for picking.

Early that morning, DM took his cotton sack from off the wooden peg inside the cotton house, threw it over his shoulder, and headed down the road to Mr. Friday's house. Mr. Friday was sitting near the barn, shucking corn to feed his mule. He could feel the warm sun on his back. It felt good to his aching muscles. When Mr. Friday saw DM coming down the dusty dirt road carrying his pick sack on his back, he wondered what the little one-arm fellow was up to.

As DM neared the barn, he called to him, "Mornin', Mr. Friday."

Mr. Friday grinned at DM as he continued pulling the dry shucks from around the corn.

"Mornin', DM. What brings ya down this way?"

DM kicked at the ground with his toe. Facing toward the bright morning sun rising in the east made it difficult for DM to see the old man clearly. He peered up at Mr. Friday with one eye closed.

"How much will ya pay me to pick your cotton for ya? I need to make some money to buy me some ice cream."

Mr. Friday's grin widened. "So ya want to pick cotton for me, huh?"

"Yep. How much do ya pay?" DM said. A large red ant was crawling along the ground in front of him. He used his big toe to crush the little creature into the soft brown dirt. In seconds it wiggled free, quickly retreating to its mound nearby.

Mr. Friday rubbed his chin with his rough, weathered hand. "Well now, let me think. How 'bout I pay ya a penny a pound?"

A penny a pound sounded good to DM. Then and there he and Mr. Friday struck a deal. DM would pick cotton, Mr. Friday would weigh it up at the end of the day and pay him a penny a pound. With visions of ice cream cones dancing in his head, DM quickly set to work. The edges of the open bolls of cotton were sharp. His small hand was soon covered with tiny cuts and streaks of blood.

An hour or so after DM had been in the field, Mrs. Friday went out to take him a cool drink of water from the well. When she saw the cuts and scrapes on DM's hand, she shook her head. Reaching into her apron pocket, she pulled out a glove from which the ends of the fingers had been cut off.

"Here, DM, put this glove on your hand," she said. "Don't ya have a glove of your own to wear when ya pick cotton?"

"No ma'am," he answered. He extended his hand forward so Mrs. Friday could help him get it on. "The only glove I've got is the one I wear durin' the winter when it's real cold. Mama would skin me alive if I was to cut the fingers out of it."

The glove was slightly larger than DM's small hand. Mrs. Friday unpinned a safety pin from the front of her apron. She gathered the extra cloth around his wrist and secured it with the pin. When she was finished, she smiled. "Well, ya got a glove now. When you're done pickin' today, ya put it in your pickin' sack so ya always know where it is. Ain't no need of gettin' your one good hand all cut up like this."

DM thanked Mrs. Friday for the glove and the water, then went straight back to work. Around noon, Mrs. Friday came to the field once again. This time she was carrying two cold biscuits filled with thin slices of fried country ham and a glass of tea. "DM," she called to him from beneath the shade of a nearby tree. "Take a break and come eat some dinner. A hard-workin' boy needs to eat."

DM gladly obliged. He was sweaty and hot. When he reached the shade tree, he sat down on the ground and laid his cotton sack down beside him. Mrs. Friday handed him the glass of tea first. Although it had no ice in it, the tea was cool and refreshing. After he quenched his thirst, he reached for the biscuits. Mrs. Friday made good biscuits; they were almost as good as his mama's biscuits. The ham inside was a real treat too.

DM took a big bite. With his mouth full of biscuit and ham, he said to her, "This ham shore is good, Mrs. Friday. We've been outta ham for nigh onto three months now. I shore will be glad when we kill another hog."

Mrs. Friday smiled. "I'm glad ya like it, DM. It's the last of what we got too. I know it don't feel like it today, but it won't be long 'fore a cold spell will be a comin'."

When DM finished off the last of his biscuit and ham, he picked up his pick sack, drank his last swallow of tea, and went straight back to work. Mrs. Friday bid him good-bye then headed back toward the house in wonderment of the little one-arm boy's determination.

When the day ended and the cotton was weighed in, DM had picked a total of ten pounds. He'd made a dime for an entire day's work. He was proud of his dime and even prouder when he was able to buy an ice cream cone for a nickel and still have money left over.

Another way DM had of making money was selling peanuts. Along about the same time peanuts came in season, a road crew was working on the roads in the area. DM took some of the peanuts Adell had parched in the wood cookstove and put them in a brown paper sack. He carried them down to where the road crew was working.

"Hey, mister," he called to one of the men. "I've got a bag of parched peanuts here. I'll sell 'em to ya for a nickel. They're real good. My mama parched 'em herself. Ain't none of 'em burnt or nothin'."

The road worker took note of the little one-arm boy holding out his bag of peanuts. He suspected by the looks of the young boy's shabby clothes and bare feet that he was most likely from a poor sharecropper family.

The road worker reached into his pocket and pulled out a nickel. "Sure, son, I'll buy your sack of peanuts." The man handed DM his nickel. DM handed him the sack of peanuts.

To DM's surprise, the man took out one peanut then handed the sack back to him. "This is all I want. I ain't much on peanuts," he said.

DM had already put the nickel in his overalls pocket. He sure hated to see it go, but if the man didn't want the peanuts, he knew he'd have to give it back. Reluctantly, he set the bag of peanuts on the ground and reached inside his pocket to retrieve the nickel.

"Oh, I don't want the nickel, son. You can keep it. Maybe

some of the other fellers on the crew would like to buy the peanuts," the man added.

DM smiled happily. "Thanks, mister." He dropped the nickel back into his pocket.

Down the road a little farther, he asked another worker about buying the sack of peanuts. The second road worker bought the peanuts too. He also took one peanut then handed DM back the sack. In all, DM sold the same bag of peanuts five times that day.

With autumn came harvesttime. A plentiful corn crop was of utmost importance. Not only did the family need the corn, so did the farm animals. The mule used for plowing, the cow used for milking, the chickens that produced the eggs, even the hog they raised for butcher shared in the eating of the corn. After splitting the crops with Mr. Patrick, their remaining share of the corn was stored in the corncrib. Some of it was shucked, and a portion of it was taken to the mill for grinding. Sacks of fine white cornmeal meant cornbread on the table.

On a farm nothing was wasted. Even the cottonseeds from the cotton crop were ground up to make cottonseed meal. The husk from the seeds was added to the feed to provide another source of nutrition for the animals.

Late fall and a few straight days of cold weather was the best time for hog killing. The menfolk took care of killing the hog, removing the intestines, and scalding it down. Adell, Imogene, Julius, Willie Charles, and even DM usually helped with scraping off the bristly hair. It was hard, tiring work, but killing a hog meant meat on the table, lard to cook with, and food to nourish the family.

Raising off a hog for hog killing time actually started back in the spring when best friends Willie Parker and Willie Bone boarded Mr. Parker's Model-A Ford for their yearly trip to the nearby community of Independence, Alabama, their destination: the home of North Ivy Davis. Their goal was to buy a meat hog for the spring and summer growing-off season.

North Ivy, a well-respected black man, was known for raising some of the finest fattening hogs around. His hogs were a mix between a Duros, a solid-red hog, and a Poulan-China, a solid-black hog. Crossbreeding of these two varieties resulted in red hogs with black spots. Both men agreed North Ivy's hogs were the preferred breed, as they fattened off quickly, thus producing large amounts of lard.

By the time the two men arrived at North Ivy's home, it was closing in on nine o'clock in the morning. North Ivy was nowhere to be seen. Mr. Parker honked his car horn. Soon, North Ivy emerged from behind his barn, carrying an empty slop bucket. North Ivy was a slight-built man but strong as an ox. He was dark-skinned with short, black, curly hair and dark-brown eyes.

"Mornin', Mr. Parker. Mornin', Mr. Bone," he said, tipping his tattered black hat. "I's been a wonderin' when ya be by ta sees me. Gots some fine piglets dis year."

Mr. Parker turned the key to the off position. The motor coughed and sputtered to a halt. "Dang motorcars," he muttered under his breath.

Mr. Bone reached into the backseat to retrieve the corn sacks they'd brought along. The sacks would be used to put the pigs in for transporting back home.

North Ivy motioned the two men to follow him. He led them around the side of the barn to his pigpen out back. There among the mud and muck lay Lois, North Ivy's prize sow. Around her scampered ten young shoals. Each weighed between thirty and forty pounds, an ideal weight for buying purposes. The two men looked over each little pig carefully until they made their decision.

Mr. Parker pointed to an almost-solid-red one. "I'll take that one there. He's a handsome feller fer' a pig."

Mr. Bone chose one with a band of black around his neck and a big black spot on his rump. One by one, North Ivy and the two men hemmed the squealing, grunting little pigs into the corner, whereupon they were stuffed inside the corn sacks. The ends of the sacks were tied into a knot then placed in the trunk of the car.

North Ivy originally asked six dollars for each of the pigs. But after a few minutes of friendly bickering back and forth, he settled on five. The two men handed North Ivy his money then shook hands to seal the deal.

Mr. Bone smiled. "Nice doin' business with ya, Mr. Davis."

North Ivy smiled a wide grin. "Nice doin' business wit' ya too, Mr. Bone."

All summer long, the family made sure the hog was well-fed. A five-gallon bucket was placed in the kitchen next to the back door. Since hogs will eat just about anything, all leftovers, such as watermelon rinds, cabbage leaves, turnip scraps, apple cores, grease, even wash water, were placed in the bucket and fed to the growing young pig.

The cow was producing up to four gallons of milk a day. That much milk was way more than the family could consume. Since there was no way to keep the milk from spoiling, short of lowering it into the well, the pig was being fed the extra milk. The goal was to produce a six-to seven-hundred-pound hog by the time the first good cold spell rolled around.

Although Willie purchased most of his pigs from North Ivy, one year he decided to purchase a young sow from Mr. Sam Hayes. Mr. Hayes and his family lived about a quarter of a mile back down behind the Patrick place. The little pig had been allowed to run loose for so long she didn't like being penned up. No sooner than they would put her in a pen, she would simply jump the fence and head back to Sam's house.

Each time she ran off, they would bring her back just to have her leave again. Willie and DM spent many a day looking for her. No sooner than they'd get her home, she'd run off again. DM decided she was one hog he was going to be glad to see frying in the skillet and hanging in the smokehouse. At least then he wouldn't have to hunt her down anymore.

Willie's corn crop had done well that year. As an answer to his problem, Willie figured the only way to keep her from running off was to fatten her up so much she wouldn't be able to jump the fence anymore. Every day he gave the young pig twenty-five ears of corn to eat. She also got scraps from the dinner table, leftover watermelons, milk, and cottonseed meal. Before long she had grown into a seven-hundred-pound hog. In fact, she was so fat she ended up having to lie down to eat.

The first cold spell of the season meant it was hog killing time. Since hog killing was such hard work, neighbors helped neighbors. When the job was done, they shared the meat with one another.

It was mid-October. When Willie sat down to eat breakfast that morning, he could feel the cold in his bones. "There's a chill in the air," he remarked. "'Spect we'll be gettin' some fire-makin' weather in the next few days. It ain't apt to last long. I figure to go talk to Mr. Friday and Willie Parker to see if they want to help us kill that hog out thar."

Imogene poured milk into her corn mush. "Bet we'll get a pile of lard outta' that old sow, Daddy."

Willie shook his head in agreement. "I do believe she's the fattest hog we've ever raised."

DM threw up his arm as though he was pointing a gun. "Can I shoot her, Daddy?" he asked anxiously.

Willie drank a swallow of coffee before answering. "I don't think you're quite old enough to shoot a hog, son. Maybe next year."

Adell got up from the table. As she reached for the pot of

coffee sitting on the stove, she spoke directly to Willie. "Ya best be gettin' some salt from old man Patrick. We're gonna need some to salt her down with."

"After I talk to Mr. Friday, I'll go on into Billingsley and pick up some. I'll catch Willie Parker on my way back," he replied.

"Can I ride to Billingsley with ya, Daddy?" Imogene begged.

"Ya best stay here and help your mama get things ready for tomorrow," answered Willie. "I'll take DM with me. He can help me load the salt onto the wagon."

"I don't never get to go nowhere," Imogene fretted. "If I was a boy, I could go with ya to Billingsley. Boys always get to go places. Girls never get to go nowhere. I don't like being a girl."

DM reached for his warm jacket. "Yeah, but if ya was a boy, you'd have to clean the guts out of the pig like us menfolk do."

"I don't care," fussed Imogene. "At least I'd get to go to town once in a while."

The next morning, everyone got up before the rooster crowed. A chill filled the room. Willie built a fire in the fireplace first then lit the kindling under the wood in the stove. While Imogene dipped some water from the water bucket into a dishpan to heat for washing dishes later, Willie went outside to start a fire under the big, black wash pot. Since it was still dark, Adell lit the kerosene lamp and placed it in the center of the table. Imogene filled the coffee pot with water. Adell put several spoonfuls of coffee grounds into the pot, then placed the pot on the stove to boil.

"By this time tomorrow," she said to Imogene, "we'll have some fresh hog meat to go with the biscuits."

Just then Willie opened the back door and hurried inside. He shivered and rubbed his hands together to warm them. "It's good and cold outside. Ain't nothin' no better than fried hog meat, fried eggs, and your cat-head biscuits, Adell." His mouth began watering at the very thought of it. DM sleepily walked into the kitchen, licking his lips. "Can we have some ribbon cane syrup with it too, Daddy?"

"Well, I 'spect Ira Huett might just have some ribbon cane syrup we could trade him for a piece of fresh hog meat," Willie answered. "He ought to be cookin' some off here in the next few days, if he ain't already. In fact, it's 'bout time we were cuttin' our sugar cane for him to cook down into syrup."

By the time breakfast was over, the sun was just beginning to rise. Willie went out to check on the fire he'd built under the black iron pot in the yard. The fire was blazing hot, and the water inside it had begun to boil.

Suddenly Mr. Friday and Willie Parker appeared around the corner of the house. Mr. Parker was wearing his heavy work coat with a gray woolen scarf around his neck. "Mornin', Willie," he called.

Willie added another log to the fire under the pot. "Mornin' to ya, Mr. Friday. Looks like it's gonna be a fine day for a hog killin'."

Willie Parker eased in close to the warm fire. "Have ya got your gun loaded and ready?"

"It's ready and waitin'," answered Willie. "Ya know, that youngest boy of mine asked if he could shoot that hog."

Mr. Friday laughed and slapped his knee. "Danged if he won't try anything. Ain't never known a boy that young to like shootin' a gun or huntin' no more than he does. Ya gonna let him shoot it?"

"Not this time," answered Willie. "He ain't old enough to realize it's different killin' something ya raised than it is shootin' a wild animal. Maybe I'll let him shoot the next one. He'll be a year older by then." Willie picked up the .22 rifle, which was leaned up against the side of the house. He and Mr. Friday walked slowly out to the hog pen.

Willie was used to killing meat animals. It was a part of life. Each animal on the farm played an important part in the family's survival. Still, looking an animal you'd raised from a baby in the eyes as you pulled the trigger to end its life was never easy, even for a hardened man like Willie. That was why he'd chosen to make DM wait another year until he was older.

When Willie reached the hog pen, the big sow rose slowly to her feet. They had withheld food from her the day before, giving her only water to drink. She was ready to be fed. She was the fattest hog Willie had raised in a long time. She was so fat she could barely walk. Willie raised his gun, pointing it directly at the center of her head. For a fleeting moment their eyes met. A single shot echoed across the fields. The hog stumbled, falling to one side. Her muscles quivered.

With everyone working, by the end of the day, the hog had been killed, cleaned, cut into pieces, and the meat salted down. After cooking off the fat, they ended up with three five-gallon buckets of lard, enough to last the year. After all the trouble they'd had with the sow about keeping her in the pen, they were glad to finally see her as a meal on their table.

During the lean years of the Depression, people did what they had to do to survive. The Bone, Parker, and Friday families were only three of many who lived during those hard times. Poor country people didn't have the luxury of going to the store to buy a steak to throw on the grill. Pork was their main source of meat. With no refrigeration readily available, there was no way to keep meat from spoiling other than canning or smoking it. Therefore, people simply enjoyed the fresh pork while it lasted. When it was gone, they waited anxiously for next year's first good cold spell, when they'd be eating high on the hog once again.

A man's ability to shoot a gun was of utmost importance. It meant wild game on the table when the pork supply ran out.

Squirrels, rabbits, coons, birds, and opossums were a welcome sight on the supper table. Younger squirrels were good for frying; older ones ended up in squirrel stew. Rabbits were prepared in much the same manner, while a big fat opossum was more likely to be baked with earth-cured sweet potatoes cooked around it.

Shells for the gun were expensive. No one could afford to waste them, so being an accurate marksman was very important. At times it could mean the difference between eating and not eating, or at the least, not having meat to eat.

Dogs were an important part of hunting too. A good hunting dog was worth its weight in gold. Willie owned a young brown and white feist dog named Nero. He was a squirrel dog used for treeing squirrel. If there was a squirrel within a mile of the place, Nero could find it.

Willie loved hunting. He loved nature. He liked being in the woods. Many winter days and nights were spent hunting with Willie Parker. In the day they hunted squirrels and rabbits. At night, when the moon was full, Willie and Mr. Parker could be seen sitting alongside Swift Creek. With their guns in hand, they waited and watched for a coon to amble down the creek bank to catch his nightly meal of crawdads and small fish.

One cool, clear night in early spring, Willie and Mr. Parker took young DM hunting with them for the first time ever. They went up to the ridge in back of the cornfield. They each found a tree stump where they could sit, relax, and enjoy the silence of the woods. The moon was full, and its radiance seemed to glow more brightly than any of them had ever seen before.

Suddenly Mr. Parker looked over at Willie. "Ya know, Mr. Bone, I don't believe I've ever seen a more beautiful moon in all my life. In fact, I do believe if I live to be a hundred, I don't think I'll ever see another moon as purdy as that one."

DM looked carefully at the huge, golden moon of which Mr. Parker had spoken. It loomed motionless in the bright, starlit sky. It seemed much bigger than usual. It was as though its brightness was all around him, pulling him closer into its magical spell. In its glow there appeared to be a huge smiling face looking down on him.

Willie looked too. "I do believe you're right, Mr. Parker," Willie agreed. "That's a mighty purdy moon all right." At that moment Willie wondered why Adell didn't understand why he enjoyed hunting so much.

Willie, Willie Parker, and friends

Hunting was an important part of survival.

Willie began taking DM hunting at an early age. At first, their trips were just to get DM used to the rules of hunting: stay quiet, keep still, and listen. When he was around eight, Willie decided it was time to give DM a gun. Adell wouldn't hear of Willie giving him a real gun. However, after much deliberation, she eventually agreed to let him have a BB gun. To DM's surprise, he got his first gun that year for Christmas, a single-shot BB gun of his very own. It was the same gun he'd wished for at Mr. Thomas's store in Billingsley.

On Christmas morning, DM was so excited about his new BB gun he could barely eat his breakfast. It wasn't like the cap gun he'd gotten the first Christmas after he'd had his arm removed. The cap gun came with only one box of caps. There was no money to buy more caps. When those were used up, he had to point the gun and just pretend to shoot.

His BB gun was a real gun with real BBs. The BBs were made of lead, so they were quite heavy for their small size. DM carried some of the BBs in his pocket; the rest he carried in his mouth. When he shot out the one in the chamber, he used his mouth to drop in another. He soon learned to shoot the gun with precise accuracy in order to not waste the BBs. When he eventually ran out, he gathered a dozen eggs to swap for a pound of BBs at Richard Thomas's store in Billingsley.

He and Imogene used his BB gun to shoot little birds that roosted in the long row of cedar trees growing along the edge of the road beside their house. They took turns shooting the birds. When one was killing the birds, the other retrieved them from where they'd fallen. Every species of bird from tiny sparrows to robins often fell prey to their hunting expeditions. However, these birds were not killed just for the fun of it.

"Eat what ya kill," Willie always said. "If ya ain't gonna eat it, there ain't no use in killin' it."

Adell would clean the birds, no matter how small, roll them up in a damp cloth, and cook them in the ashes of the fireplace for the children as a snack.

One day DM was shooting at birds alone when he spied a beautiful bluebird perched high up on the branch of a nearby oak tree. He never really expected to kill the bluebird. He thought it was too far away. However, he took careful aim and fired. The beautiful bird fell to the ground with a thud. He couldn't believe it. He had killed a bluebird. Bluebirds were one of Willie's favorite birds because they ate the insects that threatened their crops. When DM realized he'd actually killed it, he knew his daddy would give him a whipping for sure. Quickly, he retrieved the little bird and hid it under a nearby rock. It was a lesson well-learned. He never shot or even aimed at another bluebird again. In fact, he never aimed his gun at anything again unless he intended to kill it.

Christmas was a time of giving, a time when children hung their socks on the mantel in hopes they would be filled with a few nuts, some raisins, a piece of fruit, maybe even a peppermint stick. Any toys they might get were usually homemade, like DM's slingshot. There was never more than one toy given, but all the children looked forward to Christmastime and the small extras that went along with the season.

One of the best things about Christmas was Adell's hickory-nut cake. Willie always made sure there were fresh hickory nuts picked out for their special Christmas cake. Its nutty aroma as it baked in the oven filled the air, making everyone's mouth water. Although hickory nuts required a lot of work to crack and pick out, in the end it was all well worth it come Christmas morning. There was nothing like waking up to the delicious aroma of vanilla and hickory nuts combined with fresh butter, sugar, flour, eggs and home-churned buttermilk. Hickory-nut cake was something everyone in the Bone family looked forward to. It was as much a part of Christmas as the tree or even the gifts. Besides hickory nuts, the boys also gathered chestnuts from the woods to roast in the ashes of the fireplace.

One of the children's favorite places to play was down by the wet weather run. A tiny stream of water constantly trickled down the middle of two red clay embankments. Blackberry bushes and tall grass grew along its edge. Lizards, toads, and other small creatures lived in or near its cool spill. All the children had been warned about playing in the ditch due to the numerous snakes Willie had seen there. However, it was just too tempting to ignore.

Willie Charles used a stick to dig a hole at the water's edge. "It's too bad the water ain't deep enough for us to swim in."

Julius came up with a solution. "I've got an idea. We could dam it up with some rocks and stuff; then the water would be deep enough."

Everyone decided Julius's idea sounded pretty good. They began by gathering rocks and sticks and putting them into a pile in the middle of the stream. Before long, the water began backing up. The higher and thicker they made the pile, the deeper the water became. In a short time, the water was up to their knees. It wasn't deep enough to swim in, but it was certainly deep enough to play in.

As the excited children splashed around in the water, the red clay became slick. DM discovered they could easily crawl up its bank, where the ground was still dry. They could then go down to where the bank was slick, sit down, then slide down the slippery embankment and into the water. The children spent the entire afternoon sliding down the red clay bank. It was great fun. All four of them were covered in red mud. As it neared dusk, they heard Adell calling them to the house for supper. When they arrived home Adell threw a fit.

"What in the world have ya younguns been up to?" she yelled.

"We dammed up the wet weather run, Mama," DM answered proudly. "We made us a slide."

Adell couldn't believe her eyes. Their clothes were a mess. "Just look at y'all. Just look at your clothes." She turned each of them around to survey the damage. "I could scrub till the cows come home and never get these stains out. Y'all ruined your clothes. What are folks gonna think? Y'all just have to wear 'em like that, I reckon."

Just then Willie walked in the back door. "Good Lord Almighty," he said angrily. "How did ya younguns get in such a mess?"

"They've been playin' down at that wet weather run," Adell said, exasperated.

"How many times have I told y'all to stay away from there?" Willie shouted. "Haven't I told y'all there's snakes down there?"

"Yes sir," the children answered, lowering their heads.

"As bad as I hate to, I think it's time to take a trip to the woodshed," Willie said sternly. He pulled his belt from around his waist. "Maybe a good whippin' will help y'all remember when I tell ya not to do somethin'."

Willie took all four of the children out to the woodshed and gave them the whipping of their lives. They all paid dearly for their afternoon of fun.

———

Any meat, whether wild from the woods or raised on the farm, was a welcome sight on the dinner table. Willie hunted a lot during the cold winter months when their fresh meat supply was gone. It was January 24, 1939. He'd been out hunting most of the day in the woods back of their house. When he topped the ridge just north of the house, he noticed a car in the yard. Very few folks he knew owned a car, and he didn't recognize this one. A few minutes later he arrived home. Before going inside, he stomped his boots on the back porch to get the excess dirt off the soles. As he walked in the back door, he threw his brown hunting bag full of squirrels on the table. To his surprise, his brother Isaac was sitting at the kitchen table drinking a hot cup of coffee.

"How are ya, Isaac?" Willie said. He moved in close to the stove to warm himself. "What brings ya around these parts?"

Isaac placed his coffee cup back on the saucer. "I got some bad news to tell ya, Willie. Pa is dead. Died early this mornin'. I come to git ya so ya can help with the funeral and all."

"I reckon I can do that," Willie said solemnly. "I owe him that much. I suppose we'll be buryin' him at Bethany Baptist Church. They've got a lot there. Let's get some supper in us, and we'll go take care of what needs to be done."

After supper, Willie and Isaac rode back to their father's old home place. Adell sent a pot of fresh-cooked dried black-eyed peas to feed the mourners who would be sitting up with the dead. Willie would send for her and the children later after the arrangements were made. The trip was a solemn one. On the way there, Willie looked out the car window into the darkness that surrounded them. Quietly he began singing his favorite song, "Give Me the Roses While I Live":

> "Give me the roses while I live, tryin' to cheer me on. Useless are flowers that ya' give after the soul has gone. Wonderful things of folks are said when they have passed away. Roses adorn their narrow bed over their sleeping place. Let us not wait to do good deeds till they have passed away. Now is the time to sow good seeds while here on earth we stay. Kind words are useless when folks lie cold in a narrow bed. Don't wait till death to speak kind words; now should the words be said. Give me the roses while I live; don't wait until I die to spread the roses o'er my grave to see as ya pass it by."

Adell was a good cook. She learned at a young age how to make a little go a long way. She began teaching Imogene to cook at an early age too. She also taught her about canning vegetables they grew in the garden and about making jams and jellies from the fresh fruit they either grew or gathered from the woods. The jars of canned sweet peaches she and Imogene prepared in the summer were Imogene and DM's favorite after-school snack. Between the two of them, they could eat a whole quart jar of the sweet peaches right by themselves.

Their breakfast meal most often consisted of biscuits and sawmill gravy. If the hens were laying properly, there were usually enough eggs for everyone to have an egg. If the hens weren't laying and their egg supply was short, Adell would scramble what eggs they did have into the gravy.

During the fall of the year, the sugar cane was harvested and taken to the mill, where the juice was extracted and cooked into ribbon cane syrup. Ira Huett and his wife, Zadie, were some of the best syrup makers around. It was a joy to have a bucket of Ira's syrup on the table for breakfast.

Adell was beginning to be sick a lot. She would be in bed for days at a time. When Adell had one of her spells, it was left up to Imogene to prepare the family meals and take care of the duties of the house. On one such occasion when Adell was once again sick in bed, she called to Imogene, who was in the kitchen washing up the dishes from breakfast.

"Imogene."

"Yes, Mama," she answered.

"Come here a minute."

Imogene dried off her hands with the edge of her apron and went into her mama's bedroom. "What is it, Mama?"

"Take the rice left over from breakfast and make it into a rice pudding. Put ya some sugar, two or three eggs, a few tablespoons of butter, a little bit of cream, and some vanilla flavoring in a bowl. Mix it with the rice till it's beat real good. Grease that long pan I cook cakes in and put it in the oven till it gets firm and brown on top."

"Okay, Mama."

Rice was a luxury they could seldom afford. Times were few and far between when the family had rice to eat. They'd had rice with melted butter on top that morning for breakfast. Rice pudding was an even more special treat. What was left in the jar was the last they would have for a while until they could afford to buy more.

Imogene went back to the kitchen. She pulled one of the straight-back wooden chairs across the room to the row of shelves that held the jars of flour, cornmeal, sugar, dried beans, coffee, and rice. She took down the jar of rice from the shelf and carefully got down off the chair.

She had never made rice pudding before, but it sounded easy enough. She mixed together the ingredients as her mother had told her to do. The vanilla smelled so good. It made Imogene's mouth water. She loved her mama's rice pudding. She only hoped hers would be as good. When the pudding was done, she placed it in the pie keeper above the stove so it would stay warm till supper. It also helped keep the houseflies off it.

Imogene decided some chicken and broth for supper might make her mama feel better. She wanted to make some for her, but that meant having to kill a chicken. She had watched her mama wring a chicken's neck many times, but she had never actually done it herself. She thought to herself, *If Mama can do it, so can I.*

If a chicken got too old to lay, it also meant it had outlived its worth on the farm. She knew how much DM liked chasing the chickens around the yard just for the devilment of it. She would get him to catch one of the older hens that was no longer laying anymore.

Imogene went out on the back porch. DM was shooting at birds with his BB gun as they landed on top of the cotton house. "DM!" she called. "Come here a minute. I got something I want ya to do for me."

DM tried to ignore her. "Can't ya see I'm busy? I'm gonna kill us some birds for supper," he yelled.

"DM Bone," scolded Imogene. "Get your butt over here right now. I need ya to catch me one of 'em hens that ain't layin' no more. I'm gonna fix some chicken and broth for supper."

DM shouldered his BB gun and began walking toward the porch. "You're gonna fix chicken and broth?" He laughed. "Ya got to wring the chicken's neck first 'fore ya can cook it. Ya can't wring a chicken's neck."

"I can too," said Imogene defiantly. "I've seen Mama do it a thousand times. I know how it's done."

DM continued to laugh at his older sister. "Knowin' how it's done and doin' it are two different things."

"Ya just worry about catchin' the chicken," replied Imogene. "I'll worry about wringin' its neck."

DM got some cracked corn out of the barn and scattered it on the ground in front of him. "Here, chick, chick, chick," he called. "Come on, chick, chick, chick. Come to DM so I can catch ya, chick, chick, chick."

Chickens came from everywhere—little chickens, big chickens, hens, and young roosters. DM spied one of the old black-and-white-speckled hens he knew hadn't laid in months. He slowly began to move through the other chickens till he was within reach of the old hen. Like a barn cat after a rat, DM sprung into action. He grabbed the old hen before she knew what had her. He wrapped his hand around her feet and held tight as she flip-flopped around, trying desperately to get away. Proudly he walked over to the porch and handed his prize to Imogene.

"Okay, I caught her," he boasted. "Now what ya gonna do with her?"

"I'm gonna wring her neck, that's what," answered Imogene aggressively.

DM perched himself on the porch steps to watch. "This I got to see," he teased.

Imogene grabbed the hen around the neck just above her beak. Her plans were to swing the hen around as though she were swinging around a lasso. This was how she'd seen her mama do it. The goal was to break the chicken's neck, causing it to die. Then she would throw it to the ground. The chicken would flop around for a while then eventually become still as the last drop of life escaped from its body. After the chicken died, she would put it in the pot of boiling water she had heating on the stove, pick off the feathers, and finally singe it with a rolled-up burning paper bag.

With all the strength she could muster, Imogene swung the old hen around and around three or four times then tossed it to the ground. For a split second the bird was motionless. Just as Imogene decided she had succeeded in killing the chicken, it jumped to its feet and took off for the safety of the barn.

DM fell to the ground with laughter. He rolled around on the ground laughing so hard tears came to his eyes. "Now what ya gonna cook for supper, miss 'I can wring a chicken's neck,'" he teased.

Imogene felt bad that she had failed to kill the chicken. From the barn, Willie had witnessed Imogene's pitiful attempt to kill the fowl. He caught the old hen as she ran into the barn and quickly wrung her neck. He then carried the chicken across the road to Imogene.

Handing her the lifeless bird, he said, "Here ya go, Imogene. I think ya can handle the rest."

Imogene reached for the chicken. "Thanks, Daddy. I can take care of it from here."

That night there was chicken and broth, hot cornbread to crumble in the broth, and rice pudding for dessert. The old hen had cooked up good and tender, and the broth was just the right thickness. Imogene was proud when her mama and daddy bragged on how good everything tasted. When they had finished off the pot of chicken and broth, it was time to try the rice pudding. Imogene dipped out a large serving of the pudding on each person's plate. Willie scooped up a large spoonful of pudding and placed it in his mouth. Everyone else did the same. However, when they bit down on the savory pudding, it had bits of something hard and crunchy in it.

"What wrong with this puddin'?" DM asked, wrinkling his nose. "It's crunchy."

Adell tasted the pudding too. "Imogene, where did ya get the rice ya put in this puddin'?"

"I got it out of the jar on the shelf," answered Imogene. "Ya told me to use the rice we had left from breakfast. So I used what was left in the jar, like ya said."

Adell frowned. "I meant for ya to use the cooked rice we had left from breakfast. Ya make rice puddin' with cooked rice, not raw rice."

Everyone had a good laugh on Imogene. She felt bad because she had wasted the ingredients on something they couldn't even eat. When Adell realized how embarrassed Imogene felt about using the wrong rice, she consoled her by saying she reckoned that was all a part of learning to cook.

The family went to bed early that night. Shortly after dark, DM was suddenly awakened by a bright light coming from across the road. At first, he thought it must be a big truck with its headlights on, yet the only sound he heard was a crackling, popping sound. Sleepily, he got out of bed and went to the window to see what it was. To his horror, their barn across the road was on fire. Flames were burning bright orange, lighting up the night like the early morning sun. Quickly, he ran to his father's bed.

"Daddy! Daddy!" he yelled, shaking his father awake.

Startled, Willie sat upright in bed. "What is it, son?" His eyes attempted to adjust to the light.

"Daddy, the barn is on fire!"

Willie quickly jumped to his feet. When he opened the front door, he could see the blazing fire shooting out the cracks in the walls. Grabbing his pants, he called to the others.

"Everybody get up! The barn is on fire!" he yelled. "Julius, Willie Charles, get some buckets and start drawin' water from the well. Imogene, DM, y'all help tote the water out to the barn!"

Adell grabbed a blanket off the bed and followed Willie out the door. When Willie opened the door to the barn, heavy, black smoke curled out like a passing tornado. As best he could tell, most of the fire was at the back of the barn. Headlong, he rushed inside to save the animals trapped there in their stalls. Adell called after him.

"Willie!" she screamed in fear. "Don't go in there!"

It was too late; he was already inside. Willie unlatched the first stall door, grabbing Ben by his halter. The terrified mule refused to budge. Thinking quickly, Willie reached for the burlap sack draped across the gate and threw it across Ben's eyes. Pulling at the halter with all the strength he could muster, Willie was finally able to lead Ben out of the barn to safety. After he released the frightened mule, Willie went back to retrieve their only milk cow.

The children ran as fast as they could to bring water to the burning barn. They arrived just as Willie pulled the cow out the door. By now, the fire was completely out of control. All the family could do was stand there and watch as it burned to the ground.

DM looked up at his soot-covered father. "What are we gonna do now, Daddy?"

The blaze from the burning fire was mirrored in Willie's eyes. "Build a new barn and start over, son. That's all we can do," Willie answered solemnly.

When the neighbors saw what had happened, they readily came together to help Willie and his family build a new barn.

———

Visitors were always welcome in the Bone house. Babe Culpepper, Adell's youngest brother, and his wife, Ruby Lee, had come up from Montgomery for a few days to see all his folks. Their plans were to stay a day or two with Willie and Adell then head for White City to see his mama and daddy. Later, they would go over to Mountain Creek to see his sister, Carrie, and her family.

Ruby Lee was a striking woman with jet-black, wavy hair and skin the color of Chilton County peaches. She was pretty, and she knew it. She always wore the latest fashion in clothes and would never be caught dead without her high-heeled, sling-back shoes.

Babe, on the other hand, was a gentle man. He was tall—six foot four—with wavy dark-brown hair and a pleasant smile. He had served a tour in the war, where they said he'd had a mental breakdown. He enjoyed teasing Ruby Lee about how pretty she thought she was.

Everyone had decided to sit outside on the porch after supper that night. The cool autumn night was just right for visiting. Ruby Lee sat down on the front porch steps, third step from the top. She opened her black patent-leather purse, taking out a compact and her favorite color of lipstick, ruby red. It was like a scene out of a moving picture show. She leaned forward, resting her elbow on the top step, her left leg stretched out down to the bottom step. She opened the compact and surveyed her face in the mirror. Turning her head from side to side, she removed the puff and ever so gently patted the powder on her face to remove the shine from her nose. Although her lips appeared to have retained most of their color even after eating her supper, Ruby Lee added another coat of lipstick just for good measure.

Just for fun, Babe began to sing: "There's more pretty girls than one; there's more pretty girls than one. Every time I ramble around I find more pretty girls than one."

This made Ruby Lee mad as a wet settin' hen. She quickly sat upright on the steps and planted her hands firmly on her hips. "Ya should be ashamed of yourself, Babe Culpepper," she scolded. "You're a married man. Ya ain't got no business singin' about ramblin' round and pretty girls. Ya can just stop that singin' right here and now."

Everyone had a good laugh on Ruby, and it was good to laugh.

Soon winter was upon them. Droves of blackbirds darkened the sky as they flew farther south for the winter. In the winter the land lay dormant, awaiting next year's planting. Cold winter winds blew under the windowsills and through the cracks in the walls. The children brought in firewood from the back porch for the fireplace and stove wood for the stove. At night they slept under heavy quilts with a hearth-warmed iron wrapped in cloth and placed at their feet. The quilts were so heavy they could barely turn over in bed.

It was very unusual to have snow in Alabama. However, that particular winter it snowed and snowed and snowed. It began late one evening. By morning, the ground, rooftops, bushes, and trees were completely covered. DM and Imogene awoke to a winter wonderland. When DM saw all the beautiful snow, he immediately began begging to go outside. "Can we go out and play, Mama? I want to build a snowman."

"Yeah, Mama," Imogene pleaded. "Please let us go out to play. I'll gather some snow so we can have ice cream later."

Adell shivered as she stepped closer to the fire to warm her cold, stiff fingers. "It's too cold for y'all to be out," she answered, looking at Willie. "I sure hope Julius, Willie Charles, and Delene are stayin' warm at your mama's house."

Willie threw another log on the fire. "I'm sure they are," he assured her.

"Please, Mama, please," they begged. "We'll put on our coats."

Willie backed up to the roaring fire to warm his backside. "Let 'em go out, Adell. We don't get snow round these parts much. Let 'em enjoy it while it's here."

"If I let ya two go out, will ya promise to come back in if ya start gittin' too cold?" asked Adell.

Imogene and DM rushed to get their coats before Adell could change her mind. "We promise," they said, beaming with excitement.

Soon they were bundled up with all the clothes Adell could find to put on them. Seconds afterward, they rushed out the front door. The bitter-cold wind whipped across the porch, sending swirls of fluffy, white flakes dancing across the length of the porch. It was the most beautiful sight they had ever seen. Everything was so gleaming white it almost hurt their eyes to look at it.

As Imogene gathered snow for ice cream, DM made snowballs. He threw them at their dog, Nero, and at the side of the house, splattering snow everywhere. It was such fun he never wanted to stop. Before long, DM could no longer feel his fingers. He looked at his hand. His fingers were beet red.

Willie walked over to the window to watch his children as

they played. The big cedar tree at the edge of the yard moaned and crackled with the weight of the heavy, wet snow. He was afraid the branches on the tree were going to break and fall on the house. "I'd better do something 'bout that snow on the cedar tree," he said to Adell. Willie reached for his hat hanging from a nail beside the door. He pulled it down over his ears as best he could and buttoned up his coat. The air outside was crisp and cold, but it smelled fresh and clean like sun-dried clothes on wash day. Using a long cane pole, he knocked the snow off the tree as best he could. Several times that day he repeated the procedure in order to save the big cedar from breaking.

Before long, the extremely cold temperature got to Imogene. "Let's go in now," she called to her brother. "It's gettin' too cold out here."

DM tossed a snowball at one of the cats curled up under the front porch. "I don't want to go in yet," he yelled back.

"Fine," she said. "Stay out here and freeze. I'm goin' inside, where it's warm."

As DM played in the snow, Nero chased the tiny sparrows pecking at the snow. DM wished the snow would stay forever. Everything was so white and beautiful. He played until he could no longer feel his hand. Reluctantly, he decided it was time for him to go in too. As soon as he entered the house, he headed for the warmth of the fire. The logs burned brightly in the fireplace. DM placed his cold hand near the hot blaze; instantly it began to sting and hurt.

"My hand hurts," he said and began to cry.

"I told ya to come in," Imogene told him. "I knew your hand was gonna hurt, but ya wouldn't listen."

Adell wrapped her hands around DM's hand, rubbing it between her hands to try to warm it. DM cried for close to ten minutes before his hand finally thawed out.

When DM stopped crying, Adell put the snow Imogene had gathered into a large china bowl. She added fresh cream, sugar, vanilla, and eggs, beating the ingredients until the mixture was blended and ice cold.

"Are ya younguns ready for some snow ice cream?" she asked.

Imogene gathered up several bowls and some spoons from the cupboard. "I am. I am," she said gleefully.

DM grabbed one of the bowls from Imogene's hands and pushed it at his mama to fill. "Me too! Me too!" he yelled.

Willie took his seat at the table. "Sounds mighty good to me too," he added.

Adell divided the snow ice cream into the bowls. Ice cream was a real treat, and snow ice cream was the best of all. The pure vanilla flavor mixed with sweet cream and sugar was delicious, although it chilled them to the bone as they ate.

DM put a spoonful of ice cream into his mouth. "I wish it would snow in the summertime so we could have snow ice cream when it's hot," he said.

Imogene giggled. "It can't snow in the summertime, silly. It's not cold enough to snow."

DM continued to shovel the cold, sweet cream into his mouth until his tongue felt numb. "If we had one of them electric iceboxes we could save the ice cream till it got hot weather and then eat it. Couldn't we, Mama?"

"We don't even have electric lights in the house, much less an electric icebox," said Adell. "Besides, we can barely afford what bills we've got now, much less an electric bill."

DM sat up straight and bowed out his chest. "Well, when I get big I'm gonna have electric lights, an electric icebox, an electric stove, and even a radio too," he declared.

Willie took pride in his son's positive attitude. "I hope ya do, son. I hope ya do well in life. That's why I make sure ya younguns go to school every day. Education is the most important thing a person can have. Once ya have it, can't no one ever take it away from ya. It's yours forever. If y'all get a good education, y'all can do or be anything y'all want to be."

Imogene put a spoonful of the cold ice cream into her mouth, "Well, I'm gonna grow up to be a boy," she proclaimed. "Boys get to do more stuff than girls do, stuff like go to town on Saturday, hunt when they want to, and go fishin' all the time."

"Ya can't grow up to be a boy," DM said, laughing. "'Cause you'll always be a girl, and I'll always be a boy. Ain't that right, Mama?"

"That's right, Imogene. We are what we are," answered Adell. "But if ya study real hard, ya might can grow up to be a nurse or a teacher maybe. If ya get a good education."

Imogene licked the back of her spoon in order to get the last savory drop of sweet cream. "What if I want to be a doctor or a lawyer?"

"Girls can't be doctors or lawyers," said Adell matter-of-factly. "Girls ain't as smart as boys are."

Imogene dropped her spoon into her empty bowl and placed her hands firmly on her hips. "I'm as smart as any old boy," she protested. "I make better grades than the boys in my class at school. I can read better and faster, and I can do my math tables better than most anybody."

"That's right, Imogene," said Willie. "Ya keep studyin' real hard, and I bet ya can be anything ya want to be when ya grow up."

Willie sat his empty bowl on the table and leaned forward. With his strong, calloused hand he ruffled his young daughter's hair in jest. "Of course, I do think ya make a much prettier gal than ya would a boy."

Willie smiled as he watched his children laughing. His heart was thankful to have his family gathered around him. God had chosen to spare DM's life, and for this he was grateful. He thought of his other children. He missed his older boys, Julius and Willie Charles. They had chosen to live with their Granny Bone for a while. Delene had always lived primarily with his mother. Mrs. Bone had taken Delene in after her daughter-in-law passed away. By the time Willie and Adell married two years later, it seemed a shame to take her away from her grandma. It was hard for Willie, but he felt it was best for Delene.

Everyone laughed together as they ate the remainder of the snow ice cream. There was little time to enjoy simple pleasures like eating snow ice cream with the family, but with the fresh-fallen snow and winter temperatures in the teens, there was little else to do.

Winters were the hardest time of the year. The days were short, the nights long. Making sure there was food on the table at mealtime was a main priority. Their hunting dog, Nero, passed away from a snake bite. The family missed him very much. Willie put the word out that he was looking for another dog to take Nero's place.

The word spread quickly about Willie looking for a new squirrel dog. An old black man who lived over in the Independence community sent word that he had an older squirrel dog he wanted to get rid of. Willie hitched a ride with Mr. Friday over to the old man's house. As Mr. Friday was bringing the wagon to a stop in the front yard, a white, bench-legged feist with one dark spot on one of his ears came from under the house to meet them. An old black man opened the wooden plank door of his two-room shanty. His body was stooped over. As he began easing his way down the steps, he did so as though every bone in his body ached from years of toil.

Willie stepped down off the wagon. "Mornin'," Willie called to the old man.

Just as the old black man reached the bottom step, he felt a cold wind whip around the side of his meager home. Feeling chilled, he fumbled with the buttons of his brown, tattered coat. His snarled hands made it difficult for him to button it. "Mornin to ya too, sir," replied the old man.

Willie walked over to where the old man had stopped to try to button his coat. As he approached the old man, he reached out to shake the black man's calloused, wrinkled hand. "I heard ya got a dog ya want to get rid of."

The old man stuck out his hand and smiled a half-toothless grin. "Yes sir, I sho' do," he answered.

When the old man looked up at him, Willie noticed his dark eyes were covered with a fine, dense film. He was sure it was cataracts. Now he knew why the old man was giving his dog away. When a man can't see, neither can he hunt.

"My name be Silas Jackson. What might your name be?"

"Willie Bone," he said, smiling back at Silas.

Although they were dim, Willie liked the sincerity in the colored man's eyes. He could see a man much like himself—a man who had worked hard all his life with nothing more to show for it than a run-down shanty he called home. Releasing his hand from Silas's grip, Willie pointed to his neighbor still sitting on the wagon seat.

"This here is Mr. Friday."

Silas tipped his brown, frayed hat to Mr. Friday.

Silas pointed to the little white feist running around their feet, smelling Willie up and down. "Yes sir, dis dog right here be one of the finest squirrel dogs 'round dese parts. He's several years old now, but me and dis here dog has got us many a squirrel together. As ya can see, I ain't able to hunt no mo'. Dis here rheumatism done gots the best of me. Can't see none too good neither. Can't go huntin' like I used to. Seems a shame to waste a good huntin' dog. Jus' 'cause I can't hunt no mo' don't mean he can't. He still gots a lot of good huntin' left in 'im. Ain't scared o' nothin'. Make ya a fine huntin' dog for sho', Mr. Bone."

Willie squatted down and patted the dog on the head. "How much ya want for 'im?"

"I do believe I's takes a dollar fer 'im," answered Silas, hoping to seal the deal. "Dat's a bargain fer sho', Mr. Bone. Now ya know it is."

Willie opened the dog's mouth to inspect his teeth and gums. His gums were a rosy pink. His teeth looked solid. "A dollar sounds fair," replied Willie. "That is if he's as good as ya say he is."

Silas held his right hand up in the air like he was taking an oath. He smiled, showing several rotting teeth. "I swear to it on my mama's grave, Mr. Bone."

Willie stood up, reached in his overall pocket, and pulled out a shiny, round silver dollar. "Here ya are," he said, handing Silas the coin.

The old man took the silver dollar and stuffed it into his jacket pocket.

Willie got a rope off the wagon and tied it securely around the dog's neck. He picked him up by placing one arm around the dog's chest and the other around his hindquarters. Nodding his approval to Silas, he placed him in the back of the wagon. Just to make sure the dog couldn't jump out and go back home, he tied the other end of the rope to a sideboard.

"Does he have a name?" Willie asked Silas.

"Naw, sir. I ain't never named 'im. I jus' called him 'Dog' most de time," Silas answered.

Willie thought about it as he climbed onto the wagonseat to leave. "Well, I think we'll call 'im One Spot."

Silas reached up and patted One Spot on the head for the last time. "Ya be's a good dog fer Mr. Bone, now ya hear."

Willie tipped his hat to Silas. Mr. Friday did the same. "Thank ya, Mister Jackson," Willie said.

Mr. Friday turned the mule team around and headed back home.

Silas waved good-bye then headed slowly back up the steps and into the house. "Yes sir, Mr. Bone," he mumbled to himself. "Ya sho' 'nough got ya a fine huntin' dog." He took one last glance at his old hunting buddy then closed the door behind him.

———

When Julius and Willie Charles were around, they were constantly giving Adell a hard time. Willie's sisters, Josie and Lena, made things worse on Adell by telling the boys they didn't have to mind her because she wasn't their real mother. It made things very difficult for Adell when it came time to get the boys to do something. When Willie was at home, she let him handle disciplining the two of them. When he wasn't home, they did pretty much as they pleased.

One morning before going into Billingsley, Willie left instructions for the boys to stack some stove wood on the back porch. By noon, Adell noticed neither Willie Charles nor Julius had made any attempt to bring in the wood.

"Ya boys had better get some stove wood stacked up on this porch 'fore your daddy gets home," Adell warned them.

Julius and Willie Charles looked at their stepmother with distaste in their eyes.

"We don't have to do nothin' ya say. Ya ain't our mama," sassed Julius.

"That's right," Willie Charles added. "Aunt Josie said so."

"Fine," said Adell. "But your daddy's liable to give y'all a whippin' when he gets back."

Later that day when Willie returned home, there was still no stove wood on the porch. Willie was tired, hungry, and cold. He was also angry his boys had disobeyed him. He called both of them out into the yard.

"Why didn't y'all tote in some firewood like I told ya to

do?" he asked. Before either of them could answer, he began removing his belt from around his waist.

Desperate for an excuse, Julius answered him first. "We was goin' to, Daddy, but Adell wouldn't make Imogene or DM help us. We didn't think it was fair for us to have to do it all."

Anger welled up in Willie's eyes. "I didn't tell Imogene and DM to bring in the wood. I told the two of y'all to do it," he scolded.

Adell watched from the kitchen window as Willie grabbed Julius by the arm and raised his belt. She knew by the look on his face the two boys were in for the whipping of their life. Had the boys been her two children she might have said something, but these were his boys. Besides, she had tried to warn them. She made up her mind it was best to stay out of the situation.

Willie used the belt on Julius first as Willie Charles stood by watching. Before his daddy finished with Julius, Willie Charles had already started to cry. Then Willie turned the belt on him. Adell had never seen him whip the boys so much. She knew by how hard he was hitting them they must surely have welts starting to form on their legs and backs, yet he continued to hit them. Adell thought he was never going to stop. It was as though all the hardship and troubles he'd held deep inside him for all these years had suddenly exploded. Now his boys were taking the blame for it.

After what seemed like forever, Willie finally stopped beating them. However, Willie Charles couldn't stop crying. The more he cried the more Willie hit him. Willie ordered him several times to stop crying, but he continued to sob uncontrollably. Finally Adell had seen all she could stand. She was truly afraid Willie was going to kill his own son. Determined to talk some sense into her crazed husband, she laid down her dishrag and went out the back door and into the yard. Defiantly, she stepped in between Willie and the sobbing child. She could see an anger in his eyes she'd never seen before.

She planted her still-moist hands firmly on her hips. "That's enough, Willie," she declared.

Willie drew back the belt. "Ya better get out of my way, Adell, or I'll hit ya next," he shouted.

"Ya may hit me, Willie," Adell answered stubbornly, "but you're not gonna hit this youngun no more."

Willie stood over Adell with his belt raised in the air as though he was going to strike her too at any second. Then suddenly the anger melted from his face. It was as though he had been shocked back into reality. His arm dropped, hanging limp at his side. The belt fell to the ground. He looked at Adell and his two sobbing children then lowered his head and walked away, headed toward the barn. When he returned to the house some two hours later, a full stack of stove wood covered one end of the back porch. The incident was never mentioned again.

———

The Bone family lived at the Patrick place for seven years, when they found out there was to be a new baby in the house, another mouth to feed; Imogene was eleven, and DM was seven. Adell gave birth to a third child in late summer 1941, another boy. They named him Wilfred O'neal.

Wilfred was a beautiful baby. Imogene thought he was the prettiest baby she'd ever seen. His skin was a rosy pink. His dark hair lay in tiny curls. He was very tiny. Willie and Adell placed him between them at night in order to keep him safe while he slept.

With all the hardships they had gone through with DM, Adell prayed every night for the Lord to look over Wilfred. She was a strong woman, but even she could not imagine living through another illness like the one they had been through with DM She truly didn't know if her nerves could handle it.

Not long after Wilfred was born, Adell's nerves did in fact get the better of her. She suffered from a nervous breakdown and was hospitalized for a period of time. With Adell in the hospital, it was left up to Imogene to care for Wilfred. Although she was only eleven years old, Imogene readily stepped in and took her mother's place as caregiver to her younger siblings. Imogene grew to feel as though Wilfred was her child rather than her mother's child. As years passed, she sometimes thought of him as her own. The older they got, people would ask if Wilfred was her son. Wilfred and Adell's separation at such a young age seemed to place a wedge between him and his mother, a wedge that never completely healed.

Another cold winter passed, and soon it was spring again. Daffodils were always a welcome sight around the farm. It meant spring was just around the corner. It also meant it was time for spring planting. For the sharecropper, spring planting actually began in mid-December with the preparation of the field. Previously planted fields had to be readied for the next year's crop.

Corn was planted in the month of March. Corn was a staple crop. It was used to feed not only the family in the way of corn on the cob, pan-fried corn, and cornmeal, but to feed the livestock as well. When it came time to plant, most sharecroppers depended on neighbors and friends for help. When one man's field was plowed and planted, they went on to the next man's field. There was never a lot of money to buy fertilizer; therefore, there was an abundance of nubbins in the yield. However, the nubbins did not go to waste. They were fed to the cow and mule and for fattening the hogs.

Cotton was a sharecropper's cash crop. It was also planted in March. It was the crop that was sold back to the landowner to pay for the use of the land and the cost of the fertilizer and seed. Since planting cotton required the use of three mules walking in single file, there again, neighbors helped neighbors. Once the cotton was up, Adell and the children chopped the cotton to thin it out. This was done so the cotton plants would produce more cotton per plant.

At around the same time cotton and corn were being planted, Adell and the children were planting the garden too. Irish potatoes, sweet potatoes, green beans, cabbage, turnips, collards, and onions were planted early on. Once the ground was warm and the chance of a freeze had passed, black-eyed peas and tomatoes were planted also.

By the end of May 1942, Willie had most of the plowing and planting done. All that was left to plow was the lower field. As soon as the ground warmed up a little more, he would be ready to start planting peas and butter beans. He was plowing his last long row when he saw Adell come across the ridge carrying nine-month-old Wilfred in her arms. As she got closer, he could tell she'd been crying. Thinking something was wrong with the baby, he threw down the plow and ran to her side.

"What's the matter, Adell?" He lifted the blanket off Wilfred's sleeping face. "Is the baby okay? Is somebody hurt? Why are ya cryin'?"

"Wilfred's fine," she answered. "It's your mama. She had a stroke last night."

"Mama had a stroke?" he asked, just to make sure he'd heard right.

"Josie is up at the house. She says ya best come see her now. They ain't expectin' her to live long."

Willie unhitched Ben from the plow. He would have to finish the plowing later. Adell was halfway back across the field by the time Willie turned Ben toward the barn. As he walked along, a single tear fell from his eye and rolled down his dust-covered cheek. He knew his mama's death would be hard on everyone, especially Delene. She and her grandma were extremely close.

After wiping down Ben and giving him a bucket of feed, Willie made his way toward the house. Josie was sitting alone on the front porch. Her eyes were red and swollen. He could tell she'd been crying. He walked onto the porch and laid his hand on her shoulder. "Hey, Josie. How's Mama?"

Josie looked up at her younger brother. "Not good, Willie. We could shore use your help. I 'spect we'll be plannin' her funeral 'fore the week's out."

Adell opened the front door and walked out onto the porch. Imogene walked out behind her, carrying Wilfred in her arms. DM followed. "Me and the younguns are ready to go when y'all are," Adell said.

Josie stood up. Her knees wobbled. "I 'spect ya best drive, Willie," she said. "I ain't feelin' none too spry."

Willie helped Josie to her car. Everyone else climbed inside. It was a good twenty-mile ride to where Mrs. Bone lived with her daughter Lera and granddaughter Delene in Cooper, Alabama. Their house was right next to the railroad tracks. Trains came and went constantly up and down the tracks. With each passing train, the house and its contents rattled and vibrated.

By the time they arrived, it was past noon. As soon as Willie saw his mama, he was glad he came. She looked bad. Her right side was completely paralyzed. She tried to talk, but her words were garbled and made no sense. Deep, dark circles surrounded her eyes. Her mouth was drawn down on one side. She died exactly one week later, on the sixth day of June.

Imogene hated funerals. She hated the southern traditions associated with funerals: sitting up at night with the dead, taking pictures of the dead person in the casket, the flower girls who held and carried flowers during the funeral. She especially hated the flower girl one. As an eleven-year-old granddaughter, she knew she would be one of those flower girls.

The funeral was held at Bethany Baptist Church. The sermon was long and drawn out. Imogene thought the preacher would never hush. The week-long smell of death combined with the sickening sweet smell of the gardenia wreath she carried in her hands made her feel sick to her stomach. Her head felt dizzy. She looked at Delene standing beside her, also holding a wreath of flowers. Delene looked distorted and blurry. On the way to the gravesite, she felt as if she would surely pass out. As soon as they put her grandmother in the ground, Imogene went behind a bush and vomited. She remained sick for over a week after the funeral.

When the funeral was over, the family went back to Mrs. Bone's house beside the railroad track. People from the community brought in food to eat. The table was covered with a variety of vegetables, meats, breads, and desserts. After everyone had eaten, Willie's brothers and sisters gathered in the parlor to divide her belongings. As the youngest son, one of the things Willie was to inherit was the family Bible. However, when he went to retrieve it from its usual resting place on his mama's dresser, it was gone.

Willie walked back into the parlor. "Does anybody know where the family Bible is?" he asked.

Isaac was the first to answer. "It was on Mama's dresser this mornin'. I saw it thar."

Willie put his hands firmly on his hips. "Well, it ain't there now." Willie pointed his finger at his sisters. "Do either of y'all know where it's at?"

Josie and Lera looked away. Lera shook her head no. "I haven't seen it," she answered.

Willie didn't believe them. He knew either of them would lie in a heartbeat if it were to their benefit. He was the youngest son. The Bible was rightfully his. However, he left there that day without it.

⁓

The children had a two-mile walk to Billingsley School. It was hard at times when the weather was bad, but there was never a question as to whether they would go or not. The school was a big, white, wooden-plank building servicing grades one through twelve. It had long hardwood hallways leading from class to class. The principal's office had a big oak desk with a padded, brown-leather chair behind it. Mr. Story was the principal there. He kept a long wooden paddle leaned up against the wall in the corner of his office. It stood there as a reminder to unruly students that misbehavior would not be tolerated.

Although both Imogene and DM liked going to school, Julius and Willie Charles did not. The two of them were more than willing to find an excuse not to go. For Imogene, school was a getaway, a place where there were other children and fun things to do, a place to socialize and see her friends. Being able to do something besides farming was a release from the daily grind. To her, learning was fun. Imogene was in the fourth grade when DM started in the first.

Ms. Mabel King was the first grade teacher. She taught both Imogene and DM and would eventually be teaching Wilfred. Ms. King loved her students. She was a robust woman with short, light-brown hair. She was a good teacher who tried to make learning interesting. Often, she wore dresses with lots of beads on the bodice. She would sit one of the students in her lap and let him count the beads on her dress in order for him to learn counting. She wore glasses, which always stayed slid down near the end of her nose. Her eyes were always happy when she was around her children. Teaching young minds to read, and the doors it opened to them, made her proud to be a teacher.

DM was still little for his age when he started school. He was a handsome boy with thick, dark hair and a winning smile. Usually haircuts were left up to Adell, but Willie decided his son needed a real haircut to start his first day at school. Willie Parker was the community barber. He had his barber chair set up in a back room of his house. The day before DM was to start first grade, Willie took him to see Mr. Parker. When Willie and DM arrived at Mr. Parker's house, he was just finishing his morning coffee.

The front door was open, so Willie and DM walked inside. "Anybody home?" Willie called out.

"Is that Willie Bone?" Mr. Parker called back. "I'm here in the kitchen. Come on back."

Willie and DM made their way through the house to the kitchen. DM walked into the room first.

"Well now," Mr. Parker said. "Who might this long-haired, barefoot boy be?"

DM smiled. "It's me, Mr. Parker. It's DM Bone."

Mr. Parker lifted DM's long hair away from his eyes. "So it is," Mr. Parker said, acting surprised. "Hard to tell who it was with all that hair hanging down in your face."

"DM is starting first grade tomorrow," Willie said proudly. "We figured on gettin' him a real haircut for the occasion."

"Well then, let's go back here to my shop, and we'll give this boy a real man's haircut."

Mr. Parker placed a booster chair in the big black-leather barber chair. DM climbed onto the chair and took his seat. A large wood-framed mirror hung on the wall in front of the chair. A four-foot-long table sat beneath the mirror. On the table lay a pair of scissors, several combs, a straight razor, a shaving mug, and a pair of hand clippers. Several bottles filled with different-colored liquids set on the other end of the table.

Mr. Parker draped a cutting cloth around DM's neck then turned him away from the mirror. He picked up the pair of hand clippers and a comb. Easing his comb up the back of DM's neck, he began to clip his hair, talking nonstop from beginning to end.

Mr. Parker was a good barber. When the haircut was finished, he rubbed some hair cream between his hands and into DM's hair. Taking his comb, he parted the hair on one side and combed it neatly across DM's forehead. One tiny piece of hair in DM's crown stood up. Mr. Parker added more hair cream to slick it down. Only then did he turn DM back toward the mirror.

"There ya go, son," said Mr. Parker. "What do ya think?"

DM peered into the mirror at his new cut. He looked like a real boy now.

"Looks good, Mr. Parker," he replied, smiling broadly at his reflection.

"You'll knock 'em little gals at school slap out of their seats," teased Mr. Parker.

"He best be worried about his grades and not the gals," corrected Willie. "I'm sendin' him to school to learn, not be interested in the gals."

DM blushed. "Oh, Daddy," he said, "I ain't interested in no gals. Gals are stupid."

"Well, ya may not be interested in them now, but as handsome a boy as ya are, they'll shore be interested in you," said Mr. Parker. He removed the drape from around DM's neck. "How 'bout you, Willie? Looks like ya could use a little trim here and there."

Willie sat down in Mr. Parker's barber chair. "Guess I might as well, bein' I'm here."

DM was excited about his first day of school. He awoke early that morning. Adell had hung his clean overalls and a white cotton shirt on the bedpost the night before. He dressed, washed his face and hands, and slicked down his new haircut. He parted his dark brown hair on the side and combed it over and up, away from his forehead. One sprig at the crown of his head didn't want to lie down. He combed it over and over, trying to get it to stay, but to no avail. After a few minutes, he put the comb down and gave up on the defiant cowlick. He was too excited to worry with it anymore.

Imogene was always excited about the new schoolyear. School was an outlet for her. She loved to read, and she loved learning new things. Once school started, she hated missing even one day. She loved school so much she would go even when she wasn't feeling well.

During the summer, Adell made Imogene two new dresses. The cloth was from feedsacks. One had tiny blue flowers on it. The other had tiny yellow flowers on it. Imogene saved them special to wear to school. Although they seldom wore shoes in the summer, except maybe to church, Willie managed to buy each of the children a new pair of winter shoes.

The night before school was to start, Imogene asked her mother to curl her naturally straight hair. Looking through the cupboard, Adell retrieved the twenty-penny nail she saved back for just such an occasion. She placed the nail in the hot ashes of the fireplace. When the nail was hot, she carefully removed it with a dishtowel and wiped it clean. She parted Imogene's hair off into one-inch sections with a comb. Each section was carefully wrapped around the hot, four-inch long by one-fourth inch diameter nail and held there until it had formed into a curl. When the nail would get too cool, she would place it back in the fire to reheat it. She continued this procedure until every strand was a ringlet. Imogene slept on the uncombed curls until the next morning, when she brushed it into long, spiraling curls. She was proud of her curly hair, although she knew that by the end of the day it would surely be straight again.

At first, some of the kids at school made fun of DM because of his missing arm. Most of them who made fun were children he had never met. Those who knew him knew DM was a tough kid and could hold his own. It didn't take long before the big boys who teased him learned he wasn't one to mess with. He had only one arm, but he was strong, and when need be, he wielded a powerful punch. He learned quickly and readily made friends with the others in his class.

Adell remained very protective over DM. There were times that year when Adell thought DM should stay home when he was feeling under the weather. She lived in constant fear of something else happening to him. The memory of those long nights spent by his hospital bedside while he suffered remained fresh in her mind. However, DM was determined to go every day, regardless of how he felt. He wanted a book like Imogene had received for perfect attendance when she was in the second grade; only, he wanted to get his book his first grade year.

Imogene didn't miss a single day in her second grade year at Billingsley School. At the end of the year, her second grade teacher, Ms. Carter, had given her a book called *Snow White and the Seven Dwarfs* in honor of her perfect attendance. Imogene thought it was the prettiest book she'd ever seen. She read it over and over, again and again. In fact, her favorite subject was reading. She read every book she could find or borrow from the school library.

DM didn't want a Snow White book. He'd heard that story a thousand times. He felt sure Ms. King would choose a different book for the boys. After all, she was a pretty smart lady. She would know the kind of books boys liked. Sure enough, at the end of DM's first grade year, he too was awarded a book for perfect attendance. It was called *Raggedy Ann helps Grandpa Grasshopper*. DM really thought he had something. He was proud of his new book and for not missing one single day of school that entire year. His parents were proud of him too.

Both DM and Imogene made good grades in school. Learning came easy for them. They were happy when they could bring home good marks on their report cards. It always made their parents happy to see them doing so well. Education was important, especially to Willie. He knew what a hard time not having an education had been for him. Adell had to read everything to him. He could barely write his name. He was sure there had been times when he had been cheated out of money due to his lack of knowledge in arithmetic. He was determined his children were going to get a good education so they could do better than he had done.

DM, first grade

The Turner Place

The Bone family lived at the Patrick place for over eight years. A lot happened there—some good, some bad. DM had his arm removed and recovered. Imogene and DM started school while living there. The barn had burned down and been rebuilt. Willie and Adell's third child, Wilfred, was born there. There were many memories attached to the Patrick Place, but Willie felt it was time to move on.

Willie shared his crops with Walter Patrick for all those years yet had little to show for it. Half of everything he'd made went to Mr. Patrick, making Mr. Patrick a well-to-do man. Willie decided it was time to try farming on his own.

Along about that time, the Turner Place came up for rent. The farm was located down the road a ways from the Patrick Place. The house was practically new. Although it didn't have electricity or running water, the land was fertile and rich. The Turner Place would require a lot of hard work to get it going, but at least what they made would all belong to them. They wouldn't have to share it with the landowner.

The rent was one hundred dollars a year. One hundred dollars was a lot of money in the early 1940s. It was a huge commitment, but Willie felt if he was ever going to get ahead, he would have to try to make a go of it. The family gathered up what belongings they owned, borrowed a truck from their neighbor, Sam Hayes, and moved to the forty-acre farm.

The dirt road in front of the Turner Place wasn't a county road; therefore, the county wasn't required to grate it. When there came a big rain, the ruts in the road from the runoff made it nearly impassable. Oftentimes, anyone who came to visit or came on business would have to park their transportation at the end of the narrow lane then walk the remaining half mile to the house.

One of the local merchants in Billingsley sold Willie fertilizer and seed on credit. The storeowner agreed to carry the debt on his books until the crops were sold, at which time Willie would pay the debt off. For the first time, Willie just knew he was finally going to see a profit from farming.

Adell worried about Willie's new venture. She worried about how in the world they would ever be able to come up with one hundred dollars every year for the rent. To make matters worse, she had a disturbing dream. In her dream she was standing on the front porch of the Turner Place. As she was looking down the lane, she saw an ambulance coming. It was coming to take someone away. The next morning at the breakfast table she told Willie about her dream.

"What do ya reckon my dream means, Willie?" she asked.

"I wouldn't worry about that too much," he said. "You're just feelin' unsettled in this new place. It's gonna take some gettin' used to, that's all."

"No," Adell replied, shaking her head. "Someone is gonna be taken away from this house in an ambulance. I dreamed it plain as day. Mama says things like that get revealed to ya in your dreams iffen ya just pay a mind to 'em."

Willie took his knife from inside his overalls pocket then reached for the whetstone he kept on a small shelf above the cookstove. Securing the whetstone in the palm of his hand, he began sliding the blade along its surface to sharpen it. "Well, I just hope it ain't none of us," he said. "We've had enough sickness in this family already. We sure don't need no more bad luck no time soon."

Adell noticed Willie's coffee cup was nearly empty. She reached for the coffee pot from off the stovetop. Using the edge of her apron to protect her hand from the hot pot, she poured him another cup. Before placing the steaming-hot coffee pot back on the cookstove, she remembered something else she wanted to ask him. "When are ya gonna dig the storm pit?"

Adell was deathly afraid of storms. The first thing she always wanted Willie to do when they moved to a new place was dig a storm pit to get in when the weather was bad. It mattered not the time of day or night; when a storm came up, the family went to the storm pit. Sometimes the pit was no more than just a hole dug out in the side of a hill with a door on it. The rain would seep in around the door, filling the bottom of the pit with water. It was always damp and wet, a haven for spiders, lizards, and even an occasional snake.

"We just got here a week ago, Adell," scolded Willie. "I've got to get a pen ready for the mule. The fields need plowin'. The barn roof needs some repair work done on it. I've got to get some lumber to repair the stall for the cow. There's a lot to be done around here."

It didn't matter to Adell about how long they had been at their new place or the fact that the mule needed a pen or the barn needed repair. Being caught without a storm pit was her only concern. "Well, we need a storm pit too," she snapped. "It's liable to come up a bad storm. Then what will we do?"

"I'll get a storm pit dug just as soon as I get the time," promised Willie.

Willie depended heavily on DM to help him with things that had to be done around the farm, including helping to build a storm pit. Previously, someone had attempted to build a storm pit on the side of the hill in front of the house. Unfortunately, whoever had built it had used inferior products to build it. It had long since caved in and was filled with cans, bottles, rocks, and dilapidated timbers.

It took Willie and DM a good three or four days to get the mess cleaned up and dug back out. Once this was done, they were ready to start putting it back together. It took several days to rebuild it, but once it was complete, it was a far cry better than before. Certainly, the pit was by no means 100 percent waterproof. However, there was usually a big enough dry spot where one could sit without getting too wet.

At the first sign of an impending storm, Adell was always ready to head for the pit regardless of whether it was broad daylight or the middle of the night. With the first clap of thunder she'd wake the entire family from a sound sleep. "There's a storm a comin'," she'd say. "We'd better get to the pit."

Willie would reluctantly light the kerosene lantern, knowing all too well there was no need to argue with her. The children would get their coats or wrap a quilt around their shoulders and sleepily follow their parents out to the pit. Once they were inside, there were chairs to sit on and a hook on the ceiling where Willie hung the lantern.

None of the kids liked spending the night in the storm pit, especially Imogene. It was damp and smelled like musty earth. There were always a variety of spiders, bugs, and even an occasional snake residing in the dark corners of the underground fortress. However, there was one night in particular when everyone, Imogene included, was more than happy to head for the pit.

The storm came up quickly in the middle of the night. Heavy clouds rolled in, covering the moon and stars like a thick winter blanket. It was pitch-black dark outside as thunder began to rumble. Suddenly and with little warning, the sky seemed to explode. Lighting strikes lit up the sky as the family made a mad dash across the yard to the pit. Its flashes were so constant and bright a person could have read a newspaper by its light.

Once everyone was safely inside, the wind began to blow with such force it caused suction on the door. It seemed as though the door was being ripped off its hinges. It took both DM and Willie all the strength they could muster to hold the storm pit door closed. Outside the pit, the straight-line winds sent several large trees in the yard toppling to the ground. Others swayed aimlessly back and forth like a drunk man on a railroad track.

Rain came down in torrents and began dripping through the roof in several places. The noise from the wind, rain, thunder, and lightning was so loud the family had to shout to one another just to be heard. The raging storm seemed to drag on forever. Adell prayed a silent prayer as she held Wilfred tightly in her arms.

By early morning it was over. It had been one of the longest and scariest nights any of them had ever been through. When Adell decided it was safe, the family quickly emerged from the bowels of the man-made pit to survey the damage. What they saw was unbelievable.

Trees were down everywhere. Debris and rubbish lay strewn across the fields. Trees, with their tops broken off like mere toothpicks, stood splintered along the road into town; others blocked the road entirely.

Several homes once located across the railroad tracks were completely blown down and destroyed. Others had their roofs missing. Some of the neighbors' barns and outbuildings were leveled, pieces of them landing in trees and along fence lines.

The Bone family was among the lucky ones. Although they

did have some clean-up to do, their home was still intact and everyone was safe. After experiencing that harrowing night, one thing was for sure: when Adell said, "There's a storm a comin'," the family never again hesitated about heading for the storm pit.

———

Julius and Willie Charles were in their midteens when they both decided to quit school to work on a government job at a CC Camp. World War II had begun. Eventually the two of them lied about their ages in order to join the service. They boasted about wanting to see the world and fighting the Germans.

While the war was going on overseas, food was being rationed here at home. Families were given coupons to buy their allotted share of meat, sugar, flour, shoes, gas, and even candy. The bulk of these goods was being shipped to the soldiers fighting the war.

Around the same time, Willie took a job cutting meat at Cooter Headley's store. Cooter would buy a cow or pig then have Willie kill it and cut it up for him to sell. The better cuts of meat, like the hams and shoulders, he sent to Montgomery to sell on the black market. He could get four to five times more for it there than he could selling it in Billingsley. The scrap meat was sold to the locals when and if they could afford to buy it.

Willie was good at sharpening hoes, axes, and saws. Neighbors and family were forever bringing their cutting tools to him to sharpen. The heavy metal file he used kept all his farm tools good and sharp. Sharp tools made the work easier and faster, which was fine with DM, as he was largely responsible for helping Willie cut wood.

Willie taught DM early on to use a crosscut saw. It was the type of saw they used when cutting up logs. The saw had a handle on either end. Willie would get on one end and DM on the other. One pulled the saw through the log as the other pushed it through. It was backbreaking work, but it also helped DM build the muscles up in his one good arm.

Springtime was the best time for cutting wood. The temperatures were still cool enough to be comfortable without sweating oneself to death. Willie and DM spent several weeks cutting enough wood to last through the year till the next spring. They stacked the wood at the edge of the lower field to allow it time to dry and cure.

By the fall of that year, things around the Turner Place had begun to take shape. Willie decided it was time to lay down the sugar cane. He and DM were on their way to the sugar cane field when they noticed that some wood appeared to be missing from the wood stacks. Upon inspection of the ground around the woodpiles, they found footprints. The footprints led over to wagon tracks. The wagon tracks led to the house at the back of the Turner place.

"Daddy, do you reckon our neighbors are stealin' our wood?" DM wondered.

Willie shook his head in disbelief. "That's sure what it looks like, all right. I ain't never known 'em to steal, but there's no way we can be sure. "

"What do ya reckon we ought to do about it, Daddy?" asked DM somewhat angrily.

Willie placed his hand on DM's shoulder. "Well, son," he answered, "these folks are our neighbors. I reckon if they did steal it they needed it, or they wouldn't have taken it. We'll go get the wagon and haul the rest of the wood up to the house. We should've done it already anyway."

DM knew in his heart that if they really needed the wood and would have asked for it, his daddy would have gladly divided with them. Instead, it appeared they chose to steal it from them. However, he also knew his daddy was not one to make trouble. The two of them decided it was best to let the incident slide. However, from that point on, their supposed dishonesty made Willie and DM a bit uneasy when it came to their back-door neighbors.

Shortly after they moved to the Turner Place, the family received bad news. Adell's brothers-in-law, Lonnie Huett and Lloyd Golson, came to tell Adell about her oldest brother, Dee. He had passed away at the age of forty-three from pneumonia. He was to be buried at New Prospect Baptist Church, near the old home place.

Adell took her brother's death pretty hard. Although Dee had always drunk way more liquor than he should have, Adell loved him dearly. He was her oldest brother and the first of her four brothers and five sisters to pass away. She cried as she remembered how he loved to play music and sing. From the fiddle to the mandolin, a guitar to a banjo, there wasn't a stringed instrument he couldn't play. He could play them all. She remembered back to the time when she was young. Dee would play the fiddle while her mama and daddy danced around the room. Everyone would be laughing and clapping to the music he played. Soon, just after his funeral, she fell into a deep depression, spending day after day in the hospital or at home in bed.

Imogene was twelve years old and in the seventh grade. When her mother was sick, the responsibility fell on her to be the woman of the house. She cooked, cleaned, and cared for Wilfred. She washed the clothes for the family in black cast-iron wash pots over an open flame. She worked in the fields when needed, as well as went to school. Her responsibilities left very little time for herself. Her only true getaway was the special times she spent on Sunday afternoons with her best friend, Sarah Nell Herrod.

Sarah Nell's family lived down the road on the other side of the creek. She first met Sarah Nell down at the creek when she and DM went there to play. It had rained hard the day before, and the creek overflowed its banks. They spent all day playing in the mud puddles left by the overflow. From that day forward, Sarah Nell and Imogene became steadfast friends. They could tell each other anything. They shared their hopes and dreams for the future. They talked about boys and about what they liked and didn't like about them. It was good to have a special friend to share things with. It was good to have an occasional Sunday afternoon to escape the reality of her life, if only for a few precious hours.

Although they were few and far between, DM had his moments of playtime too. From a lizard to a rabbit, he had always liked throwing rocks at anything that moved. If it walked on legs, he'd try his best to hit it. His arm was growing stronger with each day that passed. His aim got better all the time.

The first bird he killed with a rock happened when they lived back at the Patrick Place. He and his friend G.C. Hayes were at a black woman's house, who lived just down the road. DM spied a little bird up in the oak tree beside her house. He took a good-size rock out of his pocket and flung it at the bird, hitting it square on the head. The little bird fell to the ground, dead as a doorknob. The old colored lady witnessed the poor bird's demise from her rocking chair, where she was seated on her front porch. When the bird hit the ground, she quickly let out a half-baked laugh and hollered, "I's shore 'nough hates fer you's to be throwin' rocks at me, Mr. Bone."

DM picked up the bird and placed it in his pocket. "No, Ma'am. I wouldn't do that," he said. "My daddy would whoop me good if I was to throw rocks at a person. I'm just gettin' a little supper for tonight, that's all."

There were lots of bumblebees, or as some folks called them, carpenter bees, that continually buzzed around the Turner house. The males were black with fuzzy legs and a white head. The females were solid black. They were about a half inch long in size. The bumblebees seemed to be everywhere, darting back and forth across the yard at breakneck speed. They often stopped in midair, hovered for only a moment, then quickly dashed off in the exact opposite direction. DM decided to use them for batting practice.

He began by cutting the handle off a discarded broomstick he'd found laying in the yard. The stick was about an inch in diameter and maybe three feet long. He used the broomstick like a bat, swinging it at the illusive buzzing bees as though he was swinging at a ball. Soon he learned to hit them with 95 percent accuracy, a triumph for DM, a sad day for the bumblebees. However, this activity proved to be a wonderful teaching tool in the coming years when he started playing baseball on a regular team.

DM first started playing baseball soon after they moved to the Turner Place. The whole family worked hard every day, except Sundays. Sunday was a day of rest. During the summer months, the kids in the community would get together on Sunday afternoon and play ball. The Seymours, Littles, Bentleys, and Lloyd children would get together at one or the other's house and spend all afternoon playing ball.

There was no money to buy a store-bought baseball. Adell made them one out of an old discarded rubber ball that came from a set of ball and jacks. She unraveled a pair of Willie's old worn-out socks, winding the thread around and around the rubber ball. When the ball was big enough, she secured the end of the thread by pushing it back through the ball with a needle. It wasn't a real baseball, but it served the purpose. The neighborhood kids spent many a Sunday afternoon playing with that very ball.

DM was always giving Imogene a hard time. Because she was the oldest child still living at home, Imogene's job was to see after the younger ones. DM didn't like being told what to do by his older sister. Consequently, quite often, they were at odds with one another. Fighting was not allowed, but an occasional prank worked well as payback.

There were always chickens running around the yard. Where there were chickens, there were chicken turds. Imogene walked out the back door just in time to see one of the chickens drop a load of wet manure on the ground about ten feet from the back porch. DM was playing in the yard some twenty feet away. She saw this as a perfect opportunity to get back at DM for all the hard times he'd been giving her of late.

"Hey, DM," she called to him.

DM was busy throwing rocks at one of the passing chickens. "What?" he called back, somewhat agitated about being disturbed.

"Ya want to play Indian?"

"What do ya mean 'play Indian'?" he asked, at which time he spied a green lizard racing up the fencepost behind him and quickly flung a rock at it.

Imogene set about explaining the game. "Well, ya see, an Indian can walk as straight as an arrow while still lookin' directly ahead. He doesn't even have to look down to see where he's goin'. I bet ya can't do that," she challenged.

"I bet I can too," DM said, turning to face her. "Just watch me."

DM looked straight at Imogene as he started walking toward her.

"You're not doin' it right," she told him. "Ya have to put one foot in front of the other, heel to toe, and walk a perfectly straight line."

DM carefully put one bare foot down then moved his back foot directly in front of the other. "See, I can do it," he boasted.

"Just keep comin' straight and don't look down," Imogene

said. Her insides wanted to burst out in laughter. "If ya look down, ya lose the game."

DM didn't like losing any game to Imogene, especially one as easy as the one he was playing. He continued steadfastly across the yard, looking straight at her, being extra careful not to venture off his perfectly straight line. Just as Imogene had planned, he walked directly into the middle of the wet, gooey chicken manure. The gummy feces squished up between his bare toes and oozed over the sides. Immediately, DM realized Imogene had succeeded in pulling a really nasty trick on him. It took a whole bucket of water and a good scrubbing with lye soap before the mess was successfully washed off and the smell gone. Imogene laughed until her sides hurt. It was one of the best tricks she'd ever pulled on him. Unfortunately, she also knew he would surely figure out a way to get back at her in due time.

It was always a blessing for the children when school started back in the fall. It meant a partial break from farm work. Billingsley School was just under two miles from the Turner Place. The bus didn't pick anyone up who lived less than two miles away. The bus only picked up children who lived two miles or more away from the school. As bad as the road was in front of their house, the bus couldn't have gotten down it to pick them up anyway.

There were two routes to school: the road, which took longer, or across the field and alongside the railroad tracks into Billingsley. Adell didn't like for DM and Imogene to walk the tracks. She was afraid the hobos, who were well known for riding the rails, might kidnap one of them. Imogene and DM thought it was silly to walk by way of the road when that way took twice as long to get to school. Besides, they rarely ever saw anyone except folks they already knew.

———

Although the crops on the Turner place were the best the Bone family had ever raised, it seemed bad luck continued knocking on their door. Willie was able to pay the hundred dollars rent that year, but with all the sickness that besieged his family, he could never manage to get ahead.

It was toward the end of World War II. Willie's oldest son, Julius, was serving in the military in Guam as a radio operator. His job was to direct the planes as they flew on and off base. His job was relatively safe

Being away from home in a strange country made Julius realize things weren't as bad back home as he might have thought they were at one time. He missed his family. He even missed his stepmother and the sister he'd once been so jealous of. While he was serving in Guam, he managed to send Imogene several beautiful items of clothing. The colorful native clothing made Imogene feel like a queen.

On the other hand, Willie Charles was serving in the thick of the fighting. He was barely sixteen when he was sent first to Belgium and later to France. His job was to carry the radio for his commanding officer. The radio was used to stay in touch with the other company commanders. Several times during his deployment, Willie Charles wrote home to tell his family about the radio being shot right off his back. Willie worried his next-to-oldest son might never make it home alive.

Before Willie Charles went off to serve his country, he married a girl by the name of Edna Maxie. While he was away, Edna lived a great majority of the time at the Turner place with the Bone family. She and Imogene came to be good friends.

Willie returned home from a trip to Billingsley. As soon

as he walked in the back door, Edna asked him if he'd checked for mail at the post office. Without answering her, he dropped a letter on the table in front of where Adell was sitting. "We got a letter from overseas. Will ya read it to me? I think it's from Willie Charles."

Adell picked up the letter and opened it. The envelope was postmarked Germany. She carefully unfolded the letter and began to read.

Dear Daddy and Adell,

This war is hell on earth. We were fighting on the streets of Berlin. My friend was shot and killed. Bullets were flying everywhere. As I was running through one of the bombed cut buildings, my radio was shot right off my back. I'm ready for this war to be over. I miss home. If I ever get out of this hell alive I'll never leave America again. Pray for me.

Your son,
Willie Charles

Soon after his letter arrived, the atomic bomb was dropped on Hiroshima—the war ended. Only three men out of Willie Charles' entire company made it home. The commanding officer and Willie Charles were both wounded. The other soldier was lucky in some ways. He had not been shot, but he suffered daily with serious mental problems caused by the memories of the others he'd seen die.

Willie Charles spent several weeks in a veteran's hospital before he was finally allowed to come home for thirty days. He was as nervous as a long-tail cat in a room full of rocking chairs. The military called it being shell-shocked. Anytime there was a sudden, loud noise it made him jump. Willie would catch him staring off into the distance as if he was in a trance. At times his nerves were so on edge that no one dared to walk up behind him unexpectly for fear of retaliation.

While home on leave, he told his daddy he knew what

the army had in mind. They were giving him thirty days to be home; then they planned to send him to Japan. He told Willie he wasn't going back. He'd had enough fighting to last him a lifetime.

"If they want me to go to Japan, they'll have to dig me out of the swamp first," he declared to Willie in a determined voice. "I've done my duty. I'm not goin' back."

His injuries, both mental and physical, earned him a medical discharge.

When the war ended, so did many jobs. During wartime, Willie's sister Lena and her husband, Oscar, worked in Childersburg at a powder factory. When the war ended, the factory closed. When they could no longer find work in Childersburg, they decided to come back to Autauga County with their four children, all of whom were boys.

It was early one Sunday morning in the spring of the year. Adell and Imogene were cleaning some turnip greens to cook for dinner. Wilfred played in the yard nearby. DM was busy batting at the bumblebees flying around the porch. In the distance, they could hear what sounded like an automobile coming down the lane to their house.

DM struck out down the hill toward the road. "I hear a car a comin'!" he hollered. Adell stood up to see if she could tell who it was. All too often, visitors brought bad news.

DM was fast. He was already down by the road.

"Do ya see anybody?" she yelled to him,

"It's somebody in a Model-T truck-lookin' thing," he yelled back. "Some of 'em are walkin', and some of 'em are ridin'. I can't tell who it is yet."

"Lord have mercy," Adell said. "I hope somebody else ain't died."

As the truck got closer, Oscar stuck his head out the driver's side and waved to DM

"It's Uncle Oscar and Aunt Lena," he called to his mama. "And there's a whole bunch of younguns with 'em."

Adell wiped her hands on her flour sack apron. "Oh my Lord," she moaned. "Imogene, go get your daddy. I think he's down by the barn. What in the world will we feed all them folks? I reckon we'll have to go back to the turnip green patch to get more greens."

As it turned out, there were eight of them in all: Oscar, Lena, their four boys, and two more boys who didn't actually belong to them at all. Supposedly, they'd come for a visit. "Just until we can find work," Oscar said.

Oscar and Lena were the kind of people who would sit back and let other folks wait on them if they could get by with it, and Willie knew it. However, since it was prime time to work the fields, Willie agreed to let them stay only if they would help with work around the farm. However, their so-called visit turned into weeks, and the weeks into months.

Oscar and Lena did help work the fields, but what work they did in no way compensated for the extra work it took to feed them and their brood. Imogene and DM would go to the pea patch and spend half the morning picking enough peas for dinner and supper, or so they thought. Trouble was, Oscar's family wouldn't stop eating till every pea in the pot was gone. That meant Imogene and DM would be back in the garden that same afternoon picking something else to cook for supper.

Adell was already half sick. The added strain of having to fix food for all the extra visitors eventually put her back in the hospital. This left fifteen-year-old Imogene with all the cooking and housework to do again. Imogene usually liked having company. Seeing friends and family was a real treat for everyone, as visitors were few and far between. However, having somewhat-lazy visitors who ate you out of house and home was altogether different, especially ones who never went home. When Imogene wasn't cooking or cleaning, she was in the fields working. Exhausted and weary, she felt half sick herself. Perhaps she was coming down with the flu, or so she thought.

It was late summer. Everyone was busy picking cotton. As usual, Imogene cooked breakfast, washed the dishes, and then put on a pot of butter beans to cook for dinner. While the beans were cooking, she went to the field and picked cotton till dinnertime. Just before noon, she left the field, walked up to the house, put on a pan of cornbread to cook, and set the table. While the cornbread was baking, she poured glasses of milk for everyone. When the bread was done, she put the beans and cornbread on the table then called everyone to come eat. Lena, Oscar, and their kids were the first ones to get there. By the time Willie, DM, and Wilfred came through the back door, half the pot was empty.

When everybody was through eating, Imogene washed up the dishes and went back to the field. With temperatures in the upper nineties, the hot August sun made Imogene feel as though her brains were being baked. Her muscles ached. Sweat poured from her body. She felt as though the life was being drained right out of her. She missed her mother and wished she would get better so she could come home.

As the afternoon progressed, she began to feel worse and worse. She was completely and utterly exhausted. Barely able to put one foot in front of the other, she kept on picking because she knew she had to. The family's welfare depended on getting their cotton crop to the gin. By the time Willie decided to call it a day, the sun was ready to set.

Imogene walked slowly back to the house, dropping her cotton sack at the edge of the field. Normally, Willie would have made her pick it up and carry it to the wagon, but he could tell she was looking poorly. By the time Imogene reached the back porch, she didn't even have the energy to make it up the steps. She sat down on the edge of the porch and collapsed flat on her back across the floor. Her body hurt so badly she felt as though she would never move again. She was sick. Willie and DM helped her get to the bed, where she remained for several days.

Her body hurt from one end to the other. She ran a high fever. She was cold one minute and hot the next. She became so weak she couldn't even feed herself. On the seventh day, she awoke to find she couldn't move her legs or lift her arms. Willie realized then it was more than just the flu. He knew it was time to carry her to the doctor.

Willie borrowed Oscar's car to transport her to the same clinic in Prattville where Adell was being treated. Upon examining Imogene, Dr. Newton knew without question that she had contracted infantile paralysis, more commonly known as polio. Polio was believed to be highly contagious. Anyone who caught it was immediately quarantined from the general public. He knew no hospital would take her if they knew she had polio.

Imogene spent several weeks at the Prattville clinic before being sent home. With no one there who could take care of her needs, Dr. Newton decided to contact a small hospital in Birmingham that specialized in housing people suffering with paralysis and other debilitating illnesses. At first they informed him they did not have room for her. Desperate to get help for her, he explained her desperate situation. He told them how her mother was in the hospital being treated for a nervous condition. Therefore, there was no one at home who could take proper care of her. The clinic finally agreed to take her.

As was foretold in Adell's dream, an ambulance came down the lane to their house to transport Imogene to Birmingham. Although the trip took several hours, Imogene remembered very little of it. She was still so sick that everything was a blur.

The hospital was actually a two-story house that had been converted into a full-time care facility. Those who could walk were housed upstairs. Those who could not were given a room on the first floor. Imogene was put into a downstairs room with two other girls.

One of the girls was eleven-year-old Mitsy Sparks. She had polio too. However, her polio mainly affected her arms. She had always loved playing the piano. As part of her therapy, a piano was brought in to help encourage her to use her arms. It was very sad to watch her sit at the piano, trying desperately to raise her arms enough to reach the keys.

Clinic Roommates: Mitsy Sparks, Ruth Cantrell, Imogene

While Imogene was in the hospital, back home, bad luck turned to worse luck. Wilfred was collecting eggs. It was one of his daily chores. One of the hens laid some eggs in the back of the old wagon. Wilfred had always been little but feisty. Instead of asking DM for help, he bravely climbed up on the wagon without assistance, lost his balance, and fell, thus breaking his arm.

Willie was in the barn tending the stock. DM was lugging an armload of wood into the house from the woodpile. When they heard Wilfred's frightening screams, DM immediately dropped his load of wood and hit the steps in a full run. By the time Willie got to his boys, DM was holding Wilfred's arm in his hand. The arm had a clean break just below the elbow. The tiny bone protruded out to one side, not breaking the skin.

"I think it's broke, Daddy," DM said.

Willie kneeled down to take a look. "No question about it, son," Willie declared, shaking his head in disbelief. "Go fetch Willie Parker. See if he can take us to see the doctor."

Upon arriving at the clinic, the doctor gave Wilfred a mild sedative to calm him down. The bone would have to be put back in place before a heavy plaster cast could be built around it to keep it stable. Even with the sedative, it took a nurse, Mr. Parker, and Willie to hold Wilfred still while the doctor put the bone back in place. The cast would need to remain on his arm for eight weeks.

Adell was in and out of the hospital on a regular basis. The anxiety of all the added people in the house, along with Imogene's illness, Wilfred's broken arm, and worrying about money, was too much for her. The doctors were puzzled by her illness. One doctor suggested her teeth were causing her medical problems, whereupon she had all her teeth extracted and was fitted with a pair of false teeth. Another said it was her gallbladder and suggested surgery to remove it.

Dr. Newton did not agree with the other doctors. He suggested to Willie what he thought it was. "Mr. Bone," he explained, "I still think your wife's problem has more to do with her nerves than anything else. She's under a lot of stress. Your daughter has polio. She's worried about that. I know your money situation isn't the best in the world. She's worried about that. Those are life situations we have very little control over. However, if there is anything else that you know about that could be causing her extra grief, I suggest you get rid of whatever it is if at all possible."

Willie knew exactly what the kind of added grief the doctor was talking about, but how could he tell his sister and her family they had to leave when they had no place to go?

Eight weeks passed. It was time for Wilfred's cast to be removed. He was very excited and could hardly wait. He was tired of lugging the heavy cast around. Besides, his arm itched something awful. He couldn't wait to get the cast off so he could give his arm a good scratching.

First thing on Monday morning, Willie Parker drove Wilfred and Willie back to the doctor. When the doctor removed the cast, Wilfred couldn't believe his eyes. His arm was wrinkled up like a prune. The top layer of skin was loose and peeling away. It smelled bad too. The nurse washed it good with soap and water and then applied a thin layer of cream to soothe the itching. By the time they left the doctor's office, his arm was feeling much better; even the itching was relieved.

On that same Monday afternoon, DM and Wilfred decided to go over to Willie Parker's house to thank him again for taking Wilfred to the doctor. As they were walking down the road, talking, Wilfred suddenly tripped, falling directly on his arm—the same arm that had been taken out of a cast just that morning. He immediately began to cry.

DM helped Wilfred to his feet. "Are you all right?" he asked.

"My arm, my arm. It hurts bad," he cried.

"Let me see it." As soon as DM saw his little brother's arm, he knew immediately it was broken again. "It'll be all right, Wilfred. Don't cry. Jump on my back. I'll carry ya home."

DM crouched down so Wilfred could jump on his back. DM ran as quickly as he could all the way back to the Turner place. As he was running up the hill toward the house, DM spied his daddy in the cow lot. "Daddy," he called, "Wilfred fell and hurt his arm again."

When Wilfred saw his daddy, he began to cry harder. When Willie saw Wilfred's arm, he knew without a doubt it was definitely broken. Reaching for his son, he cradled the small, frightened boy in his arms. A knot formed in Willie's stomach. *Will all the hardship never end?* he thought to himself.

Willie tried to comfort his son. "Don't cry, Wilfred. We'll take ya down to Willie Parker's house. We'll have to see if he can drive us back to the doctor. Try not to fret. It'll be all right."

Willie carried Wilfred the quarter mile to the Parkers' house. DM walked alongside them. When they arrived, Mr. Parker met them at the front porch steps.

"Howdy, Willie," he said. He looked at Wilfred's arm, which was already beginning to swell. "Looks like y'all got more trouble."

"Yelp," said Willie. "DM and Wilfred were on their way over here when he fell. I was wonderin' if ya could drive us to the doctor again."

"Sure enough, Willie," answered Mr. Parker. "I'd be glad to help ya out."

Mr. Parker reached for his hat, hanging on a peg just inside the door. He had never felt any worse for anybody in his entire life than for his friend Mr. Bone. Adell was in the hospital in Prattville. Imogene was in the hospital in Birmingham. He was sharing his home with eight extra mouths to feed. Now, for the second time in a row, his youngest boy had broken his arm. Willie Parker was a God-fearing man. He knew the Bible taught that God would never put more on a man than what he could handle. At that moment, he just couldn't see how even a man like Willie Bone could handle so much hardship all at one time.

Had Willie Bone been a lesser man, he might have folded under the weight of so many burdens. But Willie was like the mighty oak tree that stood outside his bedroom window. When the winds of fate blew hard against his heart, he would bend, but he refused to break.

Willie, Adell, and Wilfred just after Wilfred broke his arm

DM was eleven when all these tragedies seemed to be happening at the same time. Not only was it hard on his father, but it was hard on him too. He'd heard his mother repeatedly talk of dying and death. She worried about everything. His sister, whom he loved very much, was extremely sick from a disease he knew little about. His little brother had suffered two broken arms in a row. His house was full of people, which meant more work on him and his daddy.

Although bad luck seemed to have blossomed since moving to the Turner place, the land was good and the crops plentiful. Willie and DM worked the entire forty acres. Sometimes they did it alone. Other times, they had help from the neighbors.

There were ice trucks that traveled through the community selling blocks of ice. A twenty-five-pound block could be purchased for a nickel, a small price to pay for such a wonderful treat. However, even a nickel was hard to come by. It really didn't matter about the ice truck anyway. The ice truck only ran on the main dirt roads, the ones the county kept grated. The road in front of their house was usually too washed out for any vehicle to drive down. DM would have been glad to meet the ice truck at the intersection of the county road, but they seldom had an extra nickel to spend on a luxury such as ice.

The Turners, owners of the house they rented, were some of the best neighbors the Bone family had. The house in which the Turners lived was about a quarter of a mile behind where the Bone family lived. They had electricity in their house, whereas the rental house did not. In the summertime, Mrs. Turner would freeze two extra trays of ice each day. Come dinnertime, DM would run down to their house with a bowl. Mrs. Turner would empty the ice trays into his bowl. DM would smile and thank her. He would then run the quarter mile back to his house as fast as he could.

It was nice to have ice for their tea. It was even nicer having friends like Mr. and Mrs. Turner; something as simple as making a tray of ice cubes for a neighbor meant a lot to folks back then. Neighbors depended on each other for their very survival. When the world seemed to be closing in around you, neighbors were people to whom you could turn. Family and friends were all a poor man could depend on. DM thanked God every day for his family and for his friends.

On the backside of the Turner place was where Walter Little's family lived. Mr. and Mrs. Little had two boys, Walter Jr. and Randall. They also had four girls: Dorothy Jean, Sally Jo, Ruby Nell, and Bobbie Sue. They were a few years younger than DM. Quite often they played together in the woods between their houses, especially during the winter months, when chores were fairly limited.

There were several deep ditches back down in the woods where they liked to play best. The high embankment surrounding the ditches kept the cold winter winds blocked off. When the sun was shining, it was fairly comfortable for the children as they played games like tag, marbles, and stickball.

———

Not only was there an incident with the Bone family's wood being stolen, but there was also another incident when green beans came up missing from Adell's bean patch. The beans did well that year, hanging in huge clusters on the vines. They were so plentiful, Adell canned beans almost daily just to keep up. They shared beans with their neighbors and with family members who needed them.

The missing beans were discovered one morning when Adell and DM went down to the field to pick beans. To their surprise, the vines at the far end of the field had been picked clean.

"Looks like someone's been stealin' our beans, Mama," DM said, shaking his head in disbelief.

"It shore looks like it," Adell responded. "Don't see why anybody would think they need to sneak in here and steal 'em. All they need do is ask for some beans if they need some. I just don't understand folks wantin' to steal. Ya best not ever let me catch ya stealin' anything."

"I know better, Mama." DM laughed. "Daddy would tan my hide to a fare-thee-well. Who do ya reckon took 'em?"

Adell reached for a cluster of beans at the top of a vine. "I have an idea 'bout who it was but there ain't no way to know for shore. I don't reckon we ought to accuse nobody without actually seein' 'em do it."

A few days later, another one of the neighbors dropped by the Bones' house to drop off a letter he'd picked up for them at the post office. Willie offered him a mess of beans in exchange for his kindness.

"Ya must be sharin' beans with everybody in the county," he said. "I was ridin' the train back from Montgomery a day or two ago. As the train was passin' by, I saw ole' Spur pickin' beans on the lower end of the field. It was real early in the mornin'. I thought it sort of odd. I didn't know he got up that early for anything."

Adell's suspicions had been right. Spur was the one who had stolen the beans. However, rather than cause conflict, once again Willie let the incident pass.

⸺

It was nearing the Christmas holidays. Adell was finally home from the hospital. Imogene had been in the clinic in Birmingham for several months. It seemed as though it had been forever since the family had seen her. Birmingham was just under a hundred miles from Billingsley, but it might as well have been a thousand. Since Willie didn't own a car, the only way they had to get there was to borrow a car or pay someone to take them. The longer Imogene was away, the more the family longed to see her. Willie decided he would try to find a way to get her home in time for Christmas.

Cooter Headley was kind enough to loan Willie his car. It took every penny Willie had to buy gas. It would mean no money for Christmas gifts, but everyone agreed Christmas just wouldn't be the same without her there to share it with them. Three days before Christmas, Willie drove to Birmingham to get her. She still couldn't sit upright on her own, so they laid her across the backseat of the car. The trip back home took several long, often-uncomfortable hours. However, it was a joyous reunion when they finally arrived.

One of the things Imogene missed most while she was in the hospital was her mama's good cooking. All she'd had for breakfast over the past several months was wheat mush. Like all the hospital food, it was totally tasteless and bland. To Imogene's delight, the first morning after she arrived home, she awoke to the smell of Adell's homemade biscuits and canned sausage. Imogene ate like there was no tomorrow. For dinner, Adell warmed up a jar of vegetable soup mixture she and Imogene canned at the beginning of summer. She also baked a pone of cornbread to go with it. Imogene couldn't remember the last time she had had anything that tasted so good. Then, on Christmas morning, like every Christmas morning for as far back as Imogene could remember, there was also her mama's hickory nut cake.

All too soon, the week-long visit came to an end. It was time to go back to the hospital. Willie loaded her up in the back seat of Cooter's car. Hugs, kisses, and tears followed. Although the week was short-lived, it was a week Imogene would cherish the rest of her life.

December turned to January, January to February. One cold winter morning, Adell was preparing breakfast when she suddenly stopped and looked directly at Willie. "Willie," she said, "I want to go see Imogene."

"I do too," he agreed, looking rather forlorn. "I thought about askin' Oscar if he would take us up there in his truck. We'd have to pay for his gas to get there and back, but he might take us if I ask him."

Adell planted her hands firmly on her hips. "Well, he should take us. They've been here six months or longer, eatin' our food and us waitin' on 'em hand and foot."

"I know," said Willie. "I thought they'd have 'em a place of their own by now."

Adell took the coffee pot from off the stove and poured Willie a cup of hot coffee. "Ya know good and well they ain't gonna leave here till ya make 'em leave. Why should they? They've got a place to sleep and food to eat. They've got no reason to leave. I want ya to ask Oscar if he'll take us to see Imogene. If he says no, then I think it's time for him and the rest of his brood to go."

"I'll ask him this mornin'," promised Willie.

Oscar agreed to take everyone to see Imogene as long as Willie bought gas for the truck. They would leave early Sunday morning. It was also decided Wilfred would spend the day with Mr. and Mrs. Friday.

Sunday morning proved to be one of the coldest days of the year. The grown-ups rode up front in the cab of the truck, and the children huddled in the back. Adell brought along several quilts to help them stay warm, but the quilts were very little help. The cold, damp wind whipped around the sides of the truck, freezing them nearly half to death.

Most of the county roads were unpaved and often quite rough and hazardous. It was nearly noon by the time they arrived at their destination. DM was glad to finally get there. He was so looking forward to seeing Imogene, as was everyone else. However, when they tried to enter the clinic, the children were turned away.

"I'm sorry," the receptionist told them. "There are no children allowed past the lobby. We do not want to take the responsibility for these children catching any diseases. They will need to either wait in the lobby or wait outside."

DM was very disappointed, but he didn't want to catch polio either. He'd seen what it had done to his sister. He might have only one arm, but at least he could walk and run. He didn't know what he would do if he couldn't run. That was the worst thing he could possibly imagine.

Oscar and Lena sat down on a small leather couch near the entrance. Oscar wanted to remain near the door so he could go outside to smoke. DM and his cousins took a seat on the floor along the wall of the waiting area. The clinic floors were shiny and slick. DM watched as the nurses and doctors in their starched, white uniforms passed back and forth down the hall. Occasionally, a patient would roll past in a wheelchair or hobble past on crutches. In the air was the smell of disinfectant. He hated that smell. It always reminded him of the long days and nights he'd spent at Saint Margaret's Hospital.

An attendant escorted Willie and Adell down the hall to Imogene's room, which she shared with two other girls. Several nurses were busy changing the beds. Upon their entering the room, the attendant spoke to one of the nurses. "These people are here to see Imogene Bone."

A dark-haired, heavy-set nurse was busy tucking the remaining corner of the sheet in place. When she was finished, she looked up at Willie and Adell and smiled. "Imogene is in therapy at the moment. She should be back shortly. Are you her parents?"

"Yes, we are," Adell replied. "How's she doin'?"

The nurse picked up the dirty sheets, placing them in a large canvas bag. "She is able to sit up in a wheelchair now," she responded. "She began therapy last month. I know she will be thrilled to see y'all."

"What does she have to do in therapy?" Adell asked.

"Each day, her therapist takes her to the hot tubs, where she is completely emerged in hot water up to her neck," explained the nurse. "At first, the therapist had to move her legs for her. However, I'm told she is slowly beginning to regain movement for herself. She's a real fighter. Imogene's personal nurse, Mrs.

Carmack, gives her a daily massage to stimulate the blood flow in her body. I'm told she is slowly regaining her strength."

Imogene finished her therapy and was being wheeled back to her room. She always felt exhausted after her therapy session. She was just entering her room when she looked up and saw her mother and daddy standing just inside the door. Tears of joy filled her eyes. "Mama, Daddy," she called, extending open arms to greet them. "Is it really y'all?"

Adell rushed to her side, hugging her precious daughter tightly in her arms. "It's us. How's my baby doin'?"

"I'm better, Mama," she answered. The lump in her throat grew bigger as she choked back her tears of excitement. "How are y'all?"

Willie took his turn hugging her neck then kissed her on the forehead. "We're fine."

"How did y'all get here? I can't believe you're actually here."

"Lena and Oscar brought us," Willie answered. "They're in the waitin' room with the younguns. DM wanted to see ya too, but they won't let 'im."

"I can't believe y'all are here," Imogene repeated, wiping the tears from her eyes with the back of her hand. "I sure have missed everyone." Imogene pointed to her roommates. "Mama, Daddy, this is Mitsy and Ruth."

"I met 'em when I came to get ya for Christmas," Willie recalled, smiling at the girls. "How y'all doin'?"

Mitsy and Ruth smiled back. "Fine," they answered simultaneously.

The attendant and Willie helped Imogene get back into bed.

Adell sat down on the side of bed next to her daughter. "I've missed ya so bad I couldn't hardly stand it at times. We didn't have no way to get here, or we would have come before. I told Willie Oscar could bring us. He owes us that much."

"Are they still livin' there with y'all?" Imogene asked in disbelief.

Adell glanced over her shoulder at Willie, her eyebrows drawn close together in the middle of her forehead. "Ya know they won't leave till somebody makes 'em leave."

There was so much to talk about and so little time to do it. Imogene wanted to know about everything going on back home. She asked about her friend Sarah Nell. She wanted to know about school and what was happening there. She was being tutored there at the clinic so she wouldn't fall a grade behind when she returned home, but it wasn't like being in a real school. She asked about the crops that year and how they had done. She also asked about Wilfred and how his arm was doing. She showed them a picture of some flowers she was embroidering on a piece of cloth. She had never done embroidery before, but she found she liked doing it, and it also helped pass the time.

All too soon, the visit came to an end. Adell and Imogene both cried as they embraced and said their good-byes. Willie hugged his daughter and told her he loved her, promising to come back as soon as they could find or afford a way to get there.

Imogene at the clinic in Birmingham

As it turned out, with the exception of the one week during Christmas when Imogene got to go home for a visit, that one short visit to Birmingham was the only time they got to see Imogene during her entire stay at the clinic. She spent ten long months in the Birmingham clinic and saw her family only twice the entire time.

The day finally arrived when Imogene got to go home from the hospital for good. She was still using crutches to walk, but at least she was able to walk on her own again. She'd made many new friends while at the hospital, but going home was the happiest day of her life.

A few days after Imogene got home, the family went to Montgomery to see Adell's sister Emma and her family. Adell's other sister, Ruth, her husband, Lloyd, and Big Mama were also visiting Emma's house that day. Imogene was excited about seeing her aunts and uncles again. It had been almost a year since she'd seen any of them.

Imogene chose to wear a pair of tan, knee-length shorts and a white shirt. The clothes were a gift from Katherine Carmack, her personal nurse, during her stay at the hospital. She and Imogene had become very close during Imogene's confinement. Mrs. Carmack had even taken Imogene to her home for a visit. Imogene looked quite pretty for someone who'd spent ten long months inside a hospital. Her hair was curled and combed nicely. She felt happy to be walking again, even if it were with the aid of crutches. She was able to get out of the car on her on now. Slowly but proudly, she walked unaided across the yard toward her Aunt Emma's house.

As she was approaching the house, Big Mama met her at the steps of the porch. Although her grandmother had never been one of Imogene's favorite people, she was still glad to see her. "Hi, Big Mama," she said, smiling.

However, in lieu of a warm welcome, Big Mama began scolding her. "Lloyd Golson don't take kindly to women wearing them kinda clothes 'round him," she said angrily. "If ya ask me, they're disgraceful."

Lloyd wasn't one of Imogene's favorite people either. He was known for getting drunk on weekends. She also knew his own two girls, Dorothy and Zelda, wore shorts all the time. She couldn't believe the first thing her grandmother said to her after not seeing her for a whole year could be so mean. She wanted to tell her how mean she was. Instead she replied, "Well, I didn't come here to please you or Lloyd Golson." Feeling both angry and hurt, she returned to the car, where she remained for the entire visit.

After Imogene returned home, Lena and Oscars' family soon wore out their welcome. What was supposed to be a short visit had turned into nearly a year. Adell was weary of cooking and cleaning up after them. Without Imogene's help, the work had taken its toll on her. Willie finally told them it was time to go.

Oscar decided to go back to Childersburg with his family. However, as he was unable to find a job, their venture was short lived. It wasn't long before they moved back to Billingsley, whereupon they rented a house and land from Mr. Dave Tindle. The house was near where Adell and Willie were living.

Oscar knew very little about farming. Since there were no factory jobs available, the family quickly fell destitute. It was not unusual for them to run out of food. Desperate, Lena would send the four boys over to Willie and Adell's place so the boys would at least have something to eat. Willie and Adell would feed them for a while. Eventually, Adell would make Willie take them back home again. It seemed their dependency on Willie and Adell would never end. When they could no longer pay the rent, Lena and Oscar were forced to leave Mr. Tindle's place. From there they moved some fifteen miles away to the town of Cooper, Alabama.

Willie always got his supply of fertilizer in the spring of the year and stored it in the barn. One Sunday morning, the family decided to go to Cooper to visit with Lena and Oscar. When they returned that evening, they discovered someone had stolen a ton of Willie's soda, soda he used to side-dress his corn and cotton crop. The only evidence of who had taken it was the wagon tracks leading away from the barn. Unfortunately, the tracks disappeared a short distance later. The robbery was an especially hard blow to the family. They had purchased the soda on credit. The debt would have to be paid back to the mercantile regardless of the circumstances.

The next morning, Adell poured Willie a cup of strong coffee. "I prayed about our soda last night. I prayed that whoever it was who stole it would pay for their meanness. I asked the Lord to let the soda they stole burn up anything they put it on."

That year, one of their closest neighbors' corn crop dried up in the fields, failing to produce a single ear of corn.

<hr>

While living at the Patrick place, Willie purchased a .22 bolt-action Springfield rifle from Freddie Waites. Freddie decided he wanted to play football. In order to play, he would need a pair of football shoes to wear. He decided to sell his gun to get the money. When Willie heard he was selling the rifle, he went to Freddie's house.

"I heard tell ya got a Springfield rifle for sale," he said to Freddie.

"Yes sir," Freddie answered.

"How much are ya askin' for it?"

"I'll take six dollars," Freddie replied.

Six dollars was a lot of money, but Willie felt it was a good investment. A good rifle was a must-have during the winter, when the meat supply was running low. Willie reached inside his overall pocket and handed Freddie six silver dollars.

DM learned to aim and shoot with his BB gun while he was very young. As he got older, he began to beg his daddy to let him hunt with the .22. The gun weighed nearly ten pounds, much heavier than his BB gun. However, all the farm work DM was doing had made him strong. Surprisingly, he managed to hold the gun at shoulder level using his one good arm. With unbelievable accuracy he learned to shoot squirrels, rabbits, and even birds flying overhead. Even with his handicap, he killed what he aimed at the majority of the time.

Adell was always afraid he was going to hurt himself with the gun. She would visualize him accidentally shooting himself, lying somewhere out in the woods bleeding to death. When he decided to go hunting, he would try to sneak the gun out of the house without her knowing it. Otherwise, he would have to listen to a lecture on being careful.

Times began to look up for the Bone family. They had lived on the Turner place for three years. Julius had come back from service and was helping his daddy with the farmwork. Willie Charles had come home too. Edna lived with her in-laws for a time while Willie Charles was away. When he returned home he and Edna moved into a home of their own.

Imogene was home from the hospital but was limited in her ability to walk long distances; this presented the family with a new problem. Since Billingsley School was within two miles of the Turner place, the bus would not pick her up. It was decided they would have to move somewhere outside the two-mile limit in order for Imogene to qualify to ride the bus.

The Cooter Headley Place

For years, Cooter Headley worked for Walter Patrick at his store in Billingsley. When Mr. Patrick decided he was getting too old to deal with the store anymore, he sold it to Cooter. Cooter was a good businessman and soon became very successful with the store. Eventually, Cooter bought the Smedley place, which was located on the road that ran behind the town of Billingsley. On this land he built a house. After the Bone family decided they needed to move, Willie went into Billingsley to talk to Mr. Headley about renting the house.

When Willie entered the store, he tipped his tattered, gray hat to several men sitting near the front of the store playing checkers. After joking with the men for several minutes about who might be winning, he then made his way toward the back counter. A bushel basket half full of red apples was sitting beside the counter. Willie propped his foot on the edge of the basket then spoke to Cooter about renting his house. "Mr. Headley," he said, "I'm interested in rentin' that house ya built over to the Smedley place, along with the forty acres of land that surround it."

Cooter propped his foot on a crate of oranges he'd had shipped in from Florida. "Well, ya know, Willie, the house ain't completely finished on the inside yet."

Willie looked at the oranges in the crate, secretly wishing he could take some home to his family. "We need some place to move so Imogene can ride the bus to school. We've lived in worse places."

"Ya know if ya want it, it's yours," Cooter said, smiling.

Willie extended his hand to Cooter, and the two men shook on it.

Shortly after, the Bone family once again packed up their belongings and moved. Although the house was newly built, it had no electricity either. Two fireplaces heated it. The house was cold in the winter and hot in the summer. They drew their water from a well. It was nice that the house was new, but unfortunately, the land was poor. To make matters worse, an extreme drought hit the area. Although spring usually brought rain, the ground was dry as a bone, making it almost impossible to plow. Willie plowed and planted his crops in June. Come September, it was so dry his shoeprints could still be seen in the ground from when he'd walked behind the plow in June. The only thing that made even halfway decent was a patch of watermelons.

Although the sickness that seemed to plague the Bone family had subsided, times remained hard. With each failing crop, they went farther and farther in debt. Willie found what work he could from wherever he could find it. Every little bit he could make at whatever he could find to do helped to keep the family going.

A week or so before school started, Willie and Adell took

the children over to the school to get them registered for the coming school year. DM was in the sixth grade. Wilfred was just starting first grade. Imogene was about to enter the tenth grade. Imogene was very excited about starting back to her regular school. While she was in the hospital, Mrs. Fritz had been a good teacher, but it wasn't like being in a real school. She was anxious to join her old class and get back into the swing of things.

However, to her dismay, the principal, Mr. White, informed her she would not be joining her old class. "I'm sorry," Mr. White told her. "You've missed an entire year of school. You'll have to make up your ninth grade classes before entering the tenth."

Imogene never imagined she would have to repeat ninth grade. "But, Mr. White," Imogene argued, "I did my ninth grade classes. Mrs. Fritz came to my bedside every day. She taught me the same subjects I would have been taught here. She sent my grades here to the school. I passed all my classes."

Mr. White acted as though he didn't see the importance of Imogene starting back to school with her old class. "I realize Mrs. Fritz may have given you passing grades, but as far as I know, she is not an accredited teacher. Therefore, I cannot in all good conscience place you into a grade you have not earned."

Imogene was so angry she wanted to cry, but what could she do? Mr. White was the principal. However, when Julius heard about what Mr. White wanted to do, he was furious. If there was one thing being in the service had taught him, it was to stand up for what you believed in. Julius didn't believe it was fair to make Imogene repeat ninth grade, so he went above Mr. White's head, directly to the school board. Once the school board checked out Mrs. Fritz's credentials, she was indeed found to be an accredited teacher. When all was said and done, Imogene was allowed to start school with her old classmates.

Each year at Halloween, the school held a contest to help raise money for things the school needed. The students always nominated two girls to run for Halloween queen. That year they nominated Imogene and Dorothy Mims. It was the responsibility of the nominee to collect money. Each penny counted as a point toward her win. The night of the festivities, the money had to be turned in and counted by a certain time in order for it to count.

Julius and several others collected money for Imogene. The money was turned in at the table in plenty of time to be counted. However, due to unknown circumstances, Imogene's money was neither counted nor posted at the time it was turned in. Although Imogene had collected the most money, Dorothy Mims was declared the winner. After the announcement of the winner, a huge argument ensued. Several fights almost broke out. Eventually the principal promised to give everyone their money back. Since no one knew exactly how much or who had given a penny here and a penny there, the money was never actually returned. Dorothy Mims remained the proposed winner and was crowned that year's queen.

That same winter, a flu epidemic hit the area. DM fell sick. He ran a high fever. His throat felt as though he'd swallowed sandpaper. His head throbbed. His entire body hurt from his head to his toes. He could barely breathe. Food had no taste. He wouldn't eat and grew weaker by the day. None of the home remedies Adell tried seemed to help.

When Willie decided to make a trip to Billingsley, he asked DM if there was anything he could bring him.

DM felt so bad he could hardly raise his head. He could think of only one thing he wanted. "I want a Coca-Cola, Daddy," he answered weakly.

Willie brought home a six-pack carton of six-ounce Cokes. Since they had no electricity, they didn't have any ice to put in the Cokes, so DM drank them at room temperature. Between four o'clock that afternoon and bedtime that night, he drank all six Coca-Colas.

Since the onset of his illness, DM was sleeping in the bedroom, which had a fireplace. In the middle of the night he suddenly awoke from a dead sleep. The bed felt as if it was going around and around in circles. He felt lightheaded and sick to his stomach. Although he felt deathly ill, he decided not to wake his mama and daddy. He knew they were tired from all the long, sleepless nights they'd spent caring for him during his illness. He sat up on the side of the bed, pulling the chamber pot from beneath it. Leaning forward, he tried to vomit but couldn't. He tried lying back down. As soon as his head hit the pillow, the spinning in his head started again. He immediately sat back up. When he sat up the second time he began to vomit. By the time his vomiting spell was over, he'd vomited up nearly a cupful of what looked like green, slimy gall. Later that night, his fever broke and he began to feel better. Although the worst was over, it was still several weeks before he was fully recovered.

<hr />

One of the chores DM hated most was drawing water from the well for the mule and cow. It took several buckets of water to fill the five-gallon container. Each bucketful weighed between ten to fifteen pounds. Once the container was full, he had to then carry it across the road some thirty yards to the trough. The five gallons of water weighed close to fifty pounds. Fifty pounds was a heavy weight to carry even for a person with two arms, much less an eleven-year-old with only one arm.

Eventually REA brought electrical service to the area. Cooter had the electric company run wires from the main line to the house. He and Willie ran wiring from the outside line to inside the house. A hole was drilled through the wall, and a single wire was stapled to the ceiling outward to the center of the room. A single light bulb hung down and was turned on and off by pulling a cord that was attached to the socket. For the first time ever, the Bone family had electric lights in their house.

Once they had electricity, Mr. Headley decided to install an electric pump on the well so the family could have running water. With the installation of the electric pump, they could also run a pipe under the ground to pump water to the cow and mule. The next spring, Willie decided it was time to start digging the line. He wanted a ditch dug from the well, across the road, and out to the barn.

"DM," Willie said, handing him some tools, "take this here pick and shovel. I need ya to dig a trench. Make it at least twelve inches deep. It needs to run from up there at the well all the way across the road to the waterin' trough."

DM looked at the meager tools he was given and then at the hard red-clay ground beneath him. "Okay, Daddy," he replied somewhat reluctantly. "Does this mean I won't have to tote water no more?"

Willie smiled and shook his head yes. "That's what it means, son," he said. "I would do it myself, but I've got to work out of town the next few weeks."

"I'll get it done, Daddy," DM promised. "Ya know how I hate carryin' water. I'll be glad to dig that trench if it means I don't have to carry no more water."

DM worked every day on his trench from sunup to sundown. It was hard, grueling work. The ground was nothing but pure red clay. The farther he got into the ground, the harder it was to dig. At times, he would have to hammer the sticky, gummy clay several times before he could break loose even a single piece of dirt the size of his thumbnail. Regardless of how hard the task, he was bound and determined to dig that trench. When he found himself becoming the least bit disheartened, he would think about the day when he would no longer have to carry water. Upon doing so, the task seemed much less dauntless. It took him several gut-wrenching weeks to complete his job. When the trench was finally finished, Cooter and Willie laid down the pipe.

When the last section of pipe was installed, Willie called to him, "DM, would ya like the honor of turnin' on the faucet to see if it's gonna work?"

DM raced over to the faucet. "Yes sir," DM answered anxiously. Slowly he turned the handle. As he did so, the electric pump hummed as it began to pump water from deep within the well. DM could hear the water as it began to fill the pipes. Quickly, he ran across the road to wait for the water to come out the other end. He waited for what seemed to be a very long time. At first, the water ran muddy. However, once the pipes were cleaned out, cool clear water flowed freely from the pipe, filling the trough.

DM jumped up and down with joy, flinging his arm in the air. "Hooray!" he shouted. "No more totin' water. Whoopee! Hooray!"

When DM was around twelve years old, Mr. Edward Golson from the Indian Graves community decided to start a small baseball team. DM and several of the other boys in the community were asked if they would like to join it. Since most of them had no way to get to the games, Mr. Golson would take them in his car. DM was an exceptional player. His days spent throwing rocks and batting bumblebees were finally paying off. Mr. Golson assigned him as pitcher. In fact, he did most of the pitching for the team. He also turned out to be one of their leading batters.

The first year the team was formed, they won nineteen

out of twenty-one games. The other two games were tied and called at dark because there were no lights on the field. The one-arm boy's legacy grew as the Billingsley team won game after game.

The Randolph community also had a good team. However, the Billingsley boys beat the Randolph team in their first game played at Randolph's home field. They would later face them again in a return game to be played at Billingsley's home field.

One young player on the Randolph team stood out among the others. His name was Jake Wilcox. He was a big boy for his age, standing over six feet tall and weighing close to 220 pounds. He was an excellent batter, hitting home run after home run for his team.

There were two games scheduled that day, one with the older boys and one with the junior team, which DM played on. Jake stepped up to the batter's box. DM was pitching. He knew if Jake connected with the ball, it would surely mean a home run for the Randolph team. DM also knew that in an effort to keep Jake from hitting the ball clean out of the park, he would have to choose his pitches carefully. DM intentionally threw the first three pitches outside the strike zone. Unfortunately, the big boy was a good player and let them pass by.

Jake's father stood on the sidelines watching. After the umpire called, "Ball three!" he yelled to his son, "Just stand there, son. Save your strength. That one-arm freak is gonna walk ya."

Charles Jones was the pitcher for Billingsley's older team. When he heard what the man said, he yelled out to the big boy's daddy, "Say, Mister Wilcox, I'll bet ya fifty dollars DM strikes your boy out."

Mr. Wilcox laughed boldly and hollered back, "Son, ya got yourself a bet."

Up to that point, the count was three balls and no strikes. Trying to force Jake to strike at a wild ball had failed. DM decided it was time to try his curveball. The crowd fell silent as DM lined up for the next pitch. Bending over slightly at the waist, DM held the ball behind his back, carefully wrapping his fingers tightly around it. Stepping back then lunging forward with all the force he could muster, he let go a long, fast, curveball. The ball looked as if it was going to the outside then suddenly curved inward, directly across home plate.

"Strike one!" the umpire yelled.

The next two pitches DM threw were also strikes. Jake was out. Charles Jones had made a long-shot bet but was fifty dollars richer thanks to DM's outstanding pitching.

The Autaugaville team was also on Billingsley's line-up. Autaugaville's team knew they were facing Billingsley's unbeaten team and the one-arm boy would likely be pitching. They decided to put two of their older players on the junior team, hoping to end Billingsley's winning streak. It was not to be. They lost. Four times that year, Autaugaville played the Billingsley team. Each time, they added more of the older boys to their roster. However, the Autaugaville team proved to be no match for the Billingsley boys. With DM pitching each time, Billingsley won all four games.

By the time DM started the eighth grade at Billingsley High School, his reputation as a left-handed, one-arm pitcher had grown. His slow-pitch curveball left many a batter confused. His fastball was outstanding. DM loved the game. It seemed as though he lived to play ball. As an eighth grader, he began playing with Billingsley's varsity team. Usually a player could only be on the varsity upon entering the ninth grade.

Each player needed a sponsor, someone who would be responsible for buying the player a jersey to wear in the games. Bud Darnell owned a plumbing company in Montgomery and was a good friend of Willie's. He would often drive from Montgomery to Billingsley to go bird hunting with Willie during bird season. It was on one of those bird-hunting trips DM decided to ask Bud about being his sponsor.

As they trekked across the cornfield, DM nonchalantly brought the subject to mind. "Hey, Bud, how about bein' my baseball sponsor?" he asked.

Bud knew DM was a good player. He also knew that without a sponsor, DM's family could in no way afford to buy him a jersey. "What does it cost to be a sponsor?" Bud asked.

DM's enthusiasm grew. "The jerseys cost fifteen dollars. They put the name of your business on the back of the shirt. Ya get free advertisin' every time I play a game."

Bud patted DM on the shoulder. "Sounds like a good deal. Count me in."

Bud gave DM the fifteen dollars to buy a jersey. His number was fifteen. He continued to wear that same number and was sponsored by Darnell Plumbing for the next five years of his baseball career.

The first game he played with the varsity team was against Marbury High School. Preston McCord and Clackston Grant were the best players on the opposing team. They were seniors and had already signed contracts with major league teams to play on their minor leagues. After the first few endings, Marbury was ahead. It seemed McCord and Grant couldn't be stopped. With the bases loaded, the coach called timeout. He walked out to the pitcher's mound, where Charles Jones was pitching for Billingsley.

"Charles," he said, reaching for the ball, "we need to throw these boys off. I've decided to put DM in the game. I think DM's curveball may be just what we need to do it."

Charles handed the coach the ball. "I think you're right, Coach. My fastball just ain't workin' on 'em."

Coach signaled for DM to get in the game. The five-foot-tall, eighty-pound eighth grader headed onto the field. As

Charles and DM crossed paths, Charles patted DM on the shoulder and said, "Show 'em what ya got, buddy."

McCord was next at bat. DM threw the first ball. As McCord drew back to hit it, the ball suddenly took an inward curve. McCord decided not to swing.

"Strike one!" the umpire yelled.

McCord was in awe. As DM wound up to throw the second ball, McCord held a solid stance, ready to put it out of the field.

Again, the slow-pitch ball made a sudden curve just before reaching the batter.

"Strike two!" the umpire yelled a second time.

"What do ya mean, ump?" yelled McCord in protest. "That was no strike."

The umpire stood his ground as DM wound up for his next pitch. McCord was determined not to let another pitch go by. He drew back his bat. The third ball made its way across the plate. McCord swung hard but missed the ball completely.

"Strike three!" yelled the umpire. "You're out!"

The crowd in the stands roared. The thirteen-year-old, one-arm boy from Billingsley sent Preston McCord to the dugout. No one could believe it, not even DM

Then it was Grant's turn at bat. The outcome was the same. Three strikes, and he too was out. DM didn't know how he had done it, but he had struck out the two best players around. Although Marbury won the game that day, no one could ever take away the pride DM felt when he struck out two of Autauga County's best.

DM loved playing baseball. He was not only a great pitcher, but he was one of the fastest runners on the team. If he got to first base, you could bet he would end up stealing second and even third.

The Billingsley team was playing a game against Verbena's team. With a line drive down second base, DM made it to first.

When the second baseman missed catching the ball, he saw his chance and hightailed it for second base. However, just as DM was approaching the base, the shortstop managed to get hold of the ball and pitched it to the second baseman. Determined to get on base, DM fell to the ground on his left side and slid into second. He was declared safe, but the rocky ground dug deep into his leg from his knee all the way to his butt.

When DM got home from the game, Adell saw what a mess her son's leg was. Carefully, she washed the wound with soap and water to remove the dirt and grit. Unfortunately, the combination of sweat and dirt had already begun to set up an infection. By the third day, puss was visible under the scabs. When Adell saw what was happening, she immediately set to work doctoring it the only way she knew how.

"DM," she demanded, "ya go get in bed right now. I'm gonna fix some Epsom salt and warm water to put on that leg."

Instead of going to bed, DM reached for his jersey. "I ain't got time to go to bed, Mama," he protested. "We've got a game today."

"The only game you're gonna play is gettin' in bed and lettin' me doctor that infection. Do ya want the doctors to cut your leg off too?"

"No," he answered blankly.

"Then get in the bed, and I'll be back with a rag and some salt water to soak it in."

DM knew by his mama's tone of voice there was no use arguing. Adell returned shortly with a clean white cloth. She had DM turn over on his side then laid the cloth on his leg. Slowly, she spooned the warm salt water over the cloth until it was saturated. Every few minutes she would wet it again. Around noon, she removed the bandage to see if there was any improvement. The underside of the white cloth was yellow. The salt had drawn out much of the infection from the wound. She took the cloth in the kitchen and washed it thoroughly in hot, soapy water. Every few hours, she repeated the procedure. By evening, the infection was better and his leg began to heal.

———

Imogene was seventeen when she started the eleventh grade. Although she was a beautiful girl with a perfect figure and tiny waist, she had never dated much, mostly because Willie wouldn't allow her to date. He was very protective over his daughter. Once, when Imogene was fifteen, a young man from the community pretended to visit DM when in reality he was there to see Imogene. When Willie found out about his real intentions, he announced angrily, "I'll have that boy jumpin' barbwire fences as high as his head. Y'all tell him he'll have to deal with me if he comes messin' 'round my daughter ag'in."

The summer following Imogene's junior year, she decided to visit Delene and her new husband, Calvin Grant, at their residence in Montgomery. Reluctantly, Willie and Adell decided to let her go. Calvin and Delene lived in a duplex apartment next door to the Benton family.

The Benton family had several children, but one of the boys in particular caught Imogene's eye. He was a tall, handsome, dark-haired, brown-eyed young man with a beautiful smile and a slender build. His name was Hubert. Imogene was taken by his good looks and dry-witted charm. While Imogene was visiting, Delene invited Hubert to have dinner with them. It was soon obvious Hubert felt the same about Imogene. It wasn't long before he asked her out on a date. Imogene knew that had she been at home, her parents would never have consented to the date. Since she wasn't at home, she went anyway. The two of them had a wonderful time. Almost immediately, Imogene found herself falling in love.

Imogene and Hubert shortly after they met

When Imogene returned home, Hubert began driving to Billingsley to see her every opportunity he got. It didn't seem to matter to him that she'd had polio and walked with a limp. All he knew was he was in love with the most beautiful girl he'd ever seen.

Unlike the few other boys Imogene had dated, surprisingly, Willie took to Hubert right off. He was a hardworking, easygoing kind of person. He also liked hunting and fishing. He fit right in with the kind of man Willie wanted for his daughter and he wanted for a son-in-law; this pleased Imogene to no end.

When the summer ended, Imogene began her senior year of school. She and Hubert continued dating, secretly planning their future together. Summer turned to fall. Blackbirds darkened the skies overhead. Before Imogene met Hubert, she hated the coming of the blackbirds, as it meant another cold winter was on its way. Now, for some reason, the blackbirds didn't seem to bother her as badly, as she had other more important things on her mind.

Wintertime came to an end. It was once again time to start preparing for their spring garden. DM watched as Willie hitched up Ben to the plow.

"Daddy, can I see if I can plow?" DM asked, halfway expecting a no answer.

Willie pondered the question for a moment before answering, "Do ya think you're ready for the job, DM?" he asked.

DM bowed up his arm, tightening his muscle. "I'm gettin' real strong," he answered.

Seeing the well-formed muscles in his son's arm, Willie smiled. "I guess ya are at that." Willie stepped from behind the plow. "All right then, take hold of the reins. Keep the rows as straight as ya can. Ben will do the rest."

DM wrapped the reins around his hand and grabbed the handle of the plow. "Giddyup, Ben," he called to the mule.

Ben stepped forward; the plow dug into the ground. At first, it was hard to control the plow and hold the reins at the same time, but soon DM and Ben got in unison with one another. Before long, the garden was plowed and ready for planting. Once DM learned to plow, Willie left much of the plowing up to him. To make ends meet, Willie was having to pick up more and more work outside the farm.

One of the things that made DM stronger was cutting firewood from strips of slab. Slab wood is what is left over from a tree that has been cut into lumber. The strips average twelve to fifteen feet long and three to four inches wide. Willie would haul in a ton-and-a-half truckload of slab at a time. It was DM's job to cut them into pieces small enough to fit in the stove or in the fireplace. In order to do this, he would lay a piece of slab on a cutting block and chop a piece off. He would then have to put down the ax, slide the slab down to however long he wanted it, pick up the ax, then cut another piece. Most times it would take him two weeks or more to cut up the entire load, but eventually he managed to get it all cut.

To get a fire started required lightwood, or light'erd, as it was better known. This light'erd was made from pine stumps that had hardened and seasoned with time. When DM came across one of these light'erd stumps in the woods, he hitched up Frank to the ground slide and hauled the stump to the house. Frank was the mule Willie bought after Ben was too old to do his job anymore.

DM weighed about eighty pounds. A good average-size stump weighed four hundred pounds. The biggest challenge was getting the stump out of the ground and onto the slide. The chore was made easier by first splitting the pine stump with his ax. He would then cut down an oak tree about the size of his arm. Next, he sharpened the pole at one end and slipped it down into the slit. By twisting the pole around sideways, he could break the stump loose from down in the ground. The two halves were then loaded onto the ground slide, where-upon it could be hauled to the house. Once he got the stump home, he cut it into kindling to start the fires with. A stump of light'erd lasted from two to three weeks, depending on how big the stump was. Therefore, every week to two weeks, DM would need to go down in the woods and bring up another stump. Running out of kindling was not an option.

One day as DM was roaming through the pasture, he spotted several light'erd stumps just up the hill from their house. He decided it would be best to get the stumps out of the ground first then go back for Frank and the ground slide.

There were several small stumps in the same general area. DM successfully removed the smaller stumps from the ground without any problem. However, a little farther up the hill from where he'd been working was another stump, larger than the rest. It would need to be split. He would need to use his ax and an oak pole for that one. Raising the ax high over his head, he came down hard across the stump. To his surprise, a swarm of yellowjackets instantly filled the air. Without a doubt, there is nothing more ferocious than a nest of pissed-off yellow jackets. DM took off down the hill as fast as his legs would carry him, leaving his ax embedded in the stump.

When DM decided the yellowjackets had settled down, he hitched Frank to the ground slide and headed back up the hill to retrieve his collection of light'erd. He successfully loaded all the stumps onto the ground slide, with the exception of the one containing the wasps. Regardless of the danger, he knew he would have to retrieve his ax. Quickly but cautiously, he pulled the ax from the stump and hightailed it for the slide. His intentions were to throw the ax on the ground slide too. However, just as he was about to throw it, a yellow jacket stung Frank right on the flank. That mule took off like a possum with a blue tick hound on its trail, strewing light'erd stumps all the way back to the house. It took DM a good part of the day to find and gather up the scattered stumps.

Imogene was in her last year in high school. Willie and Adell were very proud of her. She was to be the first of their children to graduate from school. Julius and Willie Charles had quit school early on to join the service. After Julius got out of the service, he did go back to school under the GI Bill of Rights, where he earned a degree in law. Willie Charles never finished school. As soon as he was discharged from the army, he went to work right away. Delene married and also quit school prior to her graduation. However, despite her battle with polio, Imogene remained determined to finish school and get her diploma.

Imogene's graduation

Imogene and Hubert had been dating regularly for right at a year. They were deeply in love and ready to marry as soon as school was out. She graduated on Wednesday, and on Sunday, June 2, 1948, she and Hubert, along with their witnesses, Delene and Calvin, drove to a preacher's house in Highland Homes and tied the knot. They rented an upstairs, two-room, apartment on Harmon Street in Montgomery, near Hubert's work. Within the first year, Imogene became pregnant with their first child. The following June, a baby girl was born. They named her Teresa Ray.

After a lifetime of being without, Willie was finally able to purchase a car. It was a Ford Model-A Coupe with a stick shift in the floor. DM was fourteen at the time. Like all boys his age, he was more than ready to learn to drive. However, steering the car while changing gears at the same time using only one arm was another difficult challenge. However, he was as determined to master driving, as he had been with everything else he had ever learned to do.

By trial and error he discovered he could hold the steering wheel steady by leaning against it with his shoulder. He could then push in the clutch with his left foot, reach across with his left arm to change gears, then accelerate with his right foot. It was quite a chore, but one he soon mastered quite well.

The cotton crop had done well that year. However, with most of his children grown and gone away from home, Willie had to hire some black folks to pick it. With Willie away from home much of the time doing public work, overseeing the job was left up to DM. After the cotton was picked by the hired hands, it was taken to the gin in Billingsley and sold. With hot weather persisting, the remaining boles of unopened cotton down in the bottomland continued to open. Willie knew there was still a good amount of cotton left that could also be picked and sold. He also knew the cotton crop would have rotted in the fields if not for DM's help. He decided to give DM the opportunity to make some money of his own.

"Son," he said to DM, "if ya want to bother with picking the rest of the cotton that's opened up out there in the field, ya can have whatever money ya get from the sell of it."

DM liked having money of his own. Picking the remaining cotton sounded like a good idea to him. Every day thereafter he went to the fields to pick the leftover cotton. He picked right up to the day when Mr. Cleave Billingsley's gin was to close for the season. Dick Huett, an acquaintance of DM, had a small truck. DM hired Dick to haul the cotton to the gin for him. Although it was only a little over two miles to the gin, Dick charged DM fifteen dollars to haul it for him. Before DM left for the gin with his cotton, Willie called him aside.

"Now ya know, son, Mr. Headley is supposed to get a third of everything we make on his land. When ya sell your cotton, ya go over to Cooter's store and tell him how much ya got 'cause he's entitled to his cut. Ya tell him it was the cotton left over after the main pickin' was done and how ya picked it yourself. I don't expect he'll take any money under those circumstances, but ya have to at least offer it to him."

DM sold his cotton at the gin that day. After he paid Dick Huett his fifteen dollars, he went down to Cooter's store. DM explained to Mr. Headley about having picked the leftover cotton himself and how he had taken it to the gin to sell.

To DM's surprise, Mr. Headley raised one of his eyebrows and scratched his head. Then he spoke. "Now, DM, ya know your folks are workin' on thirds with me. I feel I'm entitled to get a third of that money ya got for that cotton. It's only right."

DM halfheartedly handed Mr. Headley a fifty-dollar bill and waited for his change. When Cooter handed him the remaining money, DM counted it. That was when he realized Cooter had given him change back for a twenty-dollar bill instead of a fifty-dollar bill.

DM looked at the money in his hand then counted it a second time just to make sure he hadn't made a mistake. Cooter was just about to walk away when DM called to him, "Mr. Headley, I gave ya a fifty-dollar bill. Ya gave me change for a twenty."

Mr. Headley quickly slammed the cash drawer closed. "Naw, DM, you're wrong. Ya gave me a twenty."

DM knew he'd given Cooter a fifty and therefore became a might agitated. "No sir, Mr. Headley," he said. "I gave ya a fifty. Ya open up that register again, and I'll show ya."

Seeing the anger growing in the young boy's eyes, Mr. Headley reluctantly opened the cash register. Sure enough, there it was, plain as day. DM had given him a fifty. Cooter's face turned a dark shade of red. "Well sir, I guess ya were right, DM," he said. "I reckon ya did give me a fifty. I shore thought it was a twenty." Cooter took the correct change from the drawer and handed it to him.

As DM was riding back home in Dick's truck, he thought about how unfair he felt Mr. Headley had been. Ordinarily, the leftover cotton would have rotted in the field had DM not picked it. DM didn't think it was right or fair. He knew Cooter was a businessman in business to make money, but he also suspected Mr. Headley had intentionally tried to jip him out of his correct change. That was something he never thought Cooter Headley would do. He reckoned his daddy was right; some folks would do things you never thought they'd do when it came to matters concerning money.

After all was said and done, DM had thirty-five dollars left from the sell of his cotton. He knew exactly how and where he wanted to spend it. The very next day, he walked over to Billingsley and hitched a ride to the Red Arrow Hardware store in Prattville. He was going to spend his hard-earned money on a brand-new gun of his own choosing. He picked out a bolt-action, 410-gauge shotgun that held five shells. He also bought two boxes of shells. He spent almost every penny of the money he'd made off his cotton, but he was proud of his new gun.

Hunting season started the next day. The first day of hunting season was always a big deal in the Bone household. Willie Charles and Edna came to the house the night before so Willie Charles could go hunting. Hubert and Imogene came too so Hubert could join in the hunt. That night after supper, DM proudly brought out his new gun to show Willie Charles and Hubert. Imogene was immediately displeased when she found out he'd spent all his money on a gun.

"DM," Imogene scolded, "ya should have bought ya some school clothes with that money instead of spendin' it all on a gun."

Hurt by her harsh words, he snapped back, "It was my money. I earned it. I wanted a gun, not new clothes."

Taking the gun from Hubert's hand, he promptly left the room, both hurt and angry.

The next morning, Imogene and Edna continued chastising DM for what they felt was a frivolous use of his money. As soon as breakfast was finished, Willie Charles, Hubert, and DM decided if they were to kill any squirrels that day, they needed to get in the woods. As for DM, he was glad to be leaving the subject of his new gun and the irresponsible use of his money behind.

When the three of them got to the edge of the swamp, they decided to split up. Hubert and Willie Charles went one way, DM another. The hunt went well for DM. The brown canvas bag he had slung on his back was full of bushy-tailed squirrels. He decided it was time to head back to the house. Before leaving, he looked around for Hubert and Willie Charles, but they were nowhere to be seen. He figured they had already gone back home or were still out hunting.

As he was making the long walk out of the woods, he was hoping Edna and Imogene would lay the subject of his gun to rest. However, the minute he walked in the door, he soon discovered he once again had two angry women to deal with.

Imogene met him at the door. Edna was right behind her. "Where's Hubert?" Imogene asked, enraged.

"And Willie Charles," added Edna, annoyed he was not with him.

DM stomped the mud off his feet just outside the door then scooted past them and into the house. "I reckon they're still in the woods," he replied. He propped his new gun upright in the corner of the room.

"I can't believe ya left the woods without them," raved Imogene.

DM removed his jacket and hung it across the back of a table chair. "We split up right after we got in the woods. I don't know where they are," he replied

"What if they get lost down there in that swamp?" a worried Edna asked.

"They're grown men," DM reasoned. "Willie Charles found his way around France and Germany. I think he should be able to find his way back home from the woods of Billingsley. Hubert has squirrel hunted all his life. Give 'em credit for havin' a little bit of sense."

Imogene angrily turned toward the window facing the woods just in time to see both Willie Charles and Hubert emerging. "There they are." She beamed.

Turning back to DM, she snapped, "Ya lucked out this time. Ya better thank your lucky stars they showed up when they did."

DM threw his sack of squirrels on the table. "Here's your supper, girls. I killed 'em; now y'all can clean 'em." *Women,* he thought to himself, *I'll never understand 'em if I live to be a hundred years old.*

DM went to his room and sat down on the bed, still angry that Imogene had fussed so about him buying his gun. In a few minutes, the back door opened. Hubert and Willie Charles were back from their hunt.

"Where's your squirrels?" he heard Imogene ask.

"Neither one of us killed a single squirrel," Hubert answered.

Alone in his room, DM smiled.

One Spot turned out to be one of the best hunting dogs in the county. Although One Spot was a small dog, he was good for just about any kind of hunting from rats to squirrels, rabbits to opossums. If he decided to get after something, he wouldn't stop until he caught whatever it was. All too often, his fearless nature got him into scuffles with other animals twice his size and a lot more ferocious. Wilfred was too young to hunt, but he and One Spot were best of friends.

There had been an infestation of rats around the county. The huge rodents were eating the seeds Willie planted right out of the ground. One Spot hated rats. Wilfred decided to take One Spot out into the field, among the terraces, and teach him how to dig up the rats from the soft, plowed dirt. It didn't take him long. Once One Spot caught on to the smell of a rat, he would dig until he found it, whereupon he killed it straightaway. One day as One Spot and Wilfred were out killing rats, DM decided to go out to the field to watch them.

"Ya know, Wilfred," warned DM, "that dog's liable to dig up more than just a rat out of the ground. What are ya gonna do when he digs up a snake?"

No sooner than DM said this, One Spot reached down into the hole he had just dug, pulling out a four-foot-long rat snake, tossing it right into Wilfred's lap. Wilfred screamed and jumped to his feet. Quickly, One Spot grabbed the snake by the back of its head with his sharp teeth, shaking it violently until it was dead. However, that experience was the end of digging up rats for Wilfred.

Later on, Willie got Brownie, a wooly looking brown dog, three-quarters shaggy feist and one-quarter bulldog. Brownie belonged to Willie Parker's daddy. When the young dog started treeing squirrels, Willie asked old man Parker if he could have the dog for hunting purposes. Sure enough, Mr.

Parker gave Brownie to him. Unfortunately, Brownie didn't like the idea of a new home. Willie had to keep him on a chain for nearly three weeks to keep him from going back home to the Parkers' house. Eventually, Brownie got used to his new home and decided to stay.

Although Brownie and One Spot had two totally different techniques for hunting bushy-tailed squirrels, they worked well together. Brownie hunted in a straightforward line, going from one tree to the next. One Spot hunted in circles around Brownie. Together they were able to cover more ground in less time. It was nothing for Willie and his two sons to come home with twenty-five or thirty squirrels in one day's time. This always meant there would be a fine meal on the table that night for supper.

Brownie wasn't much of a barker. If he could see you, he'd simply jump up on the side of the tree and wait until you got there. If he couldn't see you, he would give two short, raspy barks and patiently wait until you found him.

On the other hand, One Spot was a barker. There was never any doubt when One Spot treed a squirrel. His short, choppy yap made him easier to find than Brownie, but regardless of which dog treed, you could rest assured a bushy-tailed squirrel was sure to be somewhere in the tree.

One winter it rained for three days in a row. On the third day, the rain stopped around dinnertime and the sun came out. Willie figured he'd been cooped up in the house long enough. He shouldered his rifle and said to DM, "Come on, son. Let's go down to Misletine Branch and see if we can kill some squirrels this evenin'."

DM got his shotgun from behind his bedroom door. Soon, they were on their way, with Brownie and One Spot tight on their heels.

By the time they got to the swamp, Brownie had already treed a squirrel up a big oak tree. DM shook a vine on one side of the tree. When the squirrel moved to the other side, Willie shot and killed it. Brownie walked over to where the squirrel had fallen, carefully smelling it. He turned back to the same oak tree, jumped up on it again, and gave two raspy barks.

DM was about to walk away from the tree when Willie called to him, "Wait a minute, DM. There must be another squirrel in this tree."

Willie shook a bush on his side of the tree. Another squirrel came around, this time on DM's side. DM took aim and shot, killing that squirrel also. Brownie ran over, sniffed the squirrel, and then once again leaned up on the tree for the third time, barking his two husky barks. DM shook another bush on his side of the tree, and a third squirrel turned around on Willie's side. Willie shot the squirrel, and it too fell to the ground with a thud. This time when Brownie smelled the squirrel, he was finally satisfied. This one was the squirrel he had put up the tree to begin with. Without hesitation, he was on his way in search of yet another squirrel. Between One Spot and Brownie, they treed over fifteen squirrels that day in a matter of a few hours.

Brownie was known to be the smarter of the two dogs, but for sure, One Spot could hold his own when it came to sniffing out squirrels. One day, Willie, DM, and Adell's brother Buck decided to go hunting down off a hillside in the hollow back of where they lived. There was a long fence line that ran through the hollow, separating two farms. One Spot ran up to one of the light'erd fence posts and started barking as though he'd treed a squirrel. Willie kept calling him off the post, but every time he'd go right back to the same post and start barking again. DM and Buck laughed at One Spot for being so dumb as to tree a fencepost. However, One Spot remained determined. Finally, Willie went over to check the situation out.

Upon closer inspection, Willie discovered a hole in the top of the fencepost, going all the way down to the bottom. He took out his pocketknife and stuck it into the bottom side of the post. Out scurried a big red fox squirrel.

Uncle Buck decided One Spot wasn't so dumb after all. "Doggone it," he said, laughing. "One Spot knew there was a squirrel in that hollow fencepost all along. He was bound and determined to let us know it was there. I guess we were the dumb ones."

One of the last years the Bone family farmed, they planted oats to feed the animals. The oat crop wasn't great, but it was good enough to store in the shed. It was soon discovered a herd of wharf rats were getting in the shed, eating the oats. DM and Wilfred took Brownie down to the shed to try to kill some of the rats. As soon as they opened the shed door, they could hear rats scurrying in every direction. After surveying their surroundings, they found where the varmints were getting in and where they were hiding. It was around a post at the corner of the building where the lumber came up on each side. The rats were hiding inside a hole behind the lumber. There were so many of them they were packed in the hole like sardines in a tin can.

DM stuck a pitchfork in the bottom rat to prevent the other rats from backing out of the hole. He then used an ice pick to stab the remaining rats. After all the rats in the hole were dead, he removed the pitchfork and raked out the bloody corpses. Sometimes he dug as many as eight to ten dead rodents out of the hole at any given time.

Killing the rats was a messy, bloody job, not one either of them relished doing. However, it was reality. It was what had to be done. The rats were their enemy, robbing them of food meant for the animals. It was a part of what their life was about, living to survive.

One Spot was an older dog when Willie got him. He finally died of old age, his face scarred from his run-ins with angry opossums, skunks, stray dogs, and other wild animals.

After One Spot was gone, Willie and his boys had other hunting dogs, but none were ever as good as old One Spot and Brownie.

Mother Nature is the farmer's best friend and oftentimes his worst enemy. Too much rain, and the crops rot in the fields. Not enough rain, and the crops don't make. In high school, DM was required to raise a crop for his FFA (Future Farmers of America) project at school. He chose to plant watermelons. No sooner than the watermelon plants got little melons on the vines, a drought hit the area. Temperatures soared into the triple digits.

DM tried carrying water from the creek to water his plants. The ground was so hot and dry that the water evaporated the minute it hit the ground. DM ended up selling his watermelons for fifteen cents each. When he figured the costs of his seeds, fertilizer, and time, he'd lost two hundred dollars on his crop. It was the same scenario he'd seen happen with his daddy a hundred times over. The farmer was always at the mercy of Mother Nature.

One of DM's favorite things to do since he was just a little fellow was fish. When he lost his arm, he had to learn to bait his hook using only one hand, not an easy task when dealing with wiggly red worms, catalpa worms, crickets, and the like. Sometimes he used chicken livers, even wasp nest larva; it didn't matter. Regardless, he soon learned how to put any kind of bait on his hook that was available to him

Most of his fishing was done at night after the day's chores were finished. He and Willie would head down to Autauga

Creek, Swift Creek, Turn Pike Creek, sometimes even Little Mulberry Creek. With little time to fish before it got dark, they would usually set out a line of baited hooks across the creek then go back early the next morning to retrieve their catch. Most of the fish they caught at night were either catfish or an occasional eel. They would usually clean them at the creek then take them home for Adell to cook for breakfast.

When DM was around seventeen years old, he met a man named Lynn Bozeman down at Pake Stevens Sporting Goods. Lynn introduced DM to fishing with a spinning rod. Most of the rods they sold were set up for right-handed people to use. Lynn set up DM's rod for a left-handed retrieve. With much practice and determination, DM soon learned to cast the rod then hold it firmly between his knees to reel it back in. His favorite artificial lure was a mepps. He learned to catch everything from bream, bass, and even catfish on this kind of lure. People were always amazed to watch the young one-arm boy casting a rod and reel with so much skill.

It was not unusual for Willie and DM to come in from the fields at dinner and Willie to be out of tobacco. "Son," he'd say, handing DM some money, "run over to Billingsley and get me a can of Prince Albert."

Although "run over to Billingsley" was simply a phrase and was not meant literally, that's exactly what DM would do. He liked to run. He knew it helped him keep in shape for when he played baseball. In fact, he ran almost everywhere he went.

DM hung out a lot with the Chandler boys, Nelson and Junior; the Huett boys, Pete, Dick, and E. J.; and Wiley Frank and Sue Rawlinson. All of them smoked. Every time they went opossum hunting together in the woods, his friends would get to egging DM about starting to smoke. DM knew how opposed his mama was to smoking. He'd heard her fuss at his daddy a thousand times, trying to get him to quit.

"It ain't gonna hurt ya none," Wiley Frank would assure him. "Besides, ya ain't really a man till ya start smokin'."

Before long, DM did begin smoking. At first, he would sneak around to do it, but eventually he got brave enough to start smoking in front of his folks. As he'd expected, Adell was furious when she found out. She'd always felt it was not only a waste of good money, but bad for your health too. "Ya need to quit that smokin', DM," she'd say, scolding him. "That's how come your daddy coughs all the time. It's gonna kill him one day. It'll kill ya too. Ya need to quit it now afore it gets its' hold on ya."

Willie warned DM too. He admitted it was a bad habit to get into, but he also felt he couldn't say too much, being that he himself smoked.

Wiley Frank was a good ol' boy but was known to be two bricks short of a load. DM and the other boys found out he was afraid of the dark. Just for the meanness of it, they would pull tricks on him to scare him. DM and the Chandler boys spent a lot of time in the woods. All the boys knew where the fence lines dividing the property were, whereas Wiley Frank did not. When the mischievous boys would get about fifty yards from where they knew there was a fence, they would turn off their lights and take off running. Wiley Frank would run wildly after them, afraid he would get left alone in the dark. When they knew a fence lay ahead, they would stop, while Wiley Frank would run headlong into the barbwire. DM never understood why Wiley Frank continued to go hunting with them. Almost every time they went hunting together it was the same thing. Yet every time, Wiley Frank fell prey to their pranks. He knew if his buddies had done that to him he would have stopped going along, but not Wiley Frank.

The last year they lived at the Headley place was the last year Willie did any real farming. He lost money all three years they farmed there. The dry-weather conditions in the area had taken their toll on all the farmers. Money was tighter than ever.

To top it off, a fierce wind came blowing up out of Texas. The fields were already dry and dusty from the previous three-year drought. As the forty- to fifty-mile-an-hour winds ripped across the sun-parched ground, dust filled the air. It did little good to sweep the floors or dust the furniture. Five minutes later, everything would be covered in layer of dust again. To everyone's dismay, the harsh winds continued to blow for several days.

On the third day, the dust got so bad that Billingsley School decided to close until the windstorm was over. The children held their books against their faces to protect themselves against the stinging sand whipping across the schoolyard. Those who carried umbrellas to protect themselves against the sand and dust found them of little use. Most were blown away or turned inside out. Fighting against the wind, they raced to the buses that would take them home. Even the children who lived within the two-mile distance from the school were allowed to ride the bus to their homes.

When the buses where finally loaded, they began their slow route home. With each heavy gust of wind, the big, yellow bus swayed back and forth. At times, the driver could barely see the road in front of him. Some of the little ones were so scared they began to cry. Even the older children were afraid too, although they tried not to show their fear for the sake of the younger ones.

Just as the bus was topping the hill near Etta Rawlinson's Place, a gale-force wind hit the side of the bus so hard it tilted the bus to one side, causing the driver to lose control. The tires on one side were lifted completely off the ground. It felt as if the bus was going to roll over on its side, sending it down the steep embankment that ran alongside the road.

Several children screamed loudly. Some began to pray out loud. Others grabbed for the back of the seat in front of them, holding on so tightly the knuckles on their hands turned white. When all seemed lost, the straight-line wind subsided. The bus landed upright with a hard thud. It was finally back on all four tires. Luckily, the bus had not tipped over and no one was hurt, just scared half to death. DM and Wilfred were grateful when they arrived home safely and were back on solid ground.

Between three years of drought and the poor land at the Headley place, Willie was up past his ears in debt, making it impossible to get anything else on a credit. Desperate, he decided to ask the only person he thought might have the money available to loan him, his daughter Imogene. He hated asking her, but the loan was important. It would mean the difference between getting next season's crops in the ground and never farming again.

Summer of 1949

Left to Right: Julius, Imogene, DM, Delene,
Little Wilfred, Willie Charles

As soon as the opportunity presented itself, Willie took Imogene aside so he could talk to her in private.

"Imogene," he said, shamefully, "I can't get no more credit at the mercantile in Billingsley. Ya know yourself these last three years have been tough. What little money I've managed to make on the side ain't never enough. We've barely got enough money to get by." Willie lowered his head, not wanting to look his daughter in the eyes. "To make a long story short, I need ya to loan me the money to get this comin' year's crops in the ground."

Imogene could feel the anguish in his words. She knew how hard it must have been for him. Before answering, she thought hard about what her daddy was asking and what it would mean if she refused. She and Hubert had the money to loan him. Hubert was making good money at his construction job in Montgomery. They were doing pretty good financially. They had even managed to put a little money into a savings account at the bank, something her father had never been able to do.

She also knew farming had been a huge part of her father's life. He'd had other jobs here and there. Truth be known, the other jobs had actually been what had kept the family going. All farming had done was put them farther in debt. She believed he could do a lot better if he would stop farming altogether. What made it most difficult for her was knowing her father had never asked her for anything in his entire life. Getting up the nerve to ask her for money had to have been one of the hardest things he'd ever done. Her answer to him was going to be the hardest thing she had ever done.

"Daddy," she said, her voice cracking as she spoke, "I could loan ya the money, but I'm not goin' to. You're wastin' your time continuin' to farm. Ya know as well as I do the land here is poor. It's just plain ridiculous to keep puttin' yourself farther and farther in debt. Ya could get a full-time public job somewhere. You're good with your hands. You're a hard worker. I'm sure ya could get some work in construction. Hubert could see about gettin' ya on with the company he works for. I hate it worse than anything to turn ya down. But I have to do it for your sake, as well as the rest of the family. I just think ya would be better off to forget about farmin' and focus on makin' a livin' doin' something that has a future."

The hurt in her daddy's eyes was almost more than Imogene could bear. He looked as though the life was being sucked right out of him.

Tears welled up in her eyes. "I hope you understand, Daddy," she said. "I'm so sorry I can't do this for ya. You'll see I'm right if ya just take time to think about it."

Willie didn't answer. Instead, he laid his hand gently on her shoulder, nodded, and walked away.

Imogene cried.

Willie was not an educated man, but what he lacked in education he made up for in common sense. After pondering the situation for a day or two, he decided to take Imogene's advice; after all, he had no choice. He and Hubert hired on with Trans Continental Gas Lines. Along the gas line routes were substations. The gas lines were building houses for their employees working at the substations. Hubert and Willie were hired to put asbestos siding on the houses. They were paid five hundred dollars for each house they completed. The work kept them away from home for five to six weeks at a time, but at least there was steady money coming in. It was certainly more money than Willie had ever made farming.

Working for Trans Continental was the first of several public jobs Willie took to help the family get by. He was also appointed constable of Billingsley and special deputy for Autauga County. Although he was not on the county's payroll, he was paid mileage when he was sent to serve a warrant or pick up someone to deliver to the county jail in Prattville.

Willie in his deputy uniform

Adell was thirty-nine years old on April 20, 1950. She was beginning to go through the change of life. Around the middle of June, she realized she had missed her last two periods. She'd also been sick to her stomach several times. The smell of food first thing in the morning made her want to vomit. Willie became concerned about her.

One morning just after one of her sick stomach spells he turned to her. "Adell, what's goin' on with ya? Ya been sick on and off for weeks now. Do ya need to go to the doctor?"

"If it's what I think it is, I'd just as soon die," she replied blankly.

Willie could see the tears welling up in her eyes. "What do ya think it is?" he asked.

A steady stream of tears began rolling down her face. "I think I might be pregnant," she said blankly.

"Pregnant!" Willie said with a surprise. "That's good! Ain't it?"

"Good!" Adell lashed out, her sadness turning to anger. "I don't know what ya think is so great about it. I'm nearly forty years old. Wilfred is almost ten. I've got grandchildren, for heaven's sake. I thought I was through raisin' babies. I don't want to be pregnant. I feel ashamed. What are people gonna think?"

"Well, I'm not ashamed, Adell," Willie said, looking proud. "And I don't care what other people think. I think it would be nice to have a little one around again. Besides, if ya are pregnant, there ain't nothin' ya can do about it except have it."

From that point on, every time anyone looked at Adell, she was crying. To make matters worse, Imogene became pregnant too, a fact that seemed to make matters even more traumatic for Adell. To think she had a daughter old enough to have one child and be pregnant with another at the same time she was pregnant was just too much. In Adell's opinion, it was plain disgraceful.

~

After Willie stopped farming, DM had to find another way of making his spending money. He began by hiring himself out for two dollars a day to anyone who needed his help; one such person was Ira Huett.

Ira Huett was as backwoods country as any one man could get. He was basically a good man. He worked hard, lived hard, and played hard. He was a fair man and expected the same from others. He would do anything for you, but you sure didn't want him against you. In other words, he was not a man you wanted to cheat.

Ira was said to be one of the best syrup makers in all of Autauga and Chilton counties. Ira and his wife Zadie ran a syrup mill just outside of Billingsley out on route one, down on Sand Branch. Ira always needed help. When DM came to Ira looking for a job, he hired him as a seasonal worker. His job was feeding sugar cane into the press.

Working at the syrup mill was some of the hardest and hottest work DM had ever done. Yellow jackets constantly swarmed around him. Sometimes the wasps would sting him, leaving big, painful welts. Houseflies landing on and near the vats were thick as molasses in winter. They would light in his hair and on his clothes. The sweet, sticky juice from the cane splattered on DM's clothes and in his eyes and face. As it dried, it became stiff. When DM went home at night after having worked all day at the syrup mill, his clothes would be so stiff they would practically stand by themselves without him even being in them.

DM took on whatever jobs he could find, wherever he could find them. Anything he could do to put a little spending money in his pockets, he did. During growing season, DM helped Ira's sons work in the fields. They plowed, cropped cotton, picked cotton, and cut sugar cane, all while making and selling a little moonshine on the side.

When Rudolph Beaslecomb began cutting timber off Cooter Headley's land, DM took a job helping to saw logs and hauling them to the trucks. Once he was old enough to get his driver's license, he drove the logging truck filled with huge logs over to Billingsley. Whatever came up for him to do, he did. He had no choice. It was either do or do without.

DM and Adell were home alone one hot summer day in July. Willie had gone to Billingsley and carried Wilfred with him, which was unusual, as Willie and his youngest son didn't always see eye to eye on things. Even at the young age of nine, Wilfred butted heads with his daddy all the time. Wilfred made Willie mad because he could never sit still, and that bothered Willie. Adell decided the reason they didn't get along was because they were too much alike. Both of them were headstrong and wanted things done their way. However, that day was different. Strangely enough, he had decided to let Wilfred go with him.

Shortly after Willie and Wilfred headed out, the ice truck stopped by their house. They seldom bought ice in the past, but with Willie working at a public job, they could actually afford to buy ice occasionally. Adell decided to purchase a large block of it. As DM was carrying it into the house, an idea hit him.

"Ya know what would be good right now, Mama," he said. "A big bowl of cold ice cream. Sure wish we had some snow so we could make some."

"We can make ice cream if ya want to," Adell said. "We've got ice and fresh cream."

"Yeah, but we don't have an ice cream freezer," DM reminded her.

"We don't need an ice cream freezer. Go get the water bucket and an empty syrup bucket. I'll show ya how we used to make ice cream when I was a youngun."

DM hurried outside. The thought of cold, refreshing ice cream made his mouth water. His eyes searched the dark shed for an empty syrup bucket. In one corner was a stack of empty quart jars used for canning. In another area of the shed, several full buckets of syrup were stored on a long wooden shelf along the wall. He thought about all the hard work that had gone into making the syrup. He'd learned a lot from Mr. Huett that past fall. He'd never before realized what an art form making syrup really was. It wasn't a job he wanted to do for the rest of his life, but it was an experience he was glad to have been involved with. It had not only taught him to respect another man's work, but it had made him a little spending money too.

The empty syrup buckets were stacked on the floor at the back of the shed. Spiders had weaved their webs in and around several of the buckets. Pushing the webs aside, DM chose the cleanest one he could find. He knew his mama would wash it thoroughly before she even considered using it. An extra water bucket hung on a peg just inside the shed door. DM grabbed it as he exited then hurried back to the house. DM brought the two buckets inside, placing them on the table.

"Now watch and learn," Adell said.

Adell began by putting some chipped ice in the bottom of the water bucket. After washing the syrup bucket with soap and water, she filled it with a mixture of cream, beaten eggs, sugar, and vanilla flavoring. Just before she replaced the lid back onto the syrup bucket, she dropped in a spoon to help keep the mixture stirred. Making sure the lid was secure, she then put the syrup bucket into the water bucket on top of the chipped ice.

DM chipped more ice and used it to fill in around the syrup bucket. Adell took hold of the bail on the syrup bucket and began to turn it one way and then the other. The metal spoon inside the syrup bucket clanked loudly as it rocked back and forth. When Adell's arm got tired, DM took his turn. As the ice melted around the bucket, they added more ice. As the mixture began to thicken, the noise from the spoon began to sound muffled, a sure sign the ice cream was hardening. Each of them took turns swishing the bucket back and forth until the sweet, creamy mixture froze to a thick consistency.

"Time to try it out," Adell said, prying open the lid with the edge of a knife.

DM got each of them a bowl and spoon from the cupboard. Adell spooned the rich, creamy ice cream into the bowls. DM shoveled a big spoonful into his mouth.

"That'll make your tongue want to slap your brains out." He laughed. Quickly, he began digging his spoon in for another big bite. It was the best ice cream DM had ever tasted.

———

Although Big Springs Baptist Church was within walking distance of the Headley place, DM and his family never did too much church going. Willie and Adell tried not to work on Sunday, but they mostly used the day as a day of rest, not for going to church.

Etta Rawlinson's family lived just up the hill from the Headley Place. Les Chandler and his family lived a little farther on down the road from the Rawlinson Place. None of the adults in either of these families were churchgoers either. However, the children were. Going to church was one of the few places young people could get together to socialize. On Sunday morning, DM would meet his friends out by the road in front of his house, whereupon they would walk to church together.

A pretty young girl named Ruth Vinson was spending the summer in Billingsley with the Chandler family. She was a slender girl with long, blond, wavy hair and dimples in her rosy cheeks. DM was sweet on Ruth from the first time he met her. Just being able to walk to church with her was a good reason not to miss church on Sunday. Sometimes she would even let him hold her hand.

As new people moved into the area, Big Springs Church's membership began growing. Everyone seemed to like the new preacher there. His hellfire and brimstone way of preaching brought many downtrodden sinners to their knees. Although DM liked the preacher well enough, he didn't like the fact that he stayed on him constantly about joining the church and being baptized. DM thought the preacher a might pushy, and he wasn't going to be bullied into joining the church by anybody. Had the preacher let him join the church in his own good time, everything would have been fine. Although his body was there most Sundays, at that particular time in his life, his heart was more about Ruth than it was about receiving God as his personal Savior.

As the church membership grew, Wiley Gafford decided to donate some land across the road from the church on which to build a cemetery. Willie and DM, along with several more fellows, went over to the land to clean it up and put up a fence around it. In past years, the land had been used as a cornfield. Dried cornstalks lay scattered across it like fallen soldiers in the field. Someone had pulled up the corn and slip shucked it, which left some shucks still on the stalks. Unbeknown to any of them, wasps had built a nest inside some of the dried shucks. When DM picked up one of the stalks, the wasps attacked. In a matter of seconds he was covered with them. Angrily, they dug their stingers into his flesh. Willie and DM swatted at the wasps until they were either dead or had flown away. Instantly, he was covered with welts from his head to his toes. "It hurts bad," he said.

Willie wet some tobacco from his can of Prince Albert and applied it to the stings. The tobacco juice helped relieve the pain, but red marks remained everywhere he had been stung. Feeling a bit woozy, he lay down in the shade of a nearby tree. It was an experience he would never forget.

Although DM learned to ride a bicycle while living back at the Patrick place, he never had a bicycle of his own. G.C. Hayes had gotten a bicycle for Christmas one year. He let DM ride it whenever he wasn't riding it. However, once they moved to the Turner place, he never got the chance to ride a bicycle anymore, as no one around there had a bike. When they moved to the Headley place, his friends Nelson and Wylie Frank both had bikes. They would both let DM ride their bikes. Sometimes two of them would ride double. He learned to ride a bicycle as well as the next fellow, but never once in all his years of growing up did he have a bicycle he could call his own.

Wilfred fared better than DM in the bicycle department as well as the clothes department. He and his cousin Tommy were around the same age. Tommy was Emma and Tom Kennedy's son. Emma was Adell's younger sister. Tommy was a little bigger than Wilfred. When Tommy outgrew his clothes, Wilfred would get them. When Tommy got a new bike, Wilfred got his old one.

Wilfred was around ten years old and skinny as a rail. He was hardheaded and independent. Willie tried taking him hunting, but Wilfred would make so much noise moving around that he often scared off the game. Willie finally stopped taking him, which made Wilfred angry with his daddy.

There was seven years' difference in DM and Wilfred's ages. Wilfred wanted to go everywhere with DM, but like most older brothers, DM didn't like him tagging along. He was afraid he'd tell on him for something he'd done; there were just some things he didn't want his mama and daddy to know about.

Wilfred, age seven

Because Imogene was the oldest, she'd been responsible for watching over DM and Wilfred most of her growing-up years. She had looked after both of them for so long she felt as though she was their mother. She'd especially taken up for Wilfred at home and at school.

Wilfred was little for his age, so he got teased a lot by the older kids. Imogene had gotten into scuffles more than once with the bigger kids who picked on him for being so little. She took up for him at home as well. She felt DM had always been mean to both her and Wilfred. He'd always gotten more attention from her mama, especially after his arm had been removed. She knew her father had certainly spent more time with DM than he did with Wilfred. When he and Wilfred did spend time together, they were always at odds with one another. When she and Hubert married and moved away to Montgomery, Wilfred missed his older sister being there. He missed having someone he felt he could talk to.

DM missed Imogene too. He always looked forward to

Imogene and Hubert coming home for a visit. Hubert liked to hunt as much as he did. That winter had been especially cold and damp. Puddles of rain turned into solid ice. Icicles hung from the edge of the house like giant, frozen fingers. Despite the freezing-cold weather, DM and Hubert decided they would go hunting down in the swamps.

"It's as cold as a well digger's butt," Hubert said as they made their way through the frozen swamp.

"I know," DM replied. "It feels like it's gettin' colder by the minute."

No sooner than he spoke the words, a freezing rain started falling. Soon their hands, feet, and faces grew numb from the cold. Reluctantly, they decided to make their way back home rather than remain out in the harsh cold. By the time they got to the edge of the woods, a thin layer of ice had formed on the gun barrel.

Hubert wrapped his hand around his gun, running it down the gun barrel. "Look at this, DM," Hubert said. A layer of ice peeled up like shedding skin on a snake.

"We best be gettin' home purdy quick," said DM. "I'm ready for a warm fire myself."

Hubert's lower body felt so cold he was barely able to feel his feet beneath him.

"Me too," he agreed, quickening his pace.

As they made their way across the frozen field toward home, they both felt sad. There would be no fresh meat on the table that night.

When DM was in the tenth grade, a local insurance agent took it upon himself to make an appointment for DM with the Crippled Children's Foundation in Birmingham. After the hospital reviewed his circumstances, arrangements were made for him to be fitted for an artificial arm without any cost to the family. DM wasn't sure how he felt about wearing a prosthetic. He couldn't remember ever having an arm on that side. He was used to having only one arm. He wasn't sure about the possibility of having two arms to work with.

Proper fitting was difficult. The stump that had once held DM's arm was extremely short. In order to hold the prosthesis in place, a harness was constructed to fit around his neck and opposite shoulder. The arm was made of flesh-colored wood joined together at the elbow and wrist. It was heavy and bundlesome. There were two separate attachments that could be interchanged at the wrist. One looked like a hand, the other a two-prong hook. The hook and hand mechanism could be opened and closed by moving his left shoulder forward.

While the arm was being built, DM remained in Birmingham overnight. It was a bit scary for a poor country, farm boy to be in such a big city alone. The Crippled Children's Foundation made arrangements for DM to stay at the Salvation Army Emergency Home. The shelter was another scary situation. It was full of transients. Everyone showered together in an open-room bath facility. Rows of bunk beds held person after person. DM slept very little that night for fear someone would steal the ten dollars his father had given him to buy food. The man who lay next to him coughed constantly throughout the night. A young mother with several shabbily dressed children sat huddled together in one corner of the room. A gash over her left eye and bruises on her cheek and arms told DM she feared for her safety.

The next morning, DM took a taxi back to the clinic. The final fitting and adjustments were made. That evening, he was given a bus ticket back to Prattville, where his father and the men he rode to work with picked him up. When Willie saw him he wanted to cry. It was the first time he'd seen his son with two arms in over ten years.

Although the new arm was difficult to maneuver, DM tried desperately to get used to it. He liked the way it made him look in his clothes. Surprisingly, he liked the feeling of having two arms for the first time in a long time. Everything was beginning to work out fine until a confrontation at school made DM realize having an artificial arm could also mean not being able to help a friend.

The realization began when two of the Taylor boys, Kenneth and Perry, started a fight with one of DM's best friends, Oneal Weldon. It was two against one. Under normal circumstances DM would have jumped in to help his friend. However, on that particular day, DM was wearing the hook instead of the hand. He knew if he were to strike either of the Taylor boys with that hook it could do serious damage. All he could do was stand by and watch as his friend took a beating.

When DM got home from school that evening, he removed the arm for the last time. Adell put it away in a trunk, never to be worn again. Up until then he had lived his life with one arm and done pretty well without it. The incident with his friend and the Taylor boys made him realize something about himself. The way he looked to others was not as important as being there for those he cared about.

Young growing boys need their father. With Willie away from home so much, DM took to running with a bad crowd of boys and girls. One of them was Nelson Chandler. Although his reputation was none too good, he was DM's best friend. Nelson's family was one of the least-thought-of families in the community, mainly because Mr. Chandler was bad to drink. When he drank he got mean. His sons seemed to be following in his footsteps with both the drinking and the meanness.

DM's other running buddies were the Rawlinsons: Wiley Frank, Junior, and their sister, Sue. They also came from a rough family background. Sue was as tough as any young boy her age. DM figured she had to be tough to survive. Pete, Dick, and E.J. Huett were also in their group. They were Ira Huett's boys. When Ira wasn't making syrup, he was making moonshine. Folks said Ira's whiskey went down "like mother's milk" then blew the seat out of your britches when it hit bottom.

DM got his first real taste of the hard stuff when he was spending the night at Nelson Chandler's house. Pete brought some of Ira's whiskey to Nelson's house that night. They spent most of the night drinking the jar of moonshine and most of the next day vomiting it back up again. DM swore he'd never touch liquor again, but that didn't last long. Everytime Wiley Frank, Junior, Sue, the Huett boys, and DM got together there was usually a jug of Ira's moonshine close by. Pete made sure of that. Ira's boys were some of the roughest in the bunch. They could find trouble where there was no trouble. Despite their unfavorable reputations, all of them were DM's friends.

Neither DM nor any of his friends ever had any money to speak of. Finding a way to entertain themselves was often a challenge. However, money, or the lack thereof, never stopped them. Like most rural communities, school activities were a main source of entertainment. During basketball season, the lot of them would walk over to Billingsley School to watch the game. In order for all of them to attend the game, a plan had to be implemented.

They could usually scrape up enough money for at least one of them to get in the door. He was the lead man. He would be the one that paid to get in, while the others hid out by the boy's bathroom window. When the coast was clear, the lead man would open the bathroom window, and the others would crawl through, including Sue. Since no one was issued any kind of ticket at the door, once inside, no one could actually say they hadn't paid. Therefore, they were usually safe.

Then there was the mystery of the missing books. It all began the morning after Billingsley High School played Isabella High School in a game of basketball on Billingsley's home court. Mysteriously, every algebra book in Mr. Zimmerman's math class disappeared without a trace. The teachers and students looked everywhere—in the closets, through the desks, on top of the bookshelves, in storage bins, even the janitor's supply closet. They were simply nowhere to be found. The question was: Who would have taken them, and why? The students and faculty began to ask questions as to who would have had the opportunity and the motive. The answer seemed quite obvious.

Billingsley School did not have a dressing room for visiting players. Therefore, the Isabella team used the math room as a place to change into their uniforms. They had the opportunity. When Isabella lost the game to Billingsley, a motive was established. The conclusion was that Isabella's basketball team had either taken or hidden the books out of pure spite.

For several days, the disappearance of the books remained on everyone's mind. Gossip spread like wildfire. Accusations were flying. At lunch, the students talked about how awful it was that the students from Isabella could be so mean. The teachers talked about the poor discipline associated with students who would do such a thing. The principal at Billingsley contacted the principal at Isabella and accused the basketball team of the theft. Ill feelings between the two schools were sealed.

The whereabouts of the missing books remained a mystery for several days after the incident. Finally one of the boys in the first-period class suggested they search in the loft; perhaps the boys from Isabella had hidden them there. It was the only place they hadn't looked.

Two boys were sent to fetch a ladder from the storage shed while the others moved the desks out of the way. Once the ladder was securely in place, Clyde Mims and Harold Wallace were given a flashlight and sent up the ladder to investigate. At first, there was no sign of any missing books. As Clyde and Harold began to crawl around the loft, Clyde discovered a narrow hole next to the chimney. Pointing the flashlight down the dark hole, he saw them. There between the chimney and the wall were the missing books.

Once the books were found, the next problem became how to get them out of the hole in the wall. It was a good eight to ten feet straight down. The hole was extremely small. The only way to reach the books was to lower someone feet first down into the narrow opening. Oneal Weldon was the smallest boy in the class. It was decided he would be the one to retrieve the books.

A rope was secured to Oneal's waist. Several of the larger, stronger boys were put in charge of lowering and raising Oneal. Once Oneal was in the hole, he would then use his feet to pick up the books one at a time. It was a grueling task and took several days to complete. All the while, the Isabella basketball team was being blamed and shamed by Billingsley's students and faculty, an accusation that Isabella continued to deny.

Truth was, Isabella High School had absolutely nothing to do with hiding the books. It was all the work of several of Billingsley's more mischievous male students. They had gone into the math room during the game and decided it would be funny to hide the math books from their teacher. Nobody liked algebra anyway. Hiding the books would mean no more algebra lessons to contend with. The idea seemed pretty innocent at the time.

No doubt, the boys had full intentions of returning the books after a few days. Unfortunately, when they realized the severity of what they had done, they knew they would be in big trouble. DM and his gang knew all too well who the culprits were. All the ones involved vowed a pledge of silence. The mystery of the missing books was a secret that remained a secret.

The Etta Rawlinson Place

When Willie stopped farming, there was little need for the family to continue living at the Headley place. Cooter needed tenants who would work the farm. Without working tenants, he could not collect his third of the crops. It was time for the family to move again. Etta Rawlinson owned a place on top of a hill just off the back road leading into Billingsley. She offered to rent it to Willie and his family. "The house ain't much," Etta told him, "but it's a place to live."

The house was built off the ground on wooden posts. In the winter, the cold northern wind blew hard across the top of the hill. It blew through the cracks in the floor, lifting the red and green flowered linoleum rug like it was mere paper. Along the walls, old newspaper and rags had been stuffed into the knotholes to keep out the cold. Although the house had two fireplaces, it was the coldest house any of them could ever remember living in. It had never been painted either. Its gray, weathered boards had long since dried, leaving wide cracks you could shoot a broom straw through. There was no running water in the house. Water had to be carried in buckets from the spring at the bottom of the hill up a steep embankment. It seemed as though it took forever to get there and back. Every time Adell walked down the hill to wash the clothes, she wondered how she would make it back up the hill again in her condition. She desperately missed the running water they'd been blessed with at the Headley place.

The year was 1950, four days before Christmas. The family settled into their new home as best they could. Adell was so big from the baby growing inside her she feared her belly would surely pop. The pain in her lower back was almost unbearable. The coldness in the house chilled her to the bone. No matter how close she got to the fireplace, she could never seem to get warm. That morning at breakfast, Adell talked to Willie about going to see her daddy in Marbury. With trembling hands, she poured Willie his first cup of morning coffee.

"Willie, I want to go to Carrie's house to see Daddy," she told him.

Willie touched his hand to hers. They were cold as ice. "Are ya sure you're up to makin' the trip?" he asked, rather concerned.

Adell set the coffee pot back on the cookstove. "Cora says he's feelin' mighty poorly these days," she answered. "If I don't go see him now, I may not see him alive. He's getting on up in years. He's been goin' downhill ever since Mama left him to go live with Carrie."

Willie reached for one of the biscuits Adell placed on the table in front of him. He opened the hot, steaming biscuit, placing the two halves side by side on his plate. Adell spooned a hardy helping of sawmill gravy on top. "After breakfast I'll go out and warm up the car. We'll ride over there this mornin'," he promised.

After breakfast, Adell, Willie, DM, and Wilfred got into

the car and headed to Marbury, some twenty miles away. When they arrived at Carrie's house later that morning, they were astounded at what they found. Adell's daddy was in terrible shape, much worse shape than they could ever have imagined. He was lying in the fetal position on a small cot in the corner of the room. He looked like a skeleton. His legs and arms looked like skin draped over bones. His knees looked like twisted light'erd knots.

The house was so cold that the water bucket that was sitting on the kitchen table had a thick layer of ice on top. The wood in the fireplace had long since burned out, leaving only cold, gray ashes. DM looked around the room. There was no wood in the house at all. He looked out the window facing the backyard. There was no wood on the back porch either.

"Aunt Carrie, don't y'all have any wood to make a fire?" he asked as he stood shivering in his boots.

Carrie shook her head. "No," she answered sadly. "I told Lonnie he needed to git us up some wood. He said it was too cold to be out cuttin' wood. He's gone back to bed. I'm sorry it's so cold in here. I woulda hauled in some wood myself, but I hated to leave Daddy alone."

Willie knew there was no way they could stay in the house without some kind of warmth. He looked at DM. "Come on, son. Let's go cut some wood and bring it in. We need to get a fire started in here before we all freeze to death."

DM followed his daddy out back. The cold northern wind whipping across the hill cut to the bone. DM pulled the collar of his coat up around his ears. It took Willie a good while before he finally found an ax. It was hidden beneath a pile of burlap bags in the shed out back. Upon inspection, he realized it was as dull as a monotone preacher at a weeklong revival. "I've never met anybody as lazy as Lonnie Huett," Willie fussed. "It's no wonder there ain't no wood cut. This ax is so dull it couldn't cut hot butter. There ain't no excuse for havin' a dull ax. It ain't nothin' but pure laziness."

DM found a rusty file hanging on the wall of the shed. Willie used it to sharpen the ax as best he could. While Willie sharpened the ax, DM searched the woods surrounding the house for broken limbs and branches. Several small trees had fallen during the recent ice storm. DM dragged them out of the woods and into the yard.

Once Willie had the ax sharpened, he and DM spent most of the day chopping wood. The first load was carried into the house; the rest he stacked on the backporch. With the first load, DM quickly built a fire in the fireplace. Unfortunately, the roaring fire did little good to warm the section of the room where Adell's daddy lay dying of pneumonia. Adell placed a tattered quilt across his nearly lifeless body. All that afternoon she sat by his side, rubbing his skeletal hand and weeping. Late that evening, William Culpepper drew his last feeble breath. He had laid in the fetal position for so long it took both Willie and DM to straighten him out enough that he could fit into his pine casket. They buried him the day after Christmas in the New Prospect Church Cemetery next to his oldest son, Dee.

———

Through the week, Willie spent most of his time out of town working on houses for the gas company employees. On the weekend, he served as special deputy for Autauga County and constable of Billingsley. Whether or not he was home depended on how many drunks he would have to haul in on Saturday night. The closer time got to her due date, the more Willie feared for Adell to be alone. He decided to call Imogene from the phone at Cooter's store. He asked, and she agreed to come stay with her mama. Just in case Adell went into labor when Willie wasn't home, Imogene would be there to make sure she got to the hospital.

The day before the new Bone baby was born, it turned exceedingly cold. It was the kind of cold that stays in your bones and can't be warmed by any amount of fire in the fireplace. The bitter cold northern winds whistled through the trees, entering through every crack and crevice in the house. The rose-patterned linoleum rug flapped up and down on the kitchen floor. Adell poured Willie and Hubert a cup of coffee. Her chilled, trembling hands welcomed the warmth from the blue enamel-coated coffee pot. Coffee spilled over the sides of the cup into the saucer. The temperature in the house was so cold the spilled coffee froze almost immediately. The cup literally stuck to the saucer.

Willie took a quick gulp of the hot liquid. "I've never seen a colder day," he said. "It must be below zero outside."

Imogene entered the room. In doing so, she wrapped an extra shawl around her shoulders and took a seat at the table next to Hubert. "It feels like it's below zero in here," she said. Imogene was six months along with her second child. Teresa, who was nearing two years old, remained asleep under the covers.

Willie gulped down his coffee as quickly as he could before it had a chance to get cold. "How are ya feelin' this mornin', Adell?" he asked.

Adell rubbed her huge, protruding belly. "I think the baby has dropped. It feels like my insides could fall out on the floor. I wish ya wouldn't go to work today. Ya need to stay here in case this baby decides to come."

"Now, Adell, that's why Imogene and Hubert are here," he said. "If ya need to go to the hospital, one of them can come get me."

Adell felt anger welling up inside her. "Willie Bone, ya

wouldn't care if I dropped this baby right out here on the floor. Ya care more 'bout that sheriff job than ya do me."

Imogene tried to reason with her mama. "Now, Mama, ya know that's not true. Daddy's got a job to do. If we need him, Hubert or one of us will go get him."

After breakfast, Willie left to go into Billingsley. It was a miserable day. Everyone else remained as close to the fire as possible; however, regardless of the cold, there were chores to be done. DM needed to carry water up to the house from the branch at the bottom of the hill. As he made his way down the hill, he could feel the frozen ground crunch under his feet. When he reached the branch, he discovered it had a layer of ice all the way across it. He had to break the ice away with a rock in order to get to the water beneath. By the time he got back inside the house, his hand and feet were so cold he could barely feel them.

Willie was still in Billingsley when Adell went into labor late that Saturday evening. The contractions were sharp and painful. Imogene sent DM to find him. When he finally located his daddy, they rushed home to find Adell in full labor. They immediately put her in the backseat of Hubert and Imogene's car and drove her to the Prattville hospital.

Her labor was long and hard. The family waited in the lobby of the hospital for word from the doctor. As DM nervously flipped through a magazine, he remembered back when he was seven and Wilfred was being born. It was in the hot summertime. He recalled hearing his mother's cries of pain as he waited outside in the yard. He remembered being afraid. He had even asked Imogene if his mama was dying. She had assured him she was not. He was nearly eighteen now and no longer afraid. Still, he was glad his mama was in the hospital with a doctor at her side instead of at home.

The baby came early Sunday morning, January 28, 1951. Shortly after she was born, the family gathered at the nursery window to view the new addition to their family. The eight-pound, seven-ounce baby girl was the picture of health. She had fat, round cheeks and pudgy arms and legs with deep dimples in her hands and feet. She also had one single light-brown curl of hair on the top of her head.

The family needed to give her a name. Several names were suggested, but in the end Wilfred was the one who came up with her first name. "I don't care what y'all name her," he announced. "I'm gonna call her Nancy, after the girl in the book I'm readin' at school. It's called *Nancy and Bob on the Farm.* Y'all name her what ya want to, but I'm gonna call her Nancy."

Willie smiled at Wilfred's determination. "That sounds all right to me," he said. "My great grandmama's name was Nancy. What do ya think, Adell?"

Adell was just glad to have everything over with. She was exhausted. At that point, it didn't matter to her what they named the new baby.

Imogene put in her two cents' worth. "She needs a middle name too," she said. "I don't have a middle name, but a child needs a middle name."

Willie thought for a minute. "How 'bout Kawanna or Lavanna?" he suggested.

"Where in the world did ya get those names from?" Imogene asked.

Willie pulled off his hat and ran his fingers through his partly gray, thinning hair. "There are twin girls in Montgomery named Kawanna and Lavanna Paul. They live down the street from Emma. They are the prettiest little girls I've ever seen, and I especially like their names," he explained.

Adell opened her eyes long enough to speak up. "Well, I like Kawanna better than Lavanna," she stated wearily.

Everyone agreed. Nancy Kawanna became the last of Adell and Willie's children.

Baby Nancy

DM's senior year at Billingsley High School was one of confusion and concern. He was staring manhood in the face. He continually had thoughts about his future—how would he make a living? What was he to do after graduation? Should he go to college or a technical college? How would he pay for it? What did he want to study? Who did DM want DM to be? One thing he knew for certain, he didn't want to be a sharecropper.

There were seven girls and seventeen boys in DM's senior class. DM was one of the smallest boys, but he was also one of the strongest. Although most of the other boys were bigger, they were all about equal when it came to strength. It came to be known that the senior-class boys could pretty much handle whatever job came along that needed doing around the school.

Mr. L. C. Stanfield was the agriculture teacher at Billingsley School. He was a tall, slender, handsome man with dark hair and deep-set eyes. DM and the other boys in his class liked and respected Mr. Stanfield immensely.

The school board decided to build a football field in a pine grove back of the agriculture building. Workers were brought in to cut down trees and level the ground. After the trees were cut down, it became the responsibility of Mr. Stanfield and the senior-class boys to remove the stumps. The smaller stumps were dug out using spades and shovels. The larger stumps were removed using dynamite. A half stick of dynamite placed at the base of the stump caused enough of an explosion to lift the stump out of the ground, whereupon it could then be dragged from the field. Afterward, the hole was filled in with dirt and the area leveled.

All was going well. However, after several hours of the same routine, some of the more-adventurous boys got somewhat bored and decided to try something different. The Mims twins, Clyde and Claude, claimed to have used dynamite many times before. Of course, DM was always up to trying anything that sounded exciting. He and the twins got off to the side, where they were less likely to be detected. Clyde spied a stump sticking out of the ground at an angle. While the other boys kept Mr. Stanfield occupied, the three of them used a tapping rod about an inch and a half in diameter to make a hole in the ground beside the stump. When the hole was finished, they removed the rod and filled the hole with not a half stick, but rather several sticks of dynamite. A long fuse was added to give the boys time to get away before the dynamite exploded.

Once everything was set, Claude struck the match and lit the fuse. Immediately the three boys took off running. When Mr. Stanfield realized what the boys had done, he reacted promptly. Hurrying the boys as fast as possible, he directed them to get into one of the buses at the top of the hill. When everyone was safely inside, he stood on the steps by the door, cautiously watching as the explosives went off. The explosion shot the stump a good quarter of a mile into the air, sending rocks and debris flying. Fortunately, when all was said and done, no one was injured; however, the soaring rocks did shatter several windows in the school. A hole the size of a school bus was all that remained where the stump had once been. Several dump trucks full of dirt had to be hauled in to fill the gaping hole. Needless to say, Mr. Stanfield was not happy with his senior-class boys.

Despite their often bizarre and mischievous ways of doing things, everything from laying sidewalks around the school to cleaning out a stopped-up grease trap or septic tank was taken care of by the boys in DM's class. Anything that needed doing at the school and sometimes even in the community was taken care of by the rambunctious boys. If it was a challenge, they were there to meet it.

Jack Moore was one of the school bus drivers. He owned thirteen young bulls weighing between 1,100 and 1,300 pounds. The bulls had been allowed to run freely in the pasture all their lives, but their time had come. They needed to be castrated. Mr. Stanfield drove the boys over to Mr. Moore's house to aid in the transition. As luck would have it, the biggest bull in the bunch was rather ill tempered. It appeared he wanted no part of being either penned up or castrated. The boys decided it might be best to put him in a stall to himself and save him for last.

Pat Farley was a football player, one of the biggest boys in the bunch. When it came time to face the big fighting bull, he was the one who came up with a rather unusual idea. The boys gathered round him like they were huddling in a football game.

"Okay," he told the others, "this is what we're gonna do. One of ya open the gate. When the bull comes out, one of y'all run like hell across the pen. He's sure to chase ya. While his attention is on the runner, I'll tackle him to the ground. The rest of ya jump on him and help me hold him down while Mr. Stanfield cuts 'im."

Since DM was the fastest, it was decided he would be the runner. Inside the stall, the young bull seemed to know what was about to take place. He began snorting loudly, pawing ferociously at the ground. When the gate opened, the bull stormed out with a vengeance, his head down, his nostrils flaring. Just as expected, he headed directly at DM. DM sprinted across the lot, the angry bull right on his heels. The bull was closing in. DM could feel his hot breath on the back of his legs. DM was becoming concerned when suddenly Pat rammed the bull from the side. The stunned bovine was caught off balance and thrown to the ground.

As the mighty bull hit the ground, one of its horns caught Pat's shirt, tearing it from his body. However, the big Billingsley High School tackle managed to stay in control. Immediately the remaining boys jumped on top of the bull, pinning him down. Mr. Stanfield rushed in and quickly removed the bull's manhood, whereupon the bull was released and the job completed. It was a dangerous job, but the rugged farm boys met the challenge without hesitation.

Despite his sometimes-dangerous adventures, DM's senior year was basically an easy one. Mr. Moody, the school principal, appreciated all the work the boys did around the school. He also understood what a hard life most of these boys had at home. Since most of them had what credits they needed to graduate, it was not unusual for Mr. Moody to allow them to play hooky after lunch. Oftentimes they would use their off time to go hunting or fishing together. Other times they would just hang out down by the creek, trying to figure out a possible way to get to town.

Most of the boys rode the bus to school. However, there was one or two of them who did occasionally have access to a car. Some of the boys would slip off in one of the cars to the nearby town of Prattville. Once there, they would spend most of the day shooting pool at one of the local pool halls. However, they always made sure they headed back to Billingsley in time to take the school bus home. That way their folks would never know they had skipped school.

As children get older, they often tend to fool themselves into believing they have become smarter than the parents who raised them. They have a tendency to forget about the eyes in the back of their mama's head or their father's "been there, done that" days. In doing so, they assume they can get away with whatever mischief they so choose. Unfortunately for them, nine times out of ten, they will eventually get caught one way or another.

Such was the case on buck night at the Prattmont drive-in theater in Prattville. In order to bring in more business during the weeknights, Prattmont Drive-In occasionally featured what they called "buck night." The usual admission fee to get in was one dollar per person. On buck night admission was one dollar per carload. There was no stipulation as to the amount of people allowed admittance for a dollar as long as they could all fit in or on the car.

When the mischievous boys from Billingsley High School heard about buck night, they were more than just excited; they were intrigued. The idea of seeing how many of them they could fit into and on a car was more than enticing to their everyday, run-of-the-mill farm life. A plan to achieve this idea was promptly put into place.

As word spread silently through the hallways at school, volunteers came out of the woodwork. What began as a half dozen or so anxious young men turned into over twenty participants. First, they would need a motorcar that could possibly hold that many people. Willie had recently purchased a 1929 Model-A Ford Coupe. The ringleaders of the group, of which DM was one of the main ones, carefully inspected every inch of the motorcar for possible places where a body could be stowed. It seemed like the perfect car for the occasion.

Anticipation grew as buck night got closer. What started out as a simple idea quickly turned into reality. However, there was a problem: how to keep their parents from finding out about their plans. Buck night was always held on a weeknight, thus a school night, making it rather difficult for the young, strapping farm boys in need of a night on the town. Another plan was devised. Each participant would tell his parents he was going over to a friend's house to study for a big test. It was a great plan. Parents were always glad to see their children taking a special interest in their studies. Sure, it was a lie, but extreme circumstances often called for extreme measures. Besides, they reasoned, their parents would never know any different as long as everybody kept their mouths shut and stuck strictly to the plan. In their young, foolish minds, their parents just weren't that smart.

Buck night finally arrived. The lie was told. Under false pretenses, DM borrowed his daddy's car. Each boy bid his parents good night with the promise of being home by midnight. By dusk twenty-three anxious boys met at a field near the drive-in and proceeded to stuff themselves into and on the Model-A. It was nothing short of a sight to behold. Bodies were stacked threefold on top of one another. Some were hanging off the running boards, across the hood, and out the windows. Arms and legs stuck out in every direction.

No group of boys had ever been happier. Laughter and jubilation filled the air as the loaded-down Ford Coupe slowly made its way up the hill to the drive-in entrance. The boys knew it had to be some kind of a record. Surely no one had ever packed twenty-three people into one automobile before. They could hardly wait to see the look on the attendant's face when he had to admit twenty-three people into the drive-in for only one dollar. They thought they had really done something special.

Unfortunately for the boys, they weren't the only ones who thought they had done something really special. A reporter for the *Prattville Progress* newspaper was there to do a story on buck night at the drive-in. He thought what the boys had done was pretty special too. In fact, he thought it was so special he took a picture, a picture that later made front-page news. Although the idea had been a total success, they were busted in the aftermath.

Fortunately, the young men who ended up at the bottom of the pile were spared the brunt of the punishment. Although many of the parents in the small farm community suspected their own son's guilt, there was no real way to prove it. Their faces were either hidden beneath the outer layer of boys or smashed beyond recognition between legs and elbows. They were the lucky ones.

Those boys whose faces were clearly visible in the newspaper photo did not fair as well. The proof was in the pudding, or rather, the picture. Some of them got the worst whipping of their young lives. Others were put on restriction. All of them were given extra chores to do. However, regardless of the punishment, all the boys involved still thought it was one of the coolest things any of them had ever done. No one got hurt (except maybe the unfortunate ones who were squashed on the bottom of the pile). Everybody had a great time. Bragging rights for "the most people stuffed into a car at one time" were a part of the daily conversation at school. Despite their punishment, the boys had a great story to tell.

———

DM's baseball coach, J.L. Jones, turned out to be one of his best friends. DM was always telling Mr. Jones stories about his dog, Brownie, and what a good squirrel dog he was. One day after school, DM invited Mr. Jones to come home with him so they could go squirrel hunting together. Mr. Jones really liked hunting and accepted DM's invitation. Brownie happily went with them to the woods back of the house. With Brownie's help, they killed eight squirrels in no time at all.

Time passed quickly as they walked through the woods. It was getting close to dark and time to call it quits when Brownie treed another squirrel about five hundred yards away. DM saw an opportunity to pull a joke on Mr. Jones. Without a word, he suddenly took off running. DM knew there was a fence between them and Brownie, but of course, Mr. Jones did not. When DM got just short of the fence, he stopped; Mr. Jones did not. He hit the fence in a full run. His gun went one way, Mr. Jones another. DM nearly busted a gut laughing.

Except for his pride, neither Mr. Jones nor his gun was hurt. At first, Mr. Jones was angry at DM for letting him run into the fence. However, when he realized DM meant it in fun, he got up, brushed himself off, and began laughing too. Everybody knew what a prankster DM could be. After they had a good laugh, they crossed the fence and DM let Mr. Jones kill the last squirrel. Despite the fact DM had played a trick on him, he was proud of all the squirrels they killed, especially when DM gave all of them to him to take home to his family for supper.

Shortly thereafter, Brownie was run over and killed by a passing car. Like his longtime companion, One Spot, he too was covered in scars from rattlesnake bites, opossum attacks, and his many other adventures with animals in the wild. DM buried him beneath the shade of Brownie's favorite tree.

———

Baseball had always been the driving force behind DM's will to succeed. He pitched for Billingsley's baseball team for five years running. He not only excelled in pitching, but also in batting. During DM's senior year, he batted an average of .525, never striking out the entire season. In order to keep DM eligible to bat in every inning, he had to either pitch or play left field. With only one arm, DM was unable to use a glove; therefore, he caught with his bare hand. Playing a full game without rest was hard, but he loved it.

During his senior year, Billingsley was scheduled to play against Prattville's school. Prattville was a 6A team with four excellent pitchers. Each of them threw a hard fast-speed ball. Few teams who played against them ever scored. Their batting was exceptional too.

Since Prattville's team was used to being thrown fastballs during batting practice, DM decided the best way to pitch to them was to throw his slow ball. His fans were known to jokingly say DM could throw the ball so slow you could practically walk and keep up with it. The real secret to DM's slow pitch happened just before the ball actually reached home plate. It would suddenly curve inward, causing the batter to misjudge its' direction. His strategy proved to work well with the Prattville batters. The game ended with DM throwing a shutout. The score was nine to zero in Billingsley's favor.

DM's senior year in baseball

Six days after Nancy was born, Adell and Willie were awakened during the night. Their young baby was having a terrible coughing spell. She was coughing so hard she could barely catch her breath. Adell got out of bed, placed Nancy on her shoulder, and began patting her on her back. Adell tried giving her water, but she was coughing so hard she couldn't drink. Nothing she did helped. She began pacing back and forth, fearful her baby was choking to death.

"She's probably got pneumonia from livin' in this feezin'-cold house," she cried.

The whole time Adell was pregnant, she hadn't wanted another baby. Now that she was here, she loved her and certainly didn't want her to die. Adell prayed Nancy would live through the night. Early the next morning, they carried her to the doctor.

Doctor Newton ran a clinic on Main Street in Prattville. He was the doctor who had delivered Nancy at the newly established Prattville General Hospital. He was a big man with light-colored hair and a gentle face. Immediately upon examining the baby, he knew exactly what was wrong.

Willie looked at Dr. Newton with a worried look on his face. "Does she have pneumonia?" he asked, his voice slightly trembling.

Dr. Newton looked quite solemn. "Yes, I'm afraid so," he answered. "Double pneumonia and whooping cough. The only thing we know to do for the whooping cough is to let it run its course. I will give her a shot of penicillin for the pneumonia and a prescription for cough syrup. Bring her back in two days for another shot. The penicillin won't help the whooping cough, but it should help heal the pneumonia. Try to keep her as warm and comfortable as possible. I'm afraid you folks are in for some long, sleepless nights."

Adell gently stroked the infant's head. "Is she gonna die?" she asked, choking back the tears.

Dr. Newton laid his stethoscope around his neck and patted Adell on the shoulder. "I can't answer that question, Mrs. Bone, except to say only time will tell."

For the next several weeks, Nancy coughed. At times she coughed so hard she would lose her breath and start turning blue. Adell felt totally helpless. All she could do was hold her baby and pray. At times she felt God was punishing her for not wanting the baby. Deep down she knew that wasn't true, but it was hard to keep the thought from entering her mind. Each time Nancy had a coughing spell, Adell just knew every breath would be her baby's last.

As winter slowly turned to spring, the coughing spells got farther and farther apart. Finally one day they stopped altogether. She had recovered. Nancy proved to be a fighter just like the rest of her family.

Nancy had other problems too. Early on, she began having complications with her skin breaking out in a rash. Every time they got it cleared up she would break out again. The doctors at the clinic seemed puzzled as to what it was. Finally Dr. Newton came up with an idea.

"Mrs. Bone, I'm wondering if this baby is possibly allergic to soap."

Adell had never heard of anyone being allergic to soap. "What do ya mean 'allergic to soap'?" she questioned.

Dr. Newton picked up his prescription pad. "It is rare, but it does happen. I'm going to give you the name of a soap I want you to try. It's called Gamophene. If soap is the problem, this should do the trick and clear it up. Use it like you would any other soap, and we'll see what happens. If it works, she's likely to have to use it for the rest of her life."

The new soap could only be purchased at the drugstore. Rexall Drugstore in Prattville carried it, but to Adell's shock, it cost seventy-five cents a bar. The first time she bought it she told the druggist it was like buying medicine. However, it proved to do the trick, and Nancy's skin irritations cleared up in no time.

Soon after Nancy was born, Imogene and Hubert moved back to Montgomery. They rented a small house there and began preparing for their new baby. Teresa turned two on June 1. The doctors said Imogene's due date for the new baby was to be sometime in August.

Hubert continued to work in construction. Although the work was on again, off again, Imogene had learned to be conservative at an early age. On the weeks Hubert got a full week's pay she would put back what she could to tide them over on the weeks when work was slack. Imogene and Hubert were happy together. They were looking forward to the new baby. Hubert hoped for a boy. On August 2, 1951, their second child was born, another girl. They named her Vicky Marie.

Some years earlier, Julius had returned home from the war. It was then he decided to go back to school and finish his education. After getting his GED, he entered Jones Law School under the GI Bill. While going to school, he took a job as a shoe salesman at Cooper's store in Prattville. Shortly thereafter, he married Betty Jo Freemen. They had a son around the same time Teresa was born. They named him Travis Earl, Travis after Betty Jo's father and Earl after Julius.

Julius shortly after returning from World War II

Willie Charles married Edna Maxie while on leave from the service. When he returned home, they got a place in Montgomery. Their first child, Richard, became the oldest grandchild of Willie and Adell. Later a second child was born, a baby girl they named Lee. She had also been born around the same time Teresa was born. Willie Charles got a job as a roofer with A-1 Roofing Company, working for Virgil Rawson. It was a fairly new company, but the pay was good. They were soon able to purchase a house.

Willie Charles and his first son, Richard

Shortly after Lee was born, tragedy struck again. Doctors discovered a hole in Lee's heart. The technology needed to repair or replace her heart remained far into the future. Doctors told the couple their child would not live past the age of two. A few years later they had two more sons, David and Robin.

Delene and Calvin Grant

Shortly after Delene turned eighteen, she married Calvin Grant. After Imogene and Hubert married, they lived near Calvin and Delene. During that time, Delene and Imogene became close for the first time in their lives. They spent a lot of time at one another's houses. Imogene was glad she and Delene were getting the opportunity to know each other better.

Delene was never blessed with a child of her own, but she and Calvin loved children. In later years they adopted three orphaned brothers: Tony, Paul, and Dale.

DM graduated from high school in the spring, the second child of Willie and Adell to finish school. It was time for him to decide what he would do next. He had taken bookkeeping and shorthand in high school. Of course, he had also taken quite a bit of ribbing from the boys in his class. They teased him about taking those particular classes, as they were considered girly classes. However, he had done well and decided that perhaps he would go on to business school.

His first and foremost problem was how to pay for school. He applied and was accepted at Massey Draughn Business College. The school was located on the corner of Adams and Perry Streets in Montgomery. Because he was considered disabled, the financial advisor at the school was able to set up an account to pay for his education through the Easter Seals Foundation. DM went to Massey Draughn for a year and a half, where he excelled in both accounting and bookkeeping.

While he was in school, he lived with Imogene and Hubert on Mobile Street in Montgomery. The only money he had was what little Willie could scrape together to give him; usually that was around ten dollars a week. Out of the ten dollars he had to buy his food, school supplies, and transportation back and forth.

He often traveled back and forth on weekends from Prattville to Montgomery with Tom Powell in Tom's 1936 Ford. Once he arrived in Prattville, he would hitchhike to Billingsley or Willie would drive there to pick him up.

He usually ate breakfast and supper with Imogene and Hubert. At lunchtime he'd walk down to Chris's hot dog stand located on Dexter Avenue. His usual order was a hot dog with onions, sauerkraut, and chili. He called it his meat with three vegetables and bread. For the price of a quarter he could buy a hot dog, a drink, and a candy bar.

One day, as luck would have it, DM was walking back to the college from the hot dog stand when he happened across a familiar face. He had just rounded the corner in front of Klein's Jewelers when he looked up and there was his old friend Bud Darnell. DM was thrilled. Bud had been his friend and baseball sponsor for all the years he played baseball for Billingsley School.

When Bud saw DM he smiled broadly and immediately stuck out his hand to greet him. "Well, if it ain't the best pitcher Billingsley School has ever had," Bud said jovially. "How in the world have ya been?"

Montgomery was a big town for a small town boy like DM. It was good to see a familiar face. "Purdy good, purdy good," DM replied, smiling back and shaking Bud's hand.

Bud patted DM on the shoulder. "What are ya doin' in Montgomery?" he asked.

"I'm goin' to school over at Massey Draughn. I'm takin' a course in bookkeepin' and accountin'," DM answered.

"Is that right?" Bud responded. "Well, I just happen to need a good bookkeeper. How 'bout comin' to work for me? Ya could work for me durin' the day and finish your classes at night. I hear they have night classes now."

The job offer was the best news DM had heard in a long time. He was truly bored with college. Between the book-keeping he'd taken in high school and the college courses he'd already completed, he figured he knew all he needed to know about keeping books anyway.

DM smiled broadly. "When do ya want me to start?" he asked.

"Ya can start right away, soon as you're ready," replied Bud.

DM laughed. "I was born ready."

His starting salary was twenty-five dollars a week. It was a lot of money to a country boy who'd never had any money to speak of.

DM had stayed with Imogene and Hubert for eighteen months. Although he appreciated them giving him a place to live, he was more than ready to get out on his own. He felt he needed his privacy. He had never liked being told what and what not to do, especially by his older sister. With a new job and money to spend, he decided it was time to get a place of his own so he could go and come when he pleased.

He ended up renting a room from one of Bud's customers, Mrs. Summerlin. Her house was on Wilkinson Street. Mrs. Summerlin charged fifteen dollars a week for the room. After taxes, his net pay was twenty-three dollars. Once he gave Mrs. Summerlin fifteen dollars, he was left with only eight. The remaining money had to be spent wisely. With the eight dollars he bought food, had his clothes washed, and paid bus fare to and from work. Bus fare was a dime one way and a dime back. After all was said and done, there was little left over for anything else.

When he chose to go home on the weekends he would have to either hitch a ride or take the train. The fare for the train ride was seventy-five cents. Sometimes it became a choice between seeing his folks on the weekend or having food to eat the coming week.

DM had been working for Darnell Plumbing for a year or so when one of the guys who worked with him decided to sell his 1946 Plymouth automobile. The young man was asking 150 dollars for the car. It was a good-running car, and it looked good too, with the exception of the right rear fender. The fender looked like someone had taken a bite out of it.

In order to have enough money to buy the car, DM would have to take out a loan from the bank. Since he had never had credit before, he asked Hubert to co-sign with him on the loan. After much deliberation and a sincere promise from DM to pay the loan back, Imogene agreed to let Hubert sign with him.

DM was proud of his somewhat-used new car. Regardless of its haphazard looks, it was great to have a car of his own. It allowed him to have transportation to and from work without having to ride the bus. It also gave him a way to get home on weekends to visit his family and friends back in Billingsley.

DM as a working man

The Tindle Place

A dell disliked the Rawlinson place more than any place she could ever remember living. It was cold in the winter and hot in the summer. There was no electricity or running water in the house. Shortly after Nancy was born, the family decided to move on the other side of Billingsley to the Tindle place. The house was a narrow shotgun-style house. It was built close to the road on County Road III. A row of hedges in the shape of an L grew along the front of the house surrounding the front porch.

A year or so later, Imogene and Hubert decided to move back to Billingsley. They rented a house located just down the road within shouting distance of the Tindle place. It was a four-room white house built on a small hill on the opposite side of the road. Willie and Adell were glad to have them living close by, especially since Nancy and Vicky were so close in age. Living down the road from one another made it easier for all of them to visit one another. Imogene would put Teresa and Vicky in their big red Coaster wagon, and off they would go down the hill to their Granny Bone's house. Teresa and Vicky would play with Nancy while Imogene and Adell helped each other with the canning. Adell liked having her children close to her. She had missed Imogene a lot. She also missed DM something terrible and worried about him constantly.

Imogene was doing well. She was also pregnant with their third child. Hubert was still working in construction. Every day he traveled back and forth from Billingsley to Montgomery. It was a long drive, but he had to go where the work was.

Vicky was a pretty baby and an even-tempered child. Although she was only fourteen months old, she loved books and loved when Imogene read to her. One morning around ten o'clock, she was sitting in Imogene's lap, listening to her mother read a book to her. The night before she had run a fever and cried herself to sleep. When Imogene finished the book, Vicky eased down from her mother's lap. Her obvious intentions were to go to the bookcase to get another one.

As she was walking across the floor, her legs seemed to crumble beneath her. She fell to the floor with a thud. When she tried to get up, she was unable to stand. She began to cry. Immediately Imogene reached for her, helping her to her feet. However, each time she let go, Vicky would fall again. It was as though her legs would no longer support her weight.

Hubert and Willie were away at work. The only way Imogene had to get Vicky to the doctor was in their car, which, unfortunately, was a straight shift. Driving a straight shift was difficult for Imogene. Due to her polio, her left leg had lost a lot of muscle tone. She had to use her left hand to lift her leg in order to get her foot onto the clutch. The clutch was tight and hard to push in. She knew it would take all the strength she would muster to drive the thirty-some-odd miles into town to the doctor, but she had no choice. After dressing the children, she loaded Teresa and Vicky into the car and headed straight to her mama's house.

As soon as Adell saw what was happening with Vicky she

felt she knew exactly what was wrong. "Imogene, this baby has polio."

Imogene began to cry. "It can't be, Mama. It just can't be polio. Not my baby."

Adell began to cry too. "I know it's awful to say, Imogene, but it's the only thing it can be. Ya can see for yourself. She can't stand up by herself."

Imogene wiped the tears from her eyes and composed herself as best she could under the circumstances. "We have to get her to the doctor. Will ya go with me, Mama? Ya know I can't drive a straight shift very well. If ya ain't afraid to ride with me, I need ya to go too."

Without a moment's hesitation Adell grabbed Nancy and retrieved her purse from off the chest of drawers. "Of course I'll ride with ya, Imogene," she replied.

It was around thirty miles from Billingsley into Prattville. As soon as the doctor examined Vicky, he confirmed what Adell and Imogene already knew deep inside. It was indeed polio.

"Will she need to go to the hospital?" asked Imogene.

The doctor shook his head. "I don't see any need for that," he said. "You know as much about the kind of therapy she will need as anybody does. You've been through it yourself. You'll have to put her in hot tubs of water. Make her move her legs as much as possible. Other than that, there is very little else that can be done for her."

From that day forward Imogene worked with Vicky every day. She placed her in hot tubs of water, moving her legs up and down. She massaged her legs to increase circulation. She felt bad for Vicky, for she knew it was painful for her dear little girl. She'd been through the same therapy herself while confined in the hospital in Birmingham. However, she was grateful she could be the one to help Vicky so she didn't have to be away from home, living with strangers. Eventually all Imogene's hard work began to pay off. Slowly but surely, Vicky began to gain the use of her legs. Vicky's left leg seemed to be the one most affected by the disease. As she grew, the left leg remained smaller than the right one. It didn't function as well as her right one either. She was eventually fitted with a heavy metal brace to aid her walking.

As it neared time for Imogene to give birth to her third baby, she was unable to work with Vicky as much. She and Hubert decided it would be best if they moved back to Montgomery, where they could be close to the doctors. Afterward a therapist started coming to their house daily to help with Vicky until after the baby was born. On March 5, 1953, Imogene gave birth to yet another girl. They named her Debra Dianne.

In the meantime, DM was beginning to have trouble with his car. Several times it quit on him, leaving him stranded along the roadside. Mr. Darnell decided he should help him get another one.

"DM, I think that car of yours has seen its better day," he told DM. "I saw a 1949 Ford down on one of the lots in town. How 'bout we go take a look at it to see if it is one ya might be interested in."

DM knew he needed a more reliable car, but he was reluctant. "I do need another car for sure, Mr. Darnell. I just don't see how I can afford to buy another one right now."

Bud patted DM on the shoulder. "Let's go take a look at it anyway. We'll see how much they're askin' for it. Maybe something can be worked out."

After work that day, Mr. Darnell and DM rode down to the car lot together. The salesman quoted them a price of 750 dollars.

"What do ya think, DM?" Mr. Darnell asked.

DM lifted the hood to check the engine. "It's a nice-lookin' car all right. But honestly, Mr. Darnell, I don't see how I can afford the payments at this time."

Mr. Darnell stood silent for a moment. "Tell ya what I'll

do, DM," he offered. "I'll loan ya the money myself to buy the car. Ya can pay me back a little at a time from your check. We'll put it in your name, and it'll be your car. You're a good boy, DM. You've always been straight with me. I trust ya to pay me back."

DM was touched by Mr. Darnell's kind words of confidence. He was also overjoyed to be getting a better-running, more-dependable car. "I sure do appreciate this, Mr. Darnell. It's real nice of ya to do this for me."

Bud put his arm around DM's shoulder. "You're a good employee and a good friend. I'm glad I can help ya out."

The following weekend, DM drove his '49 Ford up to Billingsley to show his folks the new car he'd purchased. It just so happened that the outside team was playing a baseball game that very afternoon at Billingsley School. The outside team was made up of players who had already graduated from school but still liked getting together to play a game every now and again. When one of the guys on the team found out DM was home, he invited him to come play with the Billingsley team.

Willie was working part time as a deputy for Autauga County, so DM took Adell and Nancy with him to the game in his new car. In order to keep an eye on his car, he parked the Ford on the hill behind the backstop. He knew Adell and Nancy would have a good view of the game from there also.

It was a hot summer day. The concession stand, which usually sold cold drinks and snacks at the regular school games, was closed. Nancy was becoming fussy from the heat. Adell looked around to see where she might get a cool drink of water when suddenly, from out of nowhere, a young girl appeared at the window. Startled, Adell looked up. There, leaned against the edge of the car window, was a tall, slim girl with naturally curly brown hair. She was wearing dark-rimmed glasses with a row of tiny diamond-like gems along the upper edge. She smiled pleasantly then introduced herself.

"Hey. My name is Dorothy Billingsley, but everyone calls me Dot. Ain't ya Mrs. Bone, DM's mama?"

Adell had never seen the girl before now. Yet she suspected this Dot person was much more interested in her son than in meeting her. "Yes, I'm DM's mama," she answered.

"Can I sit in the car with y'all for a while? It's hot out here in the open sun," asked the young woman rather boldly.

Although it was Adell's nature to be a tad suspicious of people she'd never met before, she decided the girl looked friendly enough. "I reckon it'd be all right," she answered.

Dot went around to the driver's side of the car and got in. As she settled into the seat beside her, Adell began to ask questions. "How do ya know my son?"

Dot straightened her knee-length, gathered skirt. "Ever'body knows DM Bone," she answered. "He's one of the best ballplayers Billingsley's ever had. Does he have a girl-friend in Montgomery?"

Adell realized she'd been right about what Dot's inten-tions actually were for getting in the car with her. She also knew it had very little to do with getting out of the hot sun. It was just as hot or hotter in the car than it was out of the car. "He goes with first one then another," she said. "But he don't have nobody he's steady with that I know of."

Nancy was getting both hot and thirsty. She wanted some-thing cold to drink, so she was beginning to act up. Desper-ate for a solution, Adell turned to Dot. "Do ya know how to drive?"

Dot smiled. "I drive my daddy's truck sometimes. I don't have a license yet, but I can drive," she answered.

Adell fanned Nancy with the Independent Life Insurance fan the insurance salesman had given her. "Do ya think ya can drive us over to Ernest Moore's store so I can get this youngun' a cold drink?"

Without hesitation Dot answered, "Sure."

In a flash, Dot cranked DM's car and drove away.

DM noticed his car leaving the school grounds. He could see his mama waving to him out the window. He didn't know what was going on, but he figured there was little he could do about it, seeing he was in the middle of a game. He knew his mama couldn't drive. He wondered whom in the world she'd gotten to drive for her and where exactly it was they were going. Out the corner of his eye he watched as the car made a right turn and headed toward Moore's store. He could hardly keep his mind on the game. To his relief, a short time later the car reappeared and was parked back in the exact place from which it had left. A few minutes later, a young, dark-haired girl emerged from inside the car and headed toward the school. From a distance he was unable to tell who it was, but he knew he sure wanted to find out.

As soon as the game was over, DM went directly back to his car. He was curious to find out where his mother had been and even more curious to learn who was driving. Adell told him about the young girl who'd been nice enough to take them to the store.

"What was her name? Where did she come from?" DM asked.

Adell drank the last swallow of cold Coca-Cola from the six-ounce bottle. "She said her name was Dot Billingsley. She lives somewhere between here and Clanton. That's about all I know."

DM glanced around to see if she was anywhere to be seen. It was as though she had disappeared off the face of the earth. "Well, if ya ever see her again, Mama, hang onto her till I can meet her. She looked pretty good from where I was standin'."

In October of 1953, while DM was working for Bud Darnell, he met a young man by the name of Virgil Rawson. Mr. Rawson was getting ready to start a roofing business of his own. Mr. Rawson called on Mr. Darnell to give him a bid on some duct work for a house he was about to roof. When Mr. Darnell finished working up a price on the job, he asked DM to carry the bid to Mr. Rawson at his office.

The truth was, Mr. Rawson had been anxious to meet DM for some time. He learned through Willie Charles that DM was a bookkeeper. Willie Charles worked under Mr. Rawson as a roofer. He would later work for him at his new business. When DM arrived at his office with the bid, Mr. Rawson was standing out front. When he learned who DM was he seized the opportunity to finally talk to him.

When DM handed Mr. Rawson the bid, Mr. Rawson asked him, "Have you got a minute?"

DM couldn't imagine what Mr. Rawson would want to talk to him about, but for some reason he felt an immediate connection with him. "Sure," he answered.

Mr. Rawson smiled. "Good. Come into my office and have a seat." Mr. Rawson led DM into a small office where stacks of papers and several samples of roofing material cluttered his desk. Mr. Rawson sat down behind his desk and pointed to a chair. "I hear you're a bookkeeper."

Nervously DM pulled a cigarette from the pocket of his light blue shirt and took a seat across from Mr. Rawson's desk. "Yes sir," he replied.

Mr. Rawson leaned across his desk to light DM's cigarette. "I'm opening a roofing business come the first of the year. I could sure use a good bookkeeper. What would you think about coming to work for me?"

DM leaned forward, allowing Mr. Rawson to light the cigarette that dangled from his mouth. He inhaled deeply, held it for a moment, and then slowly exhaled gray smoke through his nose and mouth.

"Well, Mr. Rawson, right now I'm working for Bud Darnell."

DM took another long draw on his cigarette then exhaled the smoke. "I wouldn't feel right leavin' him. He's been good to me. Of course, if there ever comes a time when he can't use me anymore, I'd be glad to talk to ya about it then."

"Fair enough," Mr. Rawson said, smiling.

The two young men talked on for some time about first one thing and then another. DM liked Mr. Rawson, and Mr. Rawson seemed to like him as well. It made DM feel good to know he could possibly have a job with the new company Mr. Rawson was planning to start. Getting in on the ground floor of a new business intrigued him. Although DM didn't know it at the time, Mr. Rawson's offer would soon need to be seriously considered.

In June of the coming year, Mr. Darnell had some financial problems in his business. He had no choice but to lay off some of his workers, including DM. "I hate to do this to ya, DM," Mr. Darnell explained. "Business is off, and as bad as I hate to, I'm gonna have to let ya go. You're a really good bookkeeper. I'll be more than happy to write ya up a letter of recommendation. I'm sure ya can find another job without too much trouble."

At that point DM didn't know what he was going to do. He also knew Mr. Darnell wouldn't be letting him go if he could help it. "I understand," DM assured him. "But what about the car? I still owe ya money on my car."

Mr. Darnell looked troubled. "I know ya do, DM. I've thought about it a lot. I wish there was a way I could let ya keep it. But with things like they are now, I guess I'll have to get it back from ya and try to sell it."

DM knew the car was legally in his name. He could have refused to give it back to Mr. Darnell. He also knew, under the circumstances, the right thing to do was to give it back. Besides, he reasoned to himself, without a job there was no way he could ever afford to make the payments. He would just have to try to find some way to get another one later on down the line.

At the end of the day, DM placed what few belongings he had assembled on his desk into a small cardboard box. With sadness in his heart, he went into Mr. Darnell's office, thanked him for giving him a job, and handed him the key to what was once his car. DM could tell Mr. Darnell felt nearly as bad as he did about having to let him go. Mr. Darnell hugged DM and assured him he would give him a call if business picked back up again.

DM didn't know exactly which way to go next. He'd heard Virgil Rawson had successfully opened his business back in April. He didn't know if he still needed a bookkeeper, but he figured it wouldn't hurt to ask. All he could say was no. Besides, he had to start looking for a job somewhere. He might as well start with Mr. Rawson. On the bus ride back to his room, he decided to go see him first thing the next morning.

DM got up the next morning before daylight. He caught the first bus of the day headed for South Decatur Street. When he arrived a little before seven Mr. Rawson was talking to his crew about the job they were going to that day. As soon as he was finished talking, DM went over to him. Mr. Rawson turned to him and smiled, patting him on the shoulder. "DM, good to see you again."

DM could see Mr. Rawson was busy, so he got right down to what he had come for. "Mr. Rawson, I guess ya heard Mr. Darnell's having trouble with his business. Ya asked me a while back 'bout comin' to work for ya. I was wonderin' if ya still need somebody to keep books for ya."

Mr. Rawson looked toward the ground as though he was in deep thought. "Come inside with me," he said.

DM followed Mr. Rawson inside to his office. "Have a seat, DM."

DM took a seat on the brown leather chair directly across from Mr. Rawson's desk.

"Excuse me a minute, DM," said Mr. Rawson as he walked out of the room without commenting on DM's previous question.

DM could see Mr. Rawson through the glass pane that separated his office from the front desk and hallway. Mr. Rawson reached deep into his pocket and pulled out a handful of change. Searching through the change in his hand, he deposited two nickels into the red and white Coke machine located at the end of the hall. Reaching inside, he pulled out a small Coke then returned to his office, where DM waited anxiously.

Upon entering the room, Mr. Rawson handed the cold six-ounce bottle of Coca-Cola to DM "Well, DM, it's like this," he began to explain. "I hired an older feller who used to work for the IRS. As of right now, I don't need anybody."

DM's mouth turned as dry as a dust storm in August. He had so hoped Mr. Rawson would have a job for him. He didn't know what to say, so he took a swallow of the icy-cold drink he held in his hand. Part of him wanted to get down on his knees and beg Mr. Rawson to give him a job. However, he knew he could never do that; he had too much pride.

Mr. Rawson sat down behind his desk and leaned back in his own leather chair. By the look on his face, DM could tell he was in deep thought. After a few silent minutes he began to speak. "Truth is, DM, I'd really rather have somebody young like you who could grow with the business. Right now I'll need to figure out a way to get rid of the man I've got before I can hire you on. If you'll give me a couple of weeks or so, I'll let you know my decision."

DM didn't know why, but he liked Mr. Rawson. He knew he needed to get a job as soon as possible, but he figured he could give him two weeks. After that he'd have to look elsewhere. The two of them talked on a while longer. DM finished his soda, shook Mr. Rawson's hand, and then left with the understanding Mr. Rawson would be calling him soon.

Rather than spending the next two weeks in town, DM decided to go home to his folks' house for a while. While he was home, he and his daddy found a 1948 Nash automobile for sale. Willie agreed to go on a note with him so he could buy it. It appeared to be a good-running car. They knew he would need it if he were going to get another job.

Two weeks later, Willie Charles, Edna, and their children made a trip up to Billingsley from Montgomery to let DM know Mr. Rawson wanted to talk to him. The next day, DM drove his Nash to Montgomery to once again meet with Mr. Rawson.

A smile came over Mr. Rawson's face as DM entered his office. He came from behind his desk and greeted DM with a hardy handshake. "DM, good to see you. I guess Willie Charles gave you the message that I wanted to see you."

DM smiled back. "Yes sir, he did," he replied.

"I let my old bookkeeper go. I hope you're still interested in coming to work for me."

DM wanted to jump up and down and scream to the top of his lungs, "Yes! Yes!" Instead he smiled and calmly answered, "Yes sir, I am."

"Good," Mr. Rawson said cheerfully. "Have a seat, and we'll talk about your duties and your pay."

DM pulled up the brown leather chair close to Mr. Rawson's desk and sat down.

"I'll need you to take a look at the books," explained Mr. Rawson. "I'm not sure if my former bookkeeper knew what he was doing or not. I'll leave it up to you to set the books up like you think is best. Once you've got them set up, I'll have my auditor take a look at them."

"That sounds fine with me," said DM

"Now about your pay," Mr. Rawson continued. "I'm willing to start you off at forty-five dollars a week. If everything works out like I'm sure it will, I'll consider raising your pay after a few months."

"Forty-five a week sounds fair to me," DM replied casually, trying to make the moment seem like business as usual.

"Great. When can you start?" Mr. Rawson asked.

"Today is Thursday. How 'bout I start Monday mornin'?" DM answered.

Mr. Rawson leaned across the desk and shook DM's hand to close the deal. "Monday morning it is, then."

DM was both excited and grateful. "Thank ya, Mr. Rawson."

"Please, DM, just call me Rawson. Everybody else does."

DM smiled again. "Thanks, Rawson."

When DM left Rawson's office, he was on cloud nine. Forty-five dollars a week was almost twice what he had been making at Darnell Plumbing. As he walked out to get into his car, he remembered the words of a preacher he'd once heard preach at a Big Springs Church revival: "For every door that closes, another will open." Truly another door had opened for DM that day. While backing out of his parking place in front of A-1 Roofing, he silently thanked God for his new job.

———

Willie was still serving as constable for Billingsley. The little town of Billingsley had four small stores: Floyd Gilliland's gas station, Cooter Headley's mercantile, Bug Durden's grocery, and Richard Thomas's grocery. There was also a post office, a train depot, and of course, the eight-by-ten foot cement-block jail where Willie incarcerated an occasional Saturday-night drunk or moonshiner. The train, which at one time made daily stops in the town, no longer ran along its rusty rails. The abandoned depot leaned slightly to the right, looking as though a strong gust of wind might send it crumpling to the ground.

On the other hand, nearby Prattville was a thriving little

town. Main Street had several stores where one could purchase almost anything one might desire. There was Elmore's Five and Dime, Rexall Drugs, Cooper's Department Store, Red Arrow Hardware, and Goldfield's, just to name a few.

During the week, Willie worked with Hubert for Jehle Brother's Construction Company in Montgomery. He rode to work every day with Estus Deason and his son, Carl. They also worked for Jehle Brothers. It was a good job, and the money was consistent. However, he was beginning to have trouble with his breathing and oftentimes experienced tightness in his chest.

Early on Saturday morning, Willie, Adell, and Nancy were driving into Prattville to so some shopping when he began rubbing his chest.

"Is your chest hurtin' again?" Adell asked, concerned.

Willie burped. "A little. Must be 'em onions I ate last night for supper."

Adell scolded him. "It's more likely 'em cigarettes ya smoke. If ya'd stop smokin', ya wouldn't have that problem."

"Oh hell, Adell," Willie said defiantly. "It ain't got nothin' to do with smokin' cigarettes. A lot of folks smoke."

Adell hated cigarette smoke. "They're a waste of money, and they're gonna kill ya if ya don't quit 'em," she argued stubbornly.

Disgusted, Willie threw up his hands. "Ya don't know what you're talkin' 'bout, Adell," he protested. Still, deep inside, he knew Adell was right.

Wilfred was in the eighth grade but remained small for his age. He secretly dreamed of one day leaving the small town of Billingsley to move on to bigger and better things. He felt in his heart that he was destined to be more than a poor, farm boy. He was also smart enough to realize education was his ticket out of town. He studied hard and did well in school.

At home he continued to butt heads with his daddy. He was angry. He felt as though his parents didn't understand him. He was angry because he thought DM had always been given more attention. He was angry because his mother was sick and away much of the time while he was growing up. He was angry because he was no longer the baby of the family. He was angry because Nancy was getting so much more attention from his father than he'd ever gotten.

Willie called him hardheaded. Adell tried to do things to repair the wall between Willie and his youngest son. Unfortunately, Wilfred had long ago decided he could make it on his own. He chose to distance himself from the family, to be his own person. Willie had given up on trying to understand him. The wall between them grew higher every day.

"I don't know what's wrong with Wilfred," Willie said to Adell one morning at breakfast. "I can't seem to talk to him anymore."

Adell placed a pan of hot biscuits on the table and pulled up a chair. "That's because ya don't try to talk to him. Y'all are just alike. You're both headstrong. Ya try to make him do things your way, and he wants to do 'em his way. Neither of ya wants to give an inch."

Willie slammed his fist down hard on the table. "If I give 'im an inch, then he wants a mile," he said.

"Then give 'im a mile and see what happens. He's been raised up the best way we know how. The older he gets, the more he's gonna need ya. He's a good boy. He's smart. He's just got a mind of his own."

Willie lowered his head. "I don't know," he said. "Maybe it's best he's as independent as he is. Truth is, sometimes I feel like I might live long enough to see Wilfred grown, but I don't think I'll ever live to see Nancy grown."

Adell laid her hand on Willie's hand and looked directly into his eyes. "What in the world would make ya say such a thing?" she asked.

Willie pulled his hand away and reached for his cup of coffee. After taking a swallow he replied, "It's just a feelin' I've got."

Adell stood up. "Well, if there's something wrong with ya, then we need to take ya to the doctor."

Willie shook his head. "It ain't nothin' I can put my finger on. It's just a feelin' I've got. Don't worry 'bout me. I'm fine."

Adell reached for a shirt she'd been mending. "I worry, Willie. What would me and these younguns do if something happened to ya?"

Willie didn't answer.

———

DM liked and respected Rawson. His job of setting up the books for A-1 Roofing was a challenge. DM liked challenges. Once he finished setting them up, Rawson called him into his office.

"DM," Rawson said proudly, "you did an outstanding job on setting up the company's books. I had my auditor, Matt Piel, look them over. He said he couldn't have done a better job if he'd done them himself."

DM's chest filled with pride. "Thank ya, Rawson," he said, sitting up a little straighter in his chair.

Rawson smiled. "I've decided to give you a raise for doing such a good job. How does a ten-dollar-a-week raise sound to you?"

"Sounds real good to me," DM answered. He couldn't wait to tell his mama and daddy about his raise. They had always worried a lot about how he would make a good living on his own, having only one arm. It seemed life was working out well for him.

On one of his trips back to Billingsley, DM went over to the school that night to watch Wilfred play football. G.C. Hayes was also there that night. "Hey, DM," G.C. called out when he saw his old friend. "How's it goin'?"

He and G.C. had been friends for as far back as DM could remember. He was glad to hear his voice. DM climbed the heavy wooden bleachers to the top row and sat down next to G.C. "I'm doin' purdy good, G.C. How 'bout you?"

"I'm fair to middlin'," G.C. answered with a smile.

"Anything goin' on tonight after the game that ya know of?" DM asked.

G.C. thought a minute. "The only thing I know of is a party at Dot Billingsley's house. I hear she's havin' a bunch of folks over. I don't know who all will be there, but it might be fun."

DM remembered that name from the day at the baseball field. "I think that was the name of the gal who drove my mama and little sister to the store one time in my car. I've been wantin' to see what she looks like up close. How 'bout me and you go up there after the game?"

"Sounds good to me," agreed G.C.

After the game, DM and G.C. got into DM's car and headed out toward County Road 67. The house where Dot's family lived was several miles outside of Billingsley down a narrow, winding dirt road. In places, the land on either said of the road was nothing more than swampland. Low-hanging trees covered in Spanish moss hung over the road, forming a tunnel-like effect. About halfway down the road between her house and County Road 24 was a narrow, practically nonexistent wooden bridge that connected one side of the road to the other. During the rainy season, water from the murky swamp often flooded the road, making it impassable.

The small white farmhouse was several hundred yards back

off the road. There was a peach orchard on one side of the lane that led down to the house. An open field was on the other side of the lane. Clem and Ethel Billingsley had owned the farm most of their married life. They had two sons, Charles and Wilbert. Their only daughter was Dorothy. Everyone called her Dot.

When DM and G.C. arrived at the party they found out it was a "waist party," which meant the hostess measured your waist and whatever your waist size was what it cost to get in. Dot met DM and G.C. at the door. She smiled when she opened the door and saw who it was. "Come on in, fellers," she said.

DM opened the screen door and stepped inside. G.C. followed close behind. "Hope ya don't mind us showin' up like this uninvited like," DM said flashing Dot a mischievous grin.

Dot blushed, pushing her glasses back onto the bridge of her nose. "Naw, of course not. Ever'body's welcome. We're havin' a waist party. There's an admission fee to help pay for food and stuff. I have to measure your waist. Admission to the party costs one penny per inch."

DM laughed. "Glad I've got a little waist. I might not be able to get in if I was as big as ol' G.C. here." DM jokingly poked G.C. in the gut with his elbow.

Dot picked up a cloth tape measure from off the small table just inside the door. She blushed again as she bent down to put it around DM's waist. DM felt a tingle go down his spine as he breathed in the smell of Evening in Paris perfume.

Dot looked at the tape measure. "Twenty-nine inches," she announced.

DM reached into his pocket and pulled out the only coin he had. "Seems I only have a quarter."

Dot smiled. "That's okay. A quarter will be just fine."

Although G.C.'s waist was several inches bigger, Dot let him in for a quarter too. There was no way she was going to let a few pennies stand in the way of finally getting to spend time with DM

Dot was a little taller than DM, but that didn't seem to matter to either of them. DM thought she was the prettiest girl he'd ever seen. She had naturally curly brown hair and pretty blue eyes. All during the party, Dot made sure she stayed close by DM's side. Later that evening as people were beginning to leave, the two of them decided to take a walk down the dirt road in front of Dot's family farm. As they were walking, Dot held DM's hand. Almost instantly a special bond formed between the two of them. After that night they started dating on a regular basis.

———

There were two grocery stores in Prattville, the Piggly Wiggly and the A&P. Strangely enough, they were directly across the street from one another. Adell bought most of her groceries from the Piggly Wiggly because she felt the prices were cheaper and she liked their meats better.

Nancy loved going to the grocery store. She got to sit in the buggy while her daddy pushed it down the middle of the aisle between the rows of shelves. The shelves were stacked with cans of vegetables, fruit, cereals, candy, bags of sugar, flour, cornmeal, and coffee. Everything she saw she wanted. Adell had to watch Willie and Nancy closely to keep them from putting more in the cart than they needed or could pay for.

As they rounded the corner of the last aisle, Nancy looked up from the box of animal crackers she was eating. At the end of the aisle was a large black woman dressed in a bright-red dress with large white polka dots and a white apron. She was wearing a red and white checkered bandana tied securely around her hair. Her wide grin and shining cheekbones made Nancy feel happy.

"Good days to ya folks," the woman said, smiling at Nancy and pinching her chubby cheeks. "Would y'all likes ta try some of my Aunt Jemima syrup? It's mighty good."

The Negro woman held up a bottle of syrup for them to see. The picture on the label looked just like the woman holding the bottle. Her fat, round face, glistening cheekbones, and red-checkered bandana bore the spitting image of the woman in the store.

"I's bets dis purdy little girl would like some. Wouldn't ya, baby?"

Before Nancy could answer, the woman handed Nancy a small white paper plate. In the middle of the plate was a half-dollar-size pancake with syrup poured on top.

"I guess I's best gives ya somethin' to eats it with," the black woman said, laughing. She reached for one of the small wooden ice cream spoons laying on the table beside her. However, before she could hand the spoon to her, Nancy had picked up the syrup-covered pancake with her fingers. Abruptly she placed the entire pancake in her mouth at one time.

The woman laughed heartily when she saw what Nancy had done. "Good, ain't it, child?"

Nancy swallowed. "Yes ma'am."

"Can I's puts a bottle in yo' basket?" the Aunt Jemima look-alike asked.

Adell wanted to pass on buying the bottle of syrup. She insisted they didn't need it, as they had some of Ira Huett's syrup at home already. However, upon his little girl's insistence, Willie ended up adding a bottle of Aunt Jemima syrup, as well as a box of Aunt Jemima pancake mix, to the contents of their shopping cart.

Adell reached for a bag of White Lilly flour from off the shelf. *How different grocery shopping is now than how it used to be,* she thought to herself. Everything from sugar to wieners was prepackaged. Vegetables and fruits were sold in tin cans rather than jars. Candy and cookies were sealed up in cellophane packages and purchased by the dozen rather than two for a penny. Even the way one paid for their groceries was different. The owner of the store was usually nowhere to be seen. Instead, there were managers and cashiers dressed in white uniforms punching in the prices of an item on a cash register.

After leaving the Piggly Wiggly, they walked across the street to the A&P. Willie liked the fresh-ground coffee at the A&P better than what they sold at the Piggly Wiggly. As soon as they entered the store the aroma of fresh-ground coffee beans filled the air. Although Nancy wasn't allowed to drink coffee yet, she loved the way it smelled. Her daddy always told her it would turn little children black like the Aunt Jemima at the Piggly Wiggly store. Although Nancy almost always believed every word that came out of her daddy's mouth to be the honest-to-God truth, she was a might skeptical. After all, the rest of her family drank coffee all the time and none of them was black. She thought seriously about sneaking some one time just to see if it was so. It might be fun being black. If she looked like Aunt Jemima, she could hand out syrup and pancakes to everybody and make them happy.

After leaving the A&P, Willie stopped by the courthouse on their way home. The sheriff of Prattville gave Willie some papers to serve on one of the men living in Willie's community. Willie knew the man well. He'd served papers on him before. He also knew he didn't take kindly to law enforcement officials. He decided it was best to drop Adell and Nancy off at their house before he went to serve the papers. When they arrived home, DM's car was parked in the yard.

"Good," Willie commented. "DM is here. I think I'll see if he wants to go with me to serve these papers on Dewey Anniston. He can get pretty ornery at times."

DM heard his dad's car coming down the lane. He put down his glass of cold water he'd been drinking and ran out to

meet him at the car. He wanted to tell his folks about the raise
Mr. Rawson had given him.

DM leaned against the edge of the car window. "Hey,
Daddy," he said.

"Hey, son," Willie replied. "Ya got time to ride with me
over to Dewey Anniston's house? I've got some papers I need
to serve on him."

DM felt excited about getting a chance to spend some
one-on-one time with his father. "Sure, Daddy, I'll go with ya.
I've got some good news I wanted to tell ya about anyway. It'll
give us a chance to talk."

DM hurried around the front of the car. Adell and Nancy
were just getting out. Nancy hugged DM around the legs. DM
ruffled Nancy's light brown, wavy hair.

Adell was always glad to see her son. She tucked one corner of his blue, cotton dress shirt back into his pants. "I didn't
know ya were comin' today. Are ya gonna stay for supper?" she
asked.

"Yeah, I'll be here for supper, Mama," he answered. "I've
got some good news I want to share with y'all. I'll tell ya 'bout
tonight. I think Daddy's ready to go serve them papers. We'll
be back before ya know it. It shouldn't take us long."

DM was about to get into the car when Willie handed him
a sack of groceries. "Here, son. Put this on the porch for your
mama."

DM placed the brown bag full of groceries on the porch
then hurried back to the car.

Adell looked concerned. "Y'all be careful, DM," she
warned. "That whole Anniston bunch is crazy. Don't take no
chances with your life."

DM eased into the car and closed the door. "We'll be fine,
Mama," he assured her.

Willie put the car in reverse. "I ain't got to bring 'im in,

Adell. I'm just serving papers today. If he don't show up for his court hearin', then I'll have to go get 'im, but not today."

Fortunately, Dewey allowed Willie to serve papers on him without giving him any trouble. Willie and DM had a good visit and all was well.

That night at supper, DM told everyone about his raise and about how much he liked working for Mr. Rawson. Adell was pleased to hear her son was doing so well. She had always worried about how he was going to make a living with only one arm, but it seemed her fears had all been in vain. He was on his own and doing well.

The Norrell Place

The hedge bush around the Tindle Place was full of poison oak plants. They were also a great place for a mischievous little child to hide. Unfortunately, Nancy was highly allergic to poison oak, so allergic that eventually they would be forced to move from the Tindle Place altogether.

The Norrell place was empty. The four-room house was located several miles from Billingsley out on Highway 82. The house was equipped with electricity and running water. Several acres surrounding the house made for an excellent garden spot. There was a barn, a corn shed, and a smokehouse out back. It had a fenced-in area for the pigs and a fenced-in lot for the cow. The outhouse was located down past the pig lot and barn. Two huge black walnut trees stood alongside the edge of the field.

DM was seeing Dot Billingsley on a regular basis. He'd leave Montgomery after work on Friday night or early Saturday morning and drive up to Billingsley. With the pedal to the metal, he could get there in an hour or less. As soon as he'd caught everyone up on the news from town, he'd head out for Dot's house to spend the day with her. He would return home around midnight and go straight to bed. Sunday mornings he spent with his family. Sunday afternoon he drove back to Montgomery.

DM's relationship with Dot was intensifying to the point where DM decided it was time to take his and Dot's association to the next level. She'd worn his high school class ring long enough. It was time to give her something more official, so he bought her an engagement ring.

DM had always like messing with people's minds. He decided his proposal to Dot needed a little humor, so he devised a plan to fool her. That night he took her to the drive-in movie in Prattville. About a third of the way through the first show, DM removed his arm from around Dot's shoulder and looked at her very seriously. "Dot," he said, "I want my ring back."

To say the least, Dot was shocked. They'd been going steady for some time. She thought their romance was on the upswing, yet the love of her life was asking for his ring back. She could hardly believe what she was hearing. Tears welled up in her eyes as she removed the large, gold class ring from her hand and handed it to him. Without a word DM took the ring, put it back on his own finger, opened the car door, and got out, leaving Dot alone to stew over what had just happened.

From inside the concession stand DM watched a few minutes of the movie while turning over in his mind what a wonderful trick he was playing on her and how surprised she was going to be when she saw her engagement ring. When he felt a significant amount of time had passed, he headed back to the car to further implement his plan.

Dot was still there, looking as though the wind had been knocked out of her. DM opened the car door and slid across the seat next to her. "Give me your hand, Dot," he said to her.

Dot looked even more bewildered than before.

DM smiled. "Give me your hand, please," he repeated.

Dot extended her right hand.

DM shook his head. "No," he said, "your other hand."

Dot put out her left hand, whereupon DM pulled his own hand from inside his jacket pocket. The light from the movie screen caught the reflection of the diamond as he slid it onto her ring finger. "I thought ya might like this ring better."

Dot lit up like a Fourth of July fireworks display. Grabbing him around the neck, she hugged him with all her might. "Oh, DM," she squealed. "It's the most beautiful ring I've ever seen."

DM smiled again. "Does that mean you'll marry me?"

Dot hugged and kissed him again. "Of course I'll marry ya. Ya know that without even askin'. Just say when, and I'll be there."

Dot wouldn't graduate until the following spring. DM was new to his job. They decided to wait until she was finished with school and he was for sure things were going to work out with his job before actually tying the knot. Still, it was one of the happiest nights of his and Dot's life.

———

All the older Bone children were grown and married. DM was working and living in Montgomery. Wilfred stayed gone off with his friends most of the time. This left Nancy alone with no one except her parents to play with. It was almost like being an only child. The only time she had anyone her own age to play with was when her nieces and nephews came to visit. They were all around her age; however, their visits were few and far between.

Sometimes she got to play with a little Negro girl by the name of Lillie Mae. She was the granddaughter of North Ivey and Bell. They lived just up the road from the Norrell place. Lillie Mae was close to Nancy's age but nearly twice her size. Nancy liked Lillie Mae and they played well together.

One Saturday night, Willie and Adell decided to take Nancy to the drive-in picture show at the Prattmont drive-in. The outdoor theater was located just south of Prattville. It was a clear, cool, star-filled night. The movie was called *Tarantula*. It was about a scientific experiment gone awry. The experiment turned a small spider into a gigantic man-eating eight-legged monster. It was an extremely scary movie. Nancy spent most of the night hiding behind the seat of the car with her hands over her face.

When the movie was over, Willie unhooked the speaker that hung on his car window and started for home. Highway 82 was a long, desolate, narrow, two-lane paved road. Nancy quickly fell asleep in the backseat. Adell and Willie were talking about how the people who filmed the picture show had made the spider look so real. Suddenly, without warning, Willie slammed on the brakes and slid off the edge of the road.

"Did ya see 'im?" he shouted in horror.

Adell was startled and surprised by her husband's actions. "See who?" she asked.

Willie looked back over his shoulder at the dark road behind him. "That man," he answered. "He was standin' right in the middle of the road."

Adell was confused. She turned around in her seat to look for the man Willie had seen. As best she could tell looking into the darkness of the desolate highway, there was no one there to be seen. "I didn't see nobody then, and I don't see nobody now," she answered.

Willie got out of the car. He walked the short distance back to where he thought he'd seen the man, but there was no one. Walking slowly back to the car, he rubbed his eyes with the back of his calloused hand. He looked around one more time just to make sure there was no one there before getting back into the car. He wondered whom it was he'd seen if he had in fact seen anyone at all. As Willie got back into the driver's seat, he looked at Adell. "I could have sworn there was a man standin' in the middle of the road."

"It's that green liquid medicine Doc Campbell is givin' ya," Adell scolded. "Ever since ya started takin' it, ya been actin' strange. I don't think he knows what he's doin'. He ain't much of a doctor if ya ask me."

Willie sat there a moment before cranking up the car and putting it into gear. Before pulling away, he looked at Adell. "Well, nobody asked ya, Adell," he said sarcastically. "I feel better than I have in years since I started goin' to Doc Campbell, and that's good enough for me."

Adell folded her arms across her chest and looked at Willie with a disgusted look. "All he's doin' is keepin' ya drugged up. It's gonna kill ya if ya keep takin' that mess."

"Well, it may kill me," he spouted out, "but at least I'll die feelin' better than I've felt in a long time."

———

Financially, things were going well for the Bone family. The Depression had ended. Willie had a steady job with Jehle Brothers Construction as well as his weekend job working as constable for Billingsley. Julius was going to law school and working at Cooper's Shoe Store in Prattville. Willie Charles had a good job at A-1 Roofing, working as a roofer. DM was enjoying his job as bookkeeper for A-1 Roofing. On occasion, he was even being allowed to make bids on a few jobs here and there. Hubert was well on his way to becoming a superintendent for Jehle Brothers. Wilfred was doing well in school.

Willie rode to work every morning with his friend Estus Deason and his son, Carl. They would meet at Lofton Hilyer's grocery store before daylight and ride together to the jobsite in Montgomery. Splitting the cost of gas three ways saved all of them money. Every day they started work at daylight, worked all day, then drove back to Billingsley, getting home just before dark set in.

Before Willie would get in his car for the short drive home, he would go into the store and buy some kind of treat for Nancy. Sometimes it was a candy bar; other times a piece of bubblegum. He would hide the treat somewhere in his gray-striped work overalls. It was a game he and Nancy liked to play. He would hide it, and she would have to find it before she could have it.

Willie was proud of his little girl. He loved her very much. She made him feel young again. She was always the first person he saw when he got home. As soon as he turned into the yard, she was always there on the front porch, waiting for him to arrive. Before he could even turn off the ignition she was at the car.

"What did ya bring me today, Daddy?" she asked, smiling up at him.

Willie scooped her up in his arms. "What makes ya think I brought ya something?" he teased. "Have ya been behavin' today?"

Nancy threw her arms around her daddy's neck and kissed him on his day-old, scratchy, bearded cheek. "Yes sir," she answered. "I'm always behavin'."

Willie reached for his gray, metal lunchbox lying on the seat beside him. "Let's go inside first so I can put away my lunchbox and wash my face and hands," he said.

When Willie got to the kitchen, he stood Nancy on one of the straight-back kitchen chairs, kissed Adell on the cheek, then went out on the back porch to wash his face and hands. He unhooked the well rope and lowered the bucket down into the well. When he heard it hit bottom, he waited until the bucket had time to fill with water then slowly turned the water wheel until the bucket reached the top. He poured the water in a slightly chipped white, porcelain basin. Cupping his hands in the water, he splashed the refreshing, cool liquid onto his face then soaped up his hands, arms, and face with a bar of soap left lying in a discarded chipped saucer.

"Supper's 'bout ready," Adell called to him. "Tell Wilfred to come in and eat."

"Wilfred," Willie called. "Come on, son. Your mama's waitin' supper."

Wilfred appeared from behind the smokehouse. "Hey, Daddy," he said as he climbed the back steps two at a time. "How was work today?"

Willie laid his arm around Wilfred's shoulder. "Same as always, son: hot and tirin'. How was yours?"

Wilfred was surprised at his father's show of affection. "It was okay," he said. "Me and Ray went fishin'."

Willie opened the screen door that led into the kitchen. "Catch anything?" he asked.

"We caught two nice-size catfish," Wilfred replied proudly as he sat down at the kitchen table. "I think we're gonna see if we can find some Catawba worms to fish with before we go back in the morning."

Willie sat down in his chair at the head of the table. "There's a Catawba tree full of Catawba worms near the fence line between here and North Ivey's place."

Nancy stuck her hand into her daddy's side pocket. "Daddy, did ya forget my treat?" she interrupted.

"No I didn't forget." Willie laughed, picking her up and placing her on his knee.

"Nancy!" Wilfred yelled angrily. "Do you always have to interrupt every time me and Daddy are talking?"

"Wilfred, don't holler at your sister," Willie scolded.

"She's always interrupting," Wilfred lashed out. "You sure

wouldn't let me disrupt a conversation between adults when I was little."

"She wants her surprise, that's all," Willie said sternly. "It's a game we play."

Wilfred pushed back from the table. In an unexpected fit of anger, he kicked the table leg then stormed out the back door. "Well, it's a stupid game," he yelled as the screen door slammed behind him.

Willie started to get up and go after him. Adell put her hand on his shoulder. "Leave him be," she said. "He's just mad. He'll get over it."

"Mad 'bout what?" Willie questioned. "I can't have a single civil conversation with that boy anymore. He always acts like he hates my guts."

Adell dipped black-eyed peas onto Willie's plate. "I think he feels a little jealous, Willie."

"Jealous of what?" Willie asked.

"Jealous of your relationship with Nancy. When DM was here ya spent most of your time with him. Now that Nancy's come along, ya treat her like she's the only child ya got. He's right, ya know. Ya wouldn't have let any of our other children interrupt ya when ya was talkin'. It's like Nancy can do no wrong."

Willie dropped his head shamefully. "Maybe you're right, Adell," he said sadly. "I guess I should try to spend more time with Wilfred. But it seems like every time I try to talk to him we just end up arguin'."

⸺

Sunday, June 17, 1956, was Father's Day. Imogene, Hubert, and their three girls came up early that morning to spend the day with Willie and Adell and to give Willie his Father's Day gift. They had gone in halves with DM to buy him a new fly rod.

Adell cooked a big meal of fried chicken, fresh green beans, cornbread, and new potatoes.

Julius, Betty Jo, and their son, Travis (everyone called him Bug) were coming by later. Willie Charles, Edna, and their four children, Richard, Lee, David, and Robin, came the day before. DM came up on Friday night to spend the weekend. He left around ten that Sunday morning to go pick up Dot from her house. They were coming by after he and Dot got out of church. Wilfred was fourteen, and Nancy had just turned five in January. It was a good holiday. Willie got to see all his children over the weekend, with the exception of Calvin and Delene.

After dinner, the children played in the yard while the adults sat under the shade of the huge black walnut tree at the edge of the yard. Hubert, DM, and Wilfred made plans to go fishing with Willie the coming weekend so Willie could try out his new fishing gear.

The outhouse was located at the bottom of a long hill. The narrow path ran past the barn, alongside the pig lot, ending at a gully at the edge of the woods. Beside the outhouse there grew a huge persimmon tree.

Vicky and Nancy were about the same age. Only six months separated the two of them. They were best buddies. Where you saw one, you saw the other. Therefore, it was only natural for them to go to the outhouse together. Nancy picked up a long stick on their way there. She would use it to clear away the cobwebs from across and underneath the two holes. Cautiously she opened the gray, weathered door. Carefully, the two of them checked for snakes and other crawly creatures. When Nancy felt it was safe, they pulled their shorts down around their ankles and sat down on the smooth, worn wooden seat.

"Are the persimmons ready to eat?" Vicky asked. She loved the taste and sweet smell of the juicy, ripe persimmons.

Nancy mashed a small garden spider with a page she'd torn from the Sears and Roebuck catalog. "I think so," she replied.

Since Nancy had been raised in the country, Vicky thought she knew all the answers when it came to country life. She watched as Nancy spread open her legs and dropped the paper and the dead spider into the smelly sewage below.

"How do you know when they're ready?" Vicky asked.

Nancy brushed her hands together triumphantly, pleased she had done away with the dangerous spider. "When the animals start eatin' 'em then they're ready," she answered confidently.

"Animals?" Vicky asked in a muted voice.

"Sure," Nancy quipped nonchalantly. "Ya know, like possums, raccoons, and foxes."

Vicky had spent most of her growing-up years as a city girl. Wild animals were not something she was accustomed to hearing about. "Fox?" she questioned with concern in her voice. "Do they come out in the daytime?"

"Sure, I see them all the time," Nancy said bravely. "They come right up here beside the outhouse sometimes."

Things got very quiet. Five-year-old Nancy and soon-to-be five-year-old Vicky listened intently to the noises going on outside the enclosure. Their active imaginations began to run wild. Suddenly a twig broke and a leaf rustled.

"What was that noise?" Vicky whispered.

"I don't know," Nancy whispered back.

There was another crackle and a snap.

"I'm scared!" retorted Vicky. "I bet there's a fox out there eating persimmons right now. He can't get in here, can he?"

"Naw," Nancy said with confidence. "How could he? The door is shut."

Then she remembered that the opening at the bottom of the outhouse opened out into the gully. Quickly, she jumped up and looked down into the hole. In response, Vicky jumped up too. All their fears exploded into terror, and every corner of their minds held visions of being ripped to pieces by vicious unknown predators. Just at that very moment something hit the tin roof of the outhouse.

"Ayeeeee!" they screamed simultaneously.

Out the door they ran, shorts and panties still down around their ankles.

The two of them were quite the sight to behold as they ran up the hill screaming, yelling, and tripping on their own clothes. When the adults saw the two of them coming up the hill, they began to laugh. By the time they got to the walnut tree they were crying and screaming something about a pack of wolves down by the outhouse.

Adell and Imogene assured them both there were no wolves and then helped them get their shorts and underwear back up. The menfolks began teasing them about wolves and bears; that is, until Imogene got mad and scolded them for terrorizing the two little girls even more. Even then Wilfred continued to tease them about it when Imogene wasn't around.

Around five o'clock that afternoon, Hubert announced it was time to go home. Vicky and Nancy were having so much fun together they didn't want it to end. They begged and pleaded with Imogene and Hubert to let Vicky spend the week at her grandparents' house. Vicky had never spent the night away from home without her parents being there. She promised she wouldn't cry and that she would be good. Finally they agreed to let her stay.

On Monday morning, the day after Father's Day, Willie rose early as always to get ready for work. He dressed in his usual gray-striped work overalls and gray work shirt. Adell had biscuits in the oven and sausage frying in the skillet on top of the stove. She was also making Willie a fried apple pie to put in his lunch, just as she did every morning.

Once he was dressed, Willie went into the kitchen to put his work boots on. He kissed Adell on the cheek and sat down at the table. "Boy, that pie sure smells good," he said as he laced up one of his boots.

Adell removed the hot biscuits from the oven. "Better get washed up," she said. "Breakfast will be done in a minute."

Willie walked out onto the back porch. It was starting out to be a beautiful day. The morning sun was just beginning to peek over the hillside. Streaks of lavender, pink, and gray adorned the sky. As he was washing his hands, he looked out across the field of green, lush corn growing there. "That corn looks like it's grown a foot overnight," he said. Slowly he breathed in the fresh morning air, filling his lungs.

Adell woke Nancy and Vicky. "Time for breakfast, girls. Y'all get up so Willie can help get Vicky's leg brace on her."

The two girls tumbled out of bed and into the kitchen just as Willie was coming through the back door. "Good mornin', sleepyheads," he said. Willie took his seat at the table then picked up Vicky and placed her on his knee. Vicky gave him a big hug. When he finished strapping on Vicky's brace, he picked up Nancy and put her on his other knee. Nancy gave him a big hug too.

"How 'bout this, Adell?" he said proudly. "I've got my two favorite girls right here on either side of me."

Adell set a pan of gravy on the table. "Put them in their chairs so you'll have room to eat."

"We want to eat here by Daddy." Nancy pouted.

"Can we, Grandpa? Can we?" begged Vicky.

Willie pulled their plates in closer. "Sure ya can," he said. "I ain't sat between two such pretty girls since the day I sat between your grandma and her sister Emma."

Adell shook her head. She knew there was no need to argue. She fixed a buttered biscuit for each of the girls and placed it on their plates. Once she finished packing Willie's lunch into his lunchbox, she took her place at the table. "Y'all eat up. Willie's got to go to work. He can't be foolin' with y'all all mornin'."

Willie smiled at his girls then gulped down a swallow of coffee. "Ya know, Adell, I feel better this mornin' than I've felt in years," he said. "I slept like a log last night. I don't think I moved so much as an inch till I woke up."

Willie quickly finished his breakfast, kissed the two girls good-bye, took his lunchbox from off the table, kissed his wife, and left for work.

Adell spent her morning shelling and cooking a mess of peas, some fried okra, and hoecakes of cornbread for dinner. The girls played outside until nearly noon, when Adell called them inside to eat. They had just sat down at the table when Adell heard a car coming down the lane. She immediately got up from her chair and pulled back the kitchen curtains to see who it was. When she saw Hubert and Imogene's car she became somewhat concerned. The plan had been for Vicky to stay all week. *I hope nothin' has happened to one of the children,* she thought to herself. *Maybe they just miss Vicky and came to take her home.* Although she knew Vicky was sure going to be disappointed to leave, she hoped that was all it was. After taking some extra plates from the cupboard, Adell sat back down at the table to wait.

Imogene was the first to come through the kitchen doorway. Adell could tell she'd been crying. Hubert was standing behind her. Both of them looked extremely upset.

"What's the matter, Imogene?" Adell asked, looking alarmed.

Imogene's chin began to tremble. "Mama," she said slowly, her mouth so dry she could barely speak the words. "Daddy's dead."

Adell sat motionless. It was as though her mind wasn't registering the words Imogene had spoken.

Imogene broke down in tears. "Mama, did you hear what I said?"

Suddenly the reality of what Imogene said finally sunk in. Adell screamed. She sobbed uncontrollably. She tried to stand, but her knees buckled beneath her as though her legs were made of jelly. She felt as though her heart had been ripped from her chest. She could barely breathe. "What happened? How did he die?" she asked between sobs. "He was fine when he left this mornin'. He said he felt better than he'd felt in years. He can't be dead. Are ya sure he's dead? Tell me he's not dead."

Hubert helped Adell to her bed. "We've notified DM at his work," he said. "He should be on his way up here. Julius and Willie Charles know too. They're going to the funeral home to make arrangements for the funeral. Willie Charles is supposed to get ahold of Delene to let her know. Where's Wilfred?"

Adell buried her head in her pillow, continuing to cry uncontrollably. "He went fishin' with Ray early this mornin'. I don't know when they'll be back. Ya know how Wilfred is when the fish are bitin'. What in the world are me and these younguns gonna do without him?"

Jehle Brothers Construction Company was in the process of building a school just off Bell Street in Montgomery on Maxwell Air Force Base. Willie became ill shortly after arriving at work. Roy Gillespie, one of the other workers, was the first to notice Willie didn't look well.

After Adell calmed down a bit, Hubert explained to her as best he could what had happened. "Roy asked him if he was all right. He told Willie he was concerned because he didn't look too good. Willie said he felt kinda sick to his stomach and was a little lightheaded too. Estus asked him if he had his medicine with him. Willie told him no. He said he'd just as soon be dead as to have to carry medicine around with him everywhere he went. By that time, sweat was pourin' off his head, so he sat down on a pile of bricks. We could tell he was real sick. His skin was clammy and gray lookin'. He was sweatin' profusely, and his breathin' was labored. He assured everybody he'd be all right in a few minutes."

Hubert's eyes clouded over and tears began rolling down his cheeks as he continued telling Adell what had taken place. "Carl and Estus continued watchin' him for several more minutes. His condition was gettin' worse by the minute. It was then they decided he needed to see a doctor immediately. Estus leaned down and put his arm around Willie's shoulder. He said to him, 'Willie, let me and Carl take ya to the doctor. We can have ya at St. Margaret's Hospital in ten minutes tops.'

"But ya know how Willie is," Hubert continued. "He said he didn't want to go to the doctors in Montgomery but rather insisted on goin' to the Prattville hospital 'cause he knew the doctors there. Estus brought his station wagon around to where Willie was sitting. Roy and Carl helped him into the backseat. Estus said it took them nearly thirty minutes to drive from Maxwell Field to the hospital in Prattville. By the time they got there Willie could barely stand. Still, he insisted on walking up the brick steps and into the hospital lobby. Estus got on one side of him and Carl on the other. With their help he made it as far as the top step before collapsing. They basically carried him the rest of the way. Once they were inside, they eased him onto a large, red leather chair sitting in the corner by the admission office.

"Carl said when the office manager saw the condition Willie was in, she immediately called a Code Blue over the intercom. Within a minute, Dr. Jack Till and two nurses were at his side. Dr. Till felt for a pulse. There was none. He placed a stethoscope to Willie's chest and listened for a heartbeat. There was none.

"Shortly after Dr. Till arrived, Dr. Newton came on the scene. He'd heard the Code Blue also. When he saw who it was he ordered him to be taken to the emergency room immediately. Carl said Dr. Till told Dr. Newton he was already gone, but Dr. Newton said to him, 'I don't care. We've got to try and revive him. He's got a five-year-old little girl who needs her daddy.'

"Despite all they tried to do, there was no saving him."

The entire family took Willie's death hard, but none harder than Wilfred. He'd known something was wrong when he topped the hill above their house. There were several cars parked around the yard, and people were going in and out. He ran all the way down the hill as fast as he could get there. He stumbled on the top step as he ran into the house to find out what was going on. The screen door slammed behind him as he dropped his stringer of fish on the porch. Hubert stopped him in the front room.

Hubert held Wilfred by the shoulders. "I've got some bad news," he said to him.

Young Wilfred looked around the room at all the sad and crying faces. "What's going on, Hubert?" he asked, panicked.

"Your daddy died this mornin'," he answered as he tried to put his arms around Wilfred.

Wilfred quickly pulled away and looked at Hubert in disbelief. "What did you say?" he asked, confused.

Tears welled up once again in Hubert's eyes as he spoke. "Willie died this mornin' of a massive heart attack," he answered.

To everyone's surprise, Wilfred did not cry. Instead, he walked across the room and into his mama and daddy's room, where Adell was lying on the bed. Her eyes were red and swollen. When she saw her youngest son, she began to cry all over again.

"Come here, Wilfred." She sobbed, reaching her arms out to him.

Wilfred did not go to his mother's side. He stopped only

long enough to look at her then rushed out of the room, through the kitchen, and out the back door.

The most confused of all was Nancy. She was too young to understand death, nor did she understand why Wilfred seemed so angry when everyone else was so sad. When she looked out the kitchen window, she could see her older brother lying facedown on the ground under the black walnut tree. He was kicking his feet and beating his fists on the ground. He looked like a young child throwing a temper tantrum. She wanted to go to him. She wanted to find out what was wrong, but Imogene stopped her.

"Let him be, Nancy," she said. "He needs to be alone right now."

The day of Willie's funeral was the saddest day in the family's lives. The backbone that had held the family together was gone. He had ruled them with an iron fist. He made every decision that was made. Now he had been taken from them at the young age of fifty-four by a massive heart attack. His death certificate was signed June 18, 1956.

Adell sat on the front pew at Big Springs Baptist Church, trembling and crying. As she sat there, she recalled the words Dr. Newton had said to her about her husband's death: "His heart just burst. There was nothing anyone could do." Still, she couldn't believe what was happening. The last few days had been a blur. Friends, neighbors, and family had brought more food to the house than you could imagine. However, every time she tried to eat she felt as though she would choke. Her eyes remained red and swollen from crying more tears than she ever thought possible.

Her mind raced with questions for which there were no foreseeable answers. How would they get by? She'd never worked out in the public, only at home. Where would they live? She'd never learned to drive. Wilfred was too young to drive. DM and Imogene lived in Montgomery, too far away to be there for them. Suddenly her thoughts were interrupted by a woman's scream. She turned around in her seat to see who it was.

Josie, Willie's sister, was being escorted down the aisle of the church by her husband, Barry, Adell's oldest living brother, and their daughter, Vera. She was wailing at the top of her lungs, her arms flailing around in the air like a crazed person.

"Oh, Lord!" Josie cried. "Lord! Help us, Lord!"

When Josie got to the casket, her knees buckled under her. Vera kept her from falling, but the moans and screaming continued. Releasing herself from Vera's hold, Josie flung her body across the casket and kissed Willie's lifeless body several times on the face. "Where are his glasses?" she yelled. "He don't look natural without his glasses."

Julius made his way to the front of the church. Taking his father's glasses from his suit pocket, he handed them to Josie. Her hands were shaking as she placed the dark horn-rimmed glasses on Willie's face. Again she began to wail. Julius and Vera eventually led her away from the casket. The three of them sat down together on the front pew on the opposite side of the church from where Adell was sitting with the rest of the family.

Adell knew Willie didn't want to be buried with his glasses on. He'd told her that many times when he'd talked about dying. However, Adell knew there had always been ill feelings between her and all of Willie's family. They had never wanted Willie to marry her in the first place. Those ill feelings had made it extremely difficult for Adell to bond with her stepchildren. There had been constant conflict from the very beginning.

As she sat there, she thought back to when she and Willie first married. She remembered how Josie and Lena had told her two stepsons not to mind her because she wasn't their real mama. They had even convinced the two boys to set the house on fire while she was in it. When she asked them why they did it, they told her they were told to do it so they could be rid of her. From that day forward she never allowed herself to completely trust the boys or Willie's sisters again.

She hated to make an issue out of the glasses, but she also wanted to respect her late husband's wishes. She asked DM to make sure the glasses were removed before the casket was closed for the last time.

Willie's unexpected death affected everyone's life. Since Adell would have no means of financial support until they could get Willie's Social Security check started, Imogene and Hubert decided they would need to move in with Adell, Wilfred, and Nancy. It meant Hubert would have to travel back and forth every day from Billingsley to Montgomery. It also meant the small four-room house would be crowded. However, there was little choice in the matter. They would have to make do as best they could.

Wilfred was only fourteen. The man he had often challenged, the man who had been the strong arm of the family, who had made all the decisions, who had labored to keep the family afloat, was now gone. In the blink of an eye, Wilfred's life had changed forever. He went from thinking like a boy to thinking like a man. He told his mama he was going to quit school and go to work. Adell knew that would never do.

"Your daddy would roll over in his grave if I let ya quit school," Adell told him. "We'll get by somehow, but ya ain't gonna quit school if I can help it."

Nancy had just turned five in January. She was way too young to understand the meaning of death. She had seen her daddy in his casket. He looked like he was sleeping. She wondered why someone hadn't awakened him. Every night she would cry herself to sleep, asking where her daddy was and when he was coming home. Adell didn't know what to say to her little girl. How do you explain death to a five-year-old? How do you tell one so innocent her father is gone forever? The crying and questions continued for several weeks until one night Adell couldn't take it anymore.

"Nancy!" she screamed hysterically. "If ya don't stop cryin' over your daddy, you're gonna kill me too. Then ya won't have a mama or a daddy."

The frightened look on Nancy's small, round face told the story. It was a cruel thing to have said. Adell knew it the minute the words poured from her mouth. If only she could have taken the words back, she would have. Nancy never cried about her daddy again, at least not in front of her mother. Nor did she ever again ask when he was coming home.

DM was devastated too. He felt as though he'd lost his best friend. He had always been close to his father. They had hunted and fished together. Willie had taught him to be a man and not to let his disability stop him from doing whatever it was he wanted to do. He'd taught him to live as a one-arm boy in a two-arm world.

DM moved back home and helped out with money as best he could. He and Dot were in love. On August 31, 1956, just two months after Willie's death, they were married in a small at-home ceremony with close friends and family attending. They rented a small house on the main street of Billingsley. Ten months later, their first child, Laird, was born.

DM and Dot on their wedding day

Some six months later, the Social Security checks finally started arriving. The three of them totaled ninety dollars in all. Imogene and Hubert decided to move back to Montgomery. Since there would be no more farming, Adell decided to move from the Norrell place to a big four-room house belonging to the Hilyer family. It was located just off Highway 1. The house was within walking distance of Hilyer's grocery store. She rented the house for ten dollars a month.

Adell was going through a really rough time in her life. She had always been so dependent on Willie. He had taken care of finances and made all the decisions concerning their family. Now it was up to her. She continued to be plagued by ill health, even to the point of suffering from another nervous breakdown. She was hospitalized for close to a month, at which time DM and Dot moved from Billingsley to the Hilyer place to help take care of Wilfred and Nancy.

When Dot's father, Clem Billingsley, died a short time later, they moved into the house with Dot's mother, Ethyl. Before Clem's death, he sold the farm to DM with the promise that he would take care of Ethyl and always give her a place to live. DM kept his promise. Mrs. Billingsely lived with Dot and DM until she died.

As A-1 roofing company grew, so did DM's career. Soon he went from being a bookkeeper to becoming an estimator. Dot took over the job as bookkeeper for the company. He and Dot were able to buy a house in Capital Heights on North Capital Parkway. In eight years they had a total of five children: Laird, Charlotte, Tammy, Norman, and Steve. Mrs. Billingsley babysat for the children while Dot and DM worked.

In 1975, DM decided it was time to strike out on his own. He left A-1 Roofing Company to start his own business. He named his new business Bone Roofing. It was located on McQueen Street. Although he worked very hard throughout his lifetime, he never strayed far from his love of the great outdoors. He continued to fish and hunt, booking hunting trips to Canada and South America. Everywhere he went, people were amazed at the accuracy at which he could shoot.

The family also became very involved in the church. The children were given music and singing lessons. They attended all-day gospel singings where they began performing as the Singing Bone Family. They even recorded a gospel album. DM was chairman for many of these singings until the concept of all-day singings and dinner on the grounds fell by the wayside.

Wilfred had seen what farming could do to a man. He wanted no part of it. He knew education was the answer. In his junior year of high school he signed up to go to Devry Electronic Institute in Chicago, Illinois. He spent the following summer and all through his senior year working to save up the money he would need to get him through the two-year college.

On Wilfred's sixteenth birthday Adell took the money she'd saved in the bank from the sell of Willie's car and paid for a 1950 blue Chevy pickup truck. Wilfred used the truck to go to work part time at Loftin Hilyer's store pumping gas and for several other projects he had in the works. In June, shortly after graduation from Billingsley High School, he left the little town of Billingsley, where he'd grown up, never to return again.

Like many other families who lived and survived around and during the Great Depression, times were hard for the Bone family. However, it was those difficult times and their determination to get through them that made them strong. The principals on which Willie and Adell raised their family were forged deep into their souls. They were taught to respect those who respected them. They were taught that a job worth doing was worth doing well and with hard work anything was possible. They were taught never to make fun of those with handicaps but rather, to realize their worth. They were taught respect for God and his teachings. The children held a high respect for education, taught to them by parents who had very little education yet raised seven children to become useful and productive citizens in their communities.

For a time, the children strived to remain close after Willie's passing. However, as with many families, everyday life and the day-to-day living of it took its toll on a once-close-knit family. Although the years separated each individual family unit, there remained a bond that would bring them back together in the autumn years of their lives, the same bond that holds all families together, the bond of love.

Summer of 1991

Adell, Nancy, Wilfred, DM, Imogene, Delene, Julius
(Not pictured) Willie Charles

Epilogue

Adell Culpepper Bone never remarried, although she had several opportunities to do so. She learned to take care of herself and raised Nancy on her own. She and Willie never owned a home or property. However, in 1986, eight years before her passing, she bought and paid cash for the first home she ever owned. She passed away at the age of eighty-three on December 29, 1994, due to complications from knee replacement surgery.

After obtaining a law degree, Julius Earl Bone went to work for the Veteran's Administration in Montgomery, Alabama, as a lawyer representing the rights of the veterans of war. He and Betty Jo lived just off Highway 82 between Prattville and Billingsley in the back of their country store, J.E. Bone Grocery. He retired from the Veteran's Administration with the highest rank a civil servant can hold. They had one son, Travis Earl. Julius passed away September 7, 2002. Betty Jo followed on March 28, 2005.

Willie Charles Bone worked for Virgil Rawson at A-1

Roofing until he opened his own roofing business in Atlanta, Georgia. He and Edna had four children: Richard, Lee, David, and Robin. Willie Charles passed away in 1976 from lung cancer. Despite what the doctors had told them, their daughter, Lee, lived to be in her fifties.

Delene Bone Grant and her husband, Calvin, never had children of their own. They adopted three orphaned brothers: Tony, Paul, and Dale. Calvin passed away in 1971 from lung cancer. Delene passed away in 1993 from a stroke.

Imogene Bone Benton and her husband, Hubert, raised three girls: Teresa, Vicky, and Debra. They also had four grandchildren—LeAnna, Julie, Jennifer, and Allegra—and five great-grandchildren—Benton, Sarah, McKenzie, Drake, and Garrett. Imogene was a stay-at-home mom until the children were in school. She then went to work as a secretary/bookkeeper for Lazenby Tire Company in Montgomery. Hubert passed away on March 13, 1988, from stomach cancer. Imogene never remarried. She lives with her daughter Debra. She suffers daily from the pain of post-polio syndrome but remains strong in her will to enjoy life as best she can.

DM Bone was a successful business owner until he semi-retired at age sixty-five after selling his business to his two sons, Laird and Norman. He continued to go into work every day as a consultant for his son's company, Magnum Roofing. He retired completely in 2007 at the age of seventy-two. He and Dot had five children in all: Laird Bone, Charlotte Bone Jarrett, Tammy Bone Ewing, Norman Bone, and Steve Bone. They have seven grandchildren—Nicole, Nickolas, Syndal, Lyndsay, Kelli, Kyle, and Kirsten—and four great-grandchildren—Kate, Isabell, Christian, and Baylor. They celebrated their fiftieth wedding anniversary at a special ceremony in the auditorium of Billingsley High School on August 31, 2006. DM continues to support the athletics department at Billingsley High School. He and Dot are living out their retirement years in Billingsley in the house where Dot was raised.

Wilfred Bone married his high school sweetheart, Yvonne Mae Smith. After graduating from Devry Electronic Institute, he went from repairing TVs, radios, and washing machines for Ed Golson in Prattville to managing several TV stations. He later became one of the top salespeople in the country for electronic equipment while working for Harris Corportion. He and Yvonne had two children, Andy and Sandy. Andy died in a swimming accident at the age of eight. Sandy had one child, Michael. After his divorce from Yvonne, Wilfred married Elisha Neeley. She had one child, Lee, from a previous marriage. They reside in Montgomery.

Nancy Bone Goff became a hairstylist in 1968 while still attending high school. With the help of her mother, she bought her first hair salon in 1973. She remained in business until the year 2000. She married Gary Goff in 1977. Gary adopted Nancy's six-year-old daughter, Linda, by a previous marriage. She and Gary reside in Marbury, Alabama, where she is pursuing a career as a writer. Linda married John Majors in 2008. He adopted Linda's only child, Dalton, by a previous marriage. He is also father to four children by a previous marriage: Julia, Lyndsey, Jessica, and Brantley.

Note: After the death of Willie and his siblings, DM inquired several times about the whereabouts of the aforementioned family Bible, which was to go to Willie upon his mother's death. Everyone denied knowing who had it or if it even existed anymore. However, after Willie Charles, Delene, and Julius passed on, Delene's son, Paul, discovered it among his mother's possessions. Calvin and Delene adopted Paul, along with his biological brothers, Tony and Dale. Therefore, the contents of the Bible were of little interest to them. Paul offered to give it to DM

Due to the ill feelings brought about by the marriage of

Willie and Adell, his sisters had denied their youngest brother of his rightful claim to the Bible. For some sixty-eight years, its location remained a secret. Today, the Bone family Bible, its pages fragile, its contents dear, is being kept in a safe at the home of DM's oldest son, Laird.